SCARCITY, EXPLOITATION, AND POVERTY

Scarcity, Exploitation, and Poverty
Malthus and Marx in Mexico

by Luis A. Serrón

With a Foreword by Irving M. Zeitlin

University of Oklahoma Press : Norman

Library of Congress Cataloging in Publication Data

Serrón, Luis A
  Scarcity, exploitation, and poverty.

  Bibliography: p.
  Includes index.
  1. Poor–Mexico.   2. Poverty.   3. Malthus, Thomas
Robert, 1766–1834.   4. Marx, Karl, 1818–1883.
I. Title.
HC140.P6S44   301.44′1   79–4735

To the memory of my mother,
Ada Alejandra,
who taught me there are times
when it is necessary
"to make a heart out of guts"

Contents

Illustrations

Tables

If to treat good and evil as things having no essential difference, be impartiality, such impartiality I disavow.

> From *History of the Commonwealth of England*, by William Godwin.

On few subjects can any theory be pronounced just, that has not stood the test of experience.

> From *An Essay on the Principle of Population*, by Thomas Robert Malthus.

When moderation shapes the character of the investigation, it is more a sign of shying away from the truth than from untruth. It is a drag on every step I take. *In an investigation it is a prescription for fear of discovering the result*, a means of keeping one from the truth.

> From "Remarks on the Latest Prussian Censorship Instruction," by Karl Marx.

Foreword

Is it scarcity of food and other essential resources that accounts for the misery of the overwhelming majority of the earth's human population? Or does the cause of this tragic state of affairs lie elsewhere— notably in the realm of social, economic, and political relations? It was the English political economist Thomas Malthus who first sought to demonstrate that overpopulation generates scarcity which in turn causes poverty. This thesis continues to prevail in scholarly circles today and appears to have captured the imagination of the "man in the street" as well. Yet there are good grounds for questioning its validity.

It is true that everything human beings need, use, and consume is finite and "scarce." The pursuit of one worthwhile or necessary end unavoidably entails the forgoing of other such ends. But does it follow from this fact that scarcity is the cause of poverty? Or, as some population theorists claim, that the tendency of populations to grow exponentially is the cause of food and other vital-resource scarcities and hence of human impoverishment?

When Malthus formulated his theory, the scientific-industrial technology of English capitalism had yet to be applied to agriculture. One would therefore suppose that the empirical-historical basis for his theory was the pre-industrial era in the history of mankind. However, even in the pre-industrial epoch, exponential population growth, in and of itself, was never the cause of poverty and starvation. Instead, what occurred were periodic crises in which the productive forces of a given community had failed for the moment to provide for the sustenance of every man, woman, and child of the community. Often this failure was the result of natural disasters such as floods, earthquakes, drought, pestilence, or bad harvests from other natural causes. But one must not suppose that only natural causes were at work. The privation, suffering, and outright starvation of large numbers of people in the pre-industrial era were frequently a direct or indirect consequence of the policies and practices of the dominant groups and classes of the society in question. A case in point is the Enclosure Movement in Malthus's own homeland, which continued for several centuries. Elsewhere in Europe prolonged and bitter warfare led to the devastation of the community's food supply and, indeed, of large numbers of the food-producers themselves. In any event, even as applied to the pre-capitalist era, Malthus's population law and its corollary of natural scarcity do not begin to do justice to the complexity of conditions responsible for the historical forms of human misery.

But if the concept of natural scarcity fails to enlighten us concerning the earlier historical epochs, it enlightens us even less when applied to the industrial-capitalist epoch. In the typical pre-capitalist crisis, production falls short of the consumption needs of the community. In capitalist crisis, in contrast, we find the precise opposite: production far exceeds the consumption needs of the population—though large numbers of people starve nevertheless. It is evident that Malthus's theory affords us no insight at all into, say, the great economic crisis and depression that began in 1929 and ended only with the Second World War. Far from being a Malthusian-type phenomenon, this was a world-wide economic disaster that expressed itself in overproduction. Crops were plowed under; food surpluses were destroyed; factories and other productive establishments were shut down or dismantled; and while warehouses bulged with food, clothing, and other goods, millions of people went hungry and failed to obtain the basic necessities of life. The conditions leading to this state of affairs were not the consequence of Malthus's law. Neither scarcity nor overpopulation had anything to do with it. For it was certainly no scarcity in the necessaries of life that led to the massive misery of the 1930's but rather a scarcity in the means of employment and, hence, in the "effective demand" of millions of men and women. To understand the causes of this phenomenon, we need totally different tools of analysis from those put forth by Malthus and his present-day followers.

Present-day Malthusians are inclined to ignore the social, economic, political, and historical causes of poverty. That the world is becoming overpopulated has become their *idée fixe*, their explanation of the extreme impoverishment of so many Third World countries. But the truth is that, if the poor nations of the world find it difficult or impossible to feed themselves, it is not owing to any absolute shortage of food. The real cause of their plight is, first, that the distribution of existing resources is grossly unequal and, second, that the economic development of these societies is slow, lopsided, or altogether nonexistent. Both of these conditions are rooted in the class and institutional structures of the societies in question.

The validity of this assertion is patiently and skillfully demonstrated in this fine study by Luis A. Serrón. He comes to grips with the full complexity of both the Malthusian and the Marxian theories and then proceeds to assess their validity in light of the Mexican case. Why Mexico? Because that country has one of the fastest population growth rates in the world and also one of the most unequal income distributions in the world. Mexico is therefore an excellent test case of the central issues. Professor Serrón provides us with a superb clarification of these issues at a time when the need for clarity has never been greater.

Irving M. Zeitlin

University of Toronto

Preface

Class-conditioned ideologies influence perception. That proposition sociologists might very well assume. Is knowledge about human life possible despite ideology? Sociologists owe themselves an answer to that question.

This work is an outgrowth of two main influences on my development. The first of these was a close and intense study of the questions dealt with in Max Weber's essays on "Ethical Neutrality" and "objectivity"—a study which later grew into a wider assessment of the current status of these questions within sociology. The second was a course on sociological theory taken under Irving M. Zeitlin, coupled with close exposure to his work for a number of years. These influences, in turn, played upon and were informed by three earlier studies done by the writer: (1) a thesis on "Institutional Developments in American Agriculture," (2) an essay on "Social Classes in Mexico," and (3) "A Comparative Study of California and Mexico: Demographic Characteristics."

Among the Weberian ideas which guided my attention in the direction of this work, the following stand out:

1. No such phenomenon as a presuppositionless investigation of empirical data exists in reality, since the investigator's very perception that a problem is meaningful *is*, in itself, a presupposition that the problem in question can and should become an object of investigation.

2. Concepts are not generalizations from empirical data but ideal-type intellectual constructs for the mastery of data.

3. What makes an economic event is not a quality which that event

possesses objectively but, rather, a quality which arises out of our cognitive interests wherever we are faced with the problem of scarcity of means for the satisfaction of our needs.

4. There is no absolutely objective analysis of socio-cultural phenomena which is independent of one-sided points of view.

5. Science must henceforth be prepared to create new knowledge by studying known facts from known points of view.

My studies under Zeitlin opened for me a perspective on sociological theory which was essential to both my conceptualization of the theoretical part of this work and my effort to view this body of theory with references to the historically specific context of one concrete social system, namely Mexico. The perspective on sociological theory developed by Zeitlin which provides the broader theoretical background for this work—stated in the simplest possible terms—is the following: Sociology did not arise as a value-free, ethically neutral, presuppositionless approach to empirical facts. Rather, the sociological ideas which are of permanent value for the understanding of modern civilization, and, perhaps, sociology's most valuable contribution to that civilization, arose during the course of an intense and protracted debate between two opposing schools of thought. The participants in this debate during its earlier phase were, on the one hand, the philosophical exponents of the ideas of the French Revolution and, on the other, the intellectual exponents of the conservative reaction to those ideas. Among the former are such *philosophes* as Charles de Secondat Montesquieu and Jean Jacques Rousseau. Among the latter were such conservative thinkers and Louis de Bonald, Joseph de Maistre, and Edmund Burke. The *philosophes*, Rousseau in particular, rejected the value of existing institutions after measuring them against a humanistic set of values and the standards of what they conceived to be man's nature. The exponents of the reaction to these ideas viewed existing institutions as necessary restraints on what they considered to be egoistic tendencies in man's nature and sought to maintain the *status quo*. Because it rejected existing institutions, the former school became known as revolutionary, critical, and negative. The latter school became known as positive or conservative because it upheld the value of those institutions.

The latter phase of this debate includes the issues and ideas formulated by, on the one hand, Karl Marx and, on the other, most of the sociologists who now form part of the classical tradition, including Max Weber, Emile Durkheim, Gaetano Mosca, Vilfredo Pareto, Robert Michels, and Karl Manheim. The work of Karl Marx stands squarely in the humanistic tradition of the *philosophes* and marks a high point in the development of that tradition. What is most important in the classical tradition of sociology rose out of the effort on the part of these sociologists to deal with the issues and ideas formulated by Karl Marx. Despite a number of historical changes which Marx's criticism of capitalist society did not foresee, the Marxian model remains the most important single critique of that society. Yet precisely because history has taken a number of turns which Marx could not predict and because the sociologists of the classical tradition sought to account for these changes, the Marxian view must be modified and enriched by this tradition. Both the vulgar Marxism, which seeks to reduce the Marxian view to a series of universal causal laws of historical development, and the "sophisticated" forms of Marxism, which seek to accommodate all historical events under Marxian theory through *ad hoc* reinterpretations of Marx's writings, are unacceptable to anyone seeking a living view and interpretation of social change. However, the effort to interpret social change from the point of view of the conditioning influence of economic factors, combined with a recognition of the existence of other relevant factors such as politics, the military, and science, remains a living and fruitful intellectual force in sociology.

Another point emphasized by Zeitlin which was influential in the design of this work is that Marx never intended his economic interpretation of history to be used as an *a priori* formula for the construction of history but rather that its formulation and application was circumscribed to the concrete and specific conditions which he found in existence in Western Europe. It was to be not a key to open all doors but rather a hypothesis to be tested under concretely specific social conditions. Marx's journalistic writings in fact show that Marx thought the establishment of socialism by parliamentary means to be a real possibility within those countries which he considered to be the most civilized on earth, England, Holland, and the United States. Hence Zeitlin pointed to a need for sociological studies which move from theory to concrete historical conditions and back again to theory.

Before my work with Zeitlin, I had done some studies on sociological and economic theory, as well as on the origins of sociology. These studies sensitized me to a phase of the theoretical encounter just sketched which I thought would be well worth studying closer. Its locus was England, beginning just before the French Revolution and continuing for nearly a century later. Its earlier phase included a fierce theoretical and ideological encounter between the critical political philosophy of William Godwin and the conservative social philosophy and political economy of Thomas Malthus. Its latter phase consisted of the relentless and thoroughgoing critical examination of Malthus's ideas undertaken by Karl Marx and Friedrich Engels, a criticism which was both destructive and constructive. What I found most engaging in this phase of the debate was the extreme polarization in explanatory standpoint with reference to the sources of poverty and misery in human life. This polarity, I thought, encompassed the fundamental questions with respect to the locus of responsibility for poverty and related problems. One side of it (the Malthusian side) placed the blame on human nature, while the other (the Godwinian and Marxian side) placed the blame on existing institutions. It is hardly possible, I thought, to polarize the argument more sharply, more clearly, or more dramatically than by placing the blame for poverty on sex and the niggardliness of nature as Malthus does and on the landed monopolies and private property over the means of productions as Godwin and Marx do. I have labeled this the "English Phase of the Modern Debate" for want of a better term and to locate it with reference to the wider work documented by Zeitlin.

Deductive reasoning on the basis of these theories led me to identification and contraposition of the basic concepts which explain poverty in the Malthusian and the Marxian traditions. These concepts are "scarcity" on the Malthusian side and "exploitation" on the Marxian side. Malthus accounts for scarcity on the basis of a supposed tendency of population to increase faster than the means of subsistence (Godwin also uses the concept of exploitation, though much less self-consciously and systematically than do Marx and Engels). Marx accounts for exploitation in terms of expropriation of unpaid labor, an expropriation which takes the form of profits for the capitalist owners of the means of production.

The familiarity with the productivity of American agriculture which I had acquired as an inevitable by-product of work on my thesis on American agriculture made it difficult for me to accept some of Max Weber's views on the nature of economic events, in particular the view that the economic quality of an event rises out of our cognitive interests when we are faced with the problem of scarcity of means for the satisfaction of our needs. It appeared to me that the development of American agriculture had been more nearly a process of multiplying the productivity of action in such a way as to minimize the input-output ratio than it had been a process of allocating scarce resources. Nevertheless, research into current definitions of the term "economics" convinced me that many definitions of that concept were framed in terms of the problem of how best to allocate *scarce* resources. This conflict between (1) my understanding of the economics of development in American agriculture (an agriculture which had been producing surpluses for several decades) and (2) the above-mentioned point from Weber's essay on "Objectivity" (coupled with the current focus on scarcity in definitions of the term "economic") combined with another experience of mine to induce me to undertake a study of the Malthusian sources of the idea of scarcity and its ideological uses.

The other experience that influenced my decision was a reading of Weber's essay on "Objectivity," which was one of three of his methodological essays that I was required to read before undertaking a reorganization of my thinking at Tulane University. The central point in this advice that I received was to change my approach to sociology from the effort to explain social reality through the study of social facts to the effort to explain it by studying the forms of thought in terms of which men approach reality. Thus the idea of scarcity was an approach that I could not accept without critical examination.

My earlier essay on "Social Classes in Mexico" had been written with a view to tracing the historical consequences of the system of landholding introduced in Mexico following the Spanish conquest. My research had shown that those consequences were summed up under what is referred to as Mexico's "Agrarian Problem." The chief historical components of this problem were: (1) a tendency for the large haciendas to grow at the expense of the small holdings of the peasantry; (2) growing destitution of the masses of the peasantry followed by civil strife, halfway measures of reform, and re-initiation of the same cycle; and (3) reliance on the army and the church for the maintenance of order. According to my research findings, Mexico's peasantry reached the depths of destitution following passage and implementation of the "Surveying Laws" under the rule of Porfirio Díaz. This situation in turn was a large contributing factor in the revolutionary upheaval of 1910–17. This revolution ended with the defeat of the revolutionary forces led by Emiliano Zapata and Pancho Villa. The upheaval had been of such major proportions that some concessions were made to placate the peasantry. The ancestral *ejidal* system of nonalienable, infrasubsistence-sized holdings, control over which carried with it only the right of usufruct, was restored. Along with the *ejidos* the law provided for the retention of a collateral system of "small," privately owned haciendas. Near the conclusion of that paper I came upon a statement made by Frank Tannenbaum to the effect that the program of land reform was encouraging population growth and was thereby compounding the very problem that it sought to relieve. Although this comment contributed to my undertaking a study of Mexico's demographic characteristics shortly afterward, my study of social classes left me convinced that Mexico had been subjected to a system of exploitation so pervasive and widespread as to have kept the overwhelming majority of its population perilously close to a bare subsistence level (and below) throughout its history.

My subsequent study of Mexico's demographic characteristics indicated that Mexico's population has experienced one of the most rapid rates of growth in the world. Data for 1970 released by the Population Reference Bureau confirms this observation. Mexico's growth rate is on a par with the average for Central America and is exceeded only by Costa Rica and Kuwait. However, my comparative study of the demographic characteristics of California and Mexico left unanswered the question of whether class exploitation or population growth is more responsible for poverty.

Since my earlier studies of Mexican society had shown that both the exploitative tendencies of Mexico's class system and the rates of growth of Mexico's population approached extreme levels, it occurred to me that Mexican data would provide an excellent testing ground for both Marxian and Malthusian explanations of poverty. Subsequent research showed that Mexico exceeded India (the example often given in support of the idea that Malthusianism still applies) in both its population growth rates and the degree of inequality in income distribution.

The purpose of this work is to determine whether or not it is possible to arrive at conclusions that clearly tend to validate or invalidate one or the other of two ideologically polar theories of poverty by examining relevant data within a social system deliberately selected because of its known tendency to emphasize the magnitude of the key variables involved in both theories.

The thesis of this work is the following: data gathered under the guidance of concepts taken from antagonistic theories of poverty will provide evidence for assessing the relative explanatory adequacy of those theories, and, therefore, the evidence will carry implications which will not be neutral as regards the relative validity of those theories.

Certain events require brief commentary because they took place after writing was completed and before the book went to press. The peso has been devalued to about half its former value. A new president, José López Portillo, has been elected without serious or noticeable opposition. The living standards of the most oppressed classes have deteriorated steadily because of inflation. Undocumented workers have been deported back to Mexico at a rate close to one million a year. There is a new official openness on the measurement of unemployment and underemployment rates, which are admitted to be as high as 40 per cent. New oil deposits have been discovered which might rival those of Saudi Arabia in magnitude. The second Latin-American Bishops' Conference took place in Puebla with the participation of a new Polish pope who finds it possible to mix a passion for justice with the traditional Catholic attitude toward population planning and control. United States foreign policy must take into account the nation's dependency on foreign sources of oil *vis-à-vis* Mexico's nationalized oil industry. A reciprocal exchange of visits by heads of state of both countries was accompanied by an agreement on Mexico's part to sell natural gas to the United States. Mexico also plans to increase crude-oil production, but with the intention of selling to a wider assortment of customers in the world market, thus relatively reducing its dependence on the United States market. Hence it does not appear likely that Mexico will agree to make up what is becoming a chronic shortfall in United States oil supplies. The exchange of visits also failed to produce any dramatic new agreements regarding the flow of undocumented migrant workers. These developments take place in the context of temporary suspension and probably permanent curtailment of the flow of oil from Iran, following the overthrow of the shah, along with increasing rates of oil consumption in the United States and rising prices from various suppliers. Potentially the most fateful and most promising of the above developments for Mexico is the discovery of new oil deposits. It could provide a badly needed source of new funds to increase Mexico's rates of investments and to improve the living standards of its people. Or the oil industry might become a captive nationalized institution whose wealth may be diverted to benefit the small native and foreign elite that has traditionally benefited from Mexico's wealth. Or it might follow a mixed path. In either of the two latter cases the bonanza will last while the oil lasts.

Finally, as 1979 draws to a close, a United States census study reportedly reveals a sharp drop in Mexico's birth rate, a drop sharp enough to reduce the rate of natural increase from 3.2 per cent to 2.5 per cent per year during the 1975–79 interval. While this reported decrease is of a totally unexpected and improbable magnitude, it is, nevertheless, in line with observed trends and stated policies during the Echevarria and Lopez Portillo administrations.

Luis A. Serrón

University of Wisconsin—Milwaukee

PART ONE

The English Phase of the Modern Debate

1.

Introduction

There where it all ends
and where it all begins
a song that has been courageous
will always be a new song.

From the song "Manifiesto,"
by Victor Jara

What is the source of poverty and misery in human society? Do
they arise out of institutions which are ill-suited to man's nature and
which prevent normal development? Are they rather rooted in human
nature itself? These questions lay at the core of the debate which
gave rise to the classical tradition in sociological theory. The questions themselves assume that knowledge about the source is a prerequisite for assessing the direction and form which corrective action—if
any—might take. The answers are politically loaded. At stake is
nothing less than man's orientation to the natural and social conditions of his existence.

Perfectibility, progress, and humanism; unalterable laws of man's
nature, struggle for existence, and positive checks; survival of the
fittest, evolution, and adjustment; class oppression, class consciousness, and revolution; all these explanatory concepts identify the
issues and the appropriate stance to be taken toward them. They also
bring to mind whole schools of thought in the history of sociological
theory.

Malthus's *Essay on Population* has meaning within the specific
context of the French Revolution. It was specifically aimed at the

intellectual devotees of that revolution: Godwin, Condorcet, and Paine. It had a far-reaching influence on Darwin, Wallace, and the Social Darwinists. It was published in a climate of repression of revolutionary ideas, and it contributed to strengthening that climate. It provided a potent ideological tool for the politically powerful. Finally, it has since become the alleged prophet of every major famine afflicting the world. The contemporary followers of Malthus bear unmistakable similarities to the Social Darwinists (Meek 1971:38–49).

The debate between Marxists and Malthusians has roots reaching back deep into the ancient world, in myths about the golden age, the fall of man, and original sin. It is also essential for understanding the social struggles of the present day (Sabine 1958:178–79; Meek 1971:46). Another reason why it is important to study the encounter between Marx and Malthus is that explanatory concepts arise and have their meanings within concrete historical conditions and intellectual contexts, and those conditions and contexts provide a matrix within which their meaning can be deduced. Marx himself regarded England as a useful case for the study of the relationship between poverty and politics, his reason being that poverty there was so widespread and so extreme (Marx 1964:100). The works of Malthus on the one hand and of Godwin and Marx on the other provide a crucial context for deducing the meanings of "scarcity," "exploitation," and "poverty." The concepts thus deduced will be used as guides for gathering information which is relevant to a re-examination of the questions at issue, within a suitable, historically specific social system.

What we are ultimately concerned with is whether the Malthusian and Marxian perspectives on poverty are as irreconcilable as they seem and whether the issues arising from the opposing views of the nature of man, and of social institutions and their implications, are as unresolvable as they seem at first.

2.

William Godwin:
The Philosopher of Justice, Virtue, and Happiness

William Godwin was an English representative of those French *philosophes* who gave form to the ideas of the French Revolution. Marx regarded him as one of the most important developers of the theory of exploitation (Marx 1964:164). Publication of his *An Enquiry Concerning Political Justice* took place a month after the execution of Louis XVI and a month before France declared war on England. Because the French Revolution found both a following and an opposition in England, and because England became the center of an intense and successful opposition to that revolution, the political and intellectual climate of the times was fraught with repression. Godwin was at the center of a circle of men who bore the brunt of the repression, and he led the opposition to that repression (Brailsford 1913:45–48; Godwin 1926:xiii).

Godwin conceived of "justice" as both a principle of reciprocity in human relations and a criterion for determining who owns what (Godwin 1949:37–62). He viewed the existence of opulent luxury and leisure side by side with destitution and health-impairing labor as fundamentally unjust (Godwin 1949:39). Established institutions— among them private property, marriage, religion, government, and law—had built into the structure of human society a very narrow form of selfishness and inequality. The masses, who were poor, had been converted into slaves and cattle for the rich. Institutions had also created a formidable roster of pensioners on the labor of the producers of necessities: producers of trinkets and luxuries, government officials, tax gatherers, courtiers, footmen, clerks, armies, fleets, and so on (Godwin 1949:55–72).

Godwin estimated that if everyone carried a share of the burden of producing necessities no one would have to work more than one-half to two hours a day, the latter estimate being a revision of the former (Godwin 1949:72–74; Brailsford 1913:137). The greatest source of evil and of misconceptions in daily life was to be found in the established property system; it was unprincipled, profligate, and contrary to justice and to the nature of human beings. The landed monopolies were responsible for the deaths of four-fifths of Europe's population in the cradle. Vast tracts of land were kept idle while people were going hungry. Hence they were a principle of limitation on population growth. Europe was capable of supporting five times as many people (Godwin 1949:52–62). The landed monopolies were also responsible for war, crime, and the overall oppression of the peasantry.

The established churches circumvented the issues with their emphasis on charity as a social virtue. The more important task, the abolition of poverty through the establishment of justice, went by default. Governments flouted reason, protected the profligacy of the rich, and legalized the exploitation of the producers of wealth. Marriage arose out of inequalities and self-love to protect inequalities and self-love. It led to thwarting, bickering, and unhappiness. It irritated and multiplied our vices and encouraged self-deception. Such institutions stood in the way of the realization of justice, the progress of reason, and the perfectibility of man. Poverty, misery, and vice had their sources in such institutions. Justice required their abolition in favor of common labor, equality, reciprocity, and free sexual unions on the basis of mutual attraction and consent (Godwin 1949:101–105).

Godwin was an anarchist in the sense that he regarded the existing social order as fundamentally irrational, and he wanted freedom to live according to reason. He opposed violence, since violence and conviction were not the same thing. Men tended to choose in terms of what their understanding recommended as being best. Hence he wanted a revolution in opinion and the removal of all obstacles to the progress of reason.

Godwin had an almost boundless trust in the capacity of the earth to support an increasing human population. Since in his time only one-fourth of the habitable globe had been brought under cultivation and since the productivity of the cultivated fourth was capable of vast improvement, he expected the earth to remain able to accommodate a growing human population for myriads of centuries (Godwin 1949:115). He also predicted that men would stop reproducing when the earth's population reached its saturation point. Science would do away with death, and rational men would stop reproducing. He thus left himself open to the Malthusian onslaught.

3.

Thomas Malthus:
On Overpopulation, Misery, and Vice

The theoretical standpoint formulated by Thomas Malthus in his *Essay on Population* shifted the focus of attention from institutions to human nature. If Godwin and the *philosophes* found the sources of poverty and misery in faulty institutions unsuited to human nature, Malthus pointed to humanity's profligate sexuality and to the niggardliness of nature as the source of the trouble. In so doing he clarified and sharpened the position taken by those who decried the revolutionary temper, ideas, and trends of the times. England was at war with France when the first edition of the *Essay* was published—a coincidence which must have had a double effect: lending volume to Malthus's voice and muffling the voice of the opposition. Hence there is merit in Proudhon's question; Can any one doubt that the Malthusian principle is the whole of the counter-revolution (Levin 1937:25)?

Malthus accused the upper classes of having misguided the lower classes: they had encouraged the belief that the sufferings of the poor during times of scarcity could be ended through revolution (Levin 1937:82; Morris 1969:69). Actually a revolution would accomplish little. The problems arising from existing institutions were mild by comparison to those arising from the unequal operation of two laws of human nature: the attraction between the sexes and the need for food. The operation of the first law made for a geometric rate of population increase, while that of the second was limited to an arithmetic rate of increase in the food supply (Malthus 1964:6–7). Assuming an original balance of two units of population and two units of food, the changes Malthus expected with each passing generation are shown in Table 1.

Table 1.   **The Malthusian Ratios**

Generations	Population Units	Units of Food
1	2	2
2	4	4
3	8	6
4	16	8
5	32	10
6	64	12

Hence Malthus spoke of the existence of a constant tendency of population growth to outstrip the capacity to produce food. He also spoke of population growth as applying a constant pressure on the means of subsistence. This constant tendency or pressure came to be known as the Malthusian law of overpopulation—a "law" which was later to provide the theoretical basis for the so-called iron law of wages in economic theory and for natural selection in evolutionary theory.

As Malthus saw the problem, Godwin had looked at flaws in distribution from the wrong perspective. The problem was not to be solved by relying on the general benevolence to see to it that food and supplies flow from where they are plentiful to where they are scarce. Rather the problem was precisely that population growth was producing an oversupply of needs to be satisfied by the available means of subsistence. In particular the problem was that the poor were producing an oversupply of laborers and were thus cheapening the value of the only property they possessed: the labor of their hands. Thus the responsibility for the poverty and the misery of the lower classes lay squarely either on the poor themselves or on the laws of nature, which are the laws of God. In either case existing governments could do nothing for the poor.

Malthus thus provided an excuse for rulers who were afraid of the doctrines of perfectibility and progress and of the revolutionary trends of the times. There was no point in meddling with the laws of nature or with the laws of God to help the poor; such meddling could not and would not help them. Moreover, the poor would be less likely to allow themselves to be misguided along the path of violence (in times of scarcity) if they were correctly informed about the true source of their problems (Bury 1955:230–31; Glass 1953:9).

Given the supposed tendency to overpopulation, what accounts for the fact that population growth tends to be kept within the limits of the means of subsistence? Godwin thought he found the source of that limitation primarily in monopolistic landholdings. Malthus now argued that such a principle was the grinding law of necessity, misery, and the fear of misery (Malthus 1961a:106).

Godwin had envisioned a just social system where private property, inequalities, marriage, overwork, towns, unhealthy occupations, luxury, and war had been abolished. Malthus now argued that such a system would have to be abandoned a short fifty years after its establishment. The reason: it was the system most likely to be conducive to rapid population growth. Unshackled intercourse would encourage early families, and the changed conditions associated with equality and the elimination of luxury would promote a healthy population (Malthus 1961a:106–108).

Malthus estimated the total size of England's population at or about the time of publication of the first edition of his *Essay* (1798) at seven million inhabitants. Given the improvements which would follow the establishment of Godwin's system, the total population could be expected to double within twenty-five years. Malthus conceded that the equalization of property in land would make it possible to reduce the length of the working day to half a day. Beyond that, however, there were problems. Given the quality of the soil and the fertility of the lands under cultivation, and given the barrenness of the lands not under cultivation, it was unlikely that food production could be increased to supply the needs of fourteen million inhabitants. Malthus reluctantly allowed that such needs might be met by plowing up grazing lands and through comparable measures (Malthus 1961a:108).

↘ During the course of the next generation Malthus expected England's total population to double again, bringing the total to twenty-eight million inhabitants. However, the very highest increase in food production possible during that same interval (judging from the unanimity of all informed opinion) would be sufficient to supply the needs of only an additional seven million inhabitants. Such a turn of events would leave seven million people unprovided for. Godwin's vision of general benevolence and happiness would vanish into thin air within two generations. Self-interest and misery would replace benevolence and health. Every form of vice and distress which degraded and saddened humanity before the changeover would return (Malthus 1961a:108). The redundant seven million would not vanish suddenly but would be subject to continuous attrition owing to the operation of the laws of nature.

Protection of the common store would require administration of the death penalty for theft, amounting to the restoration of private property. More careful consideration of the problem would lead the sharper intellects to the deeper roots of the problem: irresponsible breeding. Hence marriage would be restored along with social ostracism for women who bore out of wedlock. Women were singled out, of course, because there is never a question about who the mother is (Malthus 1961a:109–10).

Restoration of private property and marriage would mean that equality no longer existed and that a class system very similar to that prevailing before the changes would now be in operation. Malthus regarded private property and self-love as something akin to a ladder which had been essential to the passage from savagery to civilization; they were civilizing forces which it would be foolish to discard. Hence he also regarded class inequalities as inevitable (Malthus 1961b:416). Yet there is a contradiction in Malthus's comparative evaluation of systems of equality and inequality: he speaks of class society as a degeneration from equality (Malthus 1961b: 416). Are private property and marriage civilizing forces or degenerative forces?

This much Malthus felt certain of: contraception was an unnatural method of avoiding problems created by population growth; no one had a right to subsistence beyond what he could command through the labor of his hands. Condorcet was in error on the former count; Paine was in error on the latter. Man had to be moral to nature: it was unnatural to interfere with the sexual act. As regards provisions the destitute had no claims either on nature or on the rights of property.

Malthus, under criticism from Godwin, admitted the possibility of strict abstinence and late marriage as preventive checks on population growth, but he seriously doubted their effectiveness. In later years Malthus was to end on a medieval Christian note: the earth was a place of moral discipline and probation, with difficulties to be overcome and temptations to be resisted. Those who overcome the difficulties and resist the temptations are rewarded with happiness in this life and in the next one. Such was the wisdom of providence. The power of increase was not too strong. It was just strong enough. There was no God but Scarcity, and Malthus was its prophet (Malthus 1960:58–59).

In reply Godwin wrote a essay entitled *Of Population*. There he took the blame for eliciting the Malthusian onslaught and credited Malthus with some insights (Smith 1951:38). However, he pointed to the danger of confusing the historically specific with what is universally essential to order. He also summed up the essay as an apology for vice and misery and as a carefully contrived mixture of squandering by the rich and starving by the poor (Smith 1951: 123, 131).

The mechanical and irreversible operation of the ratios came under criticism even from Malthus's contemporaries (Hazlitt 1960:175). Hence later, in his *A Summary View of the Principle of Population*, Malthus made some modifications of his theory. There he acknowledged that all things which reproduce by seed or generation increase geometrically, an admission which undermines his whole theory, since, as Marx noted later, it was based on the point that people, not plants and animals, increase geometrically (Meek 1971:138). Nonetheless Malthus continued to use the expression "the unequal operation of the ratios" as a catch phrase. The assumed tendency to overpopulation was now postulated to arise from a number of factors: the scarcity of land, the barrenness of the earth's surface, and the tendency for returns on capital investments to diminish. Rates of increase in the food supply were now said to depend on the quality of land available. Food production rates could be increased fast enough to provide for the fastest rates of population growth when land was of good quality. If no limits were set on expansion and on population increase, however, the geometric rate of increase in the food supply would diminish.

～ Malthus regarded the law of private property as a positive law which had a claim to being the most natural of positive laws. In his view this law tended to promote the general good. Private property would provide an incentive to production because people were naturally indolent, and self-provision was the best incentive (Malthus 1960:34). What Malthus did not know, or could not know, was that the secret of the agricultural productivity which was to emerge in the nineteenth century lay not in any change in the intensity of hedonistic motives, but in the hundreds of ways in which science and technology radically altered the physical limitations of the human body and the human capacity to transform the natural habitat: reapers, tractors, six-bottom plows, combined harvester threshers, fertilizers, hybrids, and the rest (Serrón 1957:33–57, 100–35).

～ To Malthus human life was akin to a great lottery. A few were lucky; the rest were unlucky. A few were included among those who possessed a share of the earth and its goods; others owned nothing but the labor of their hands. The latter were unlucky children; they had been born in a world already possessed; they had drawn a blank lottery ticket. The luckless ones had a right only to what they could buy with the labor of their hands; they cheapened that right by overreproducing. Poverty existed because of overpopulation. The owners of the earth and of its goods had an unquestionable right to consume all that was produced (Keynes 1963:118–19). Malthus rejected the legitimacy of changing the property system by force, though he condoned the use of force to protect it (Malthus 1960: 55–56). To him the only legitimate means of effecting modifications on the rights of property was taxation.

What Malthus called the "positive checks" on population played an important ideological and political role in system maintenance. If the frightful death rate among the "redundant" poor could be successfully blamed on the laws of nature, then whatever institutional factors operated to produce population attraction could also operate to reduce the potential opposition to existing institutions under the cover of natural law. If wars and other excesses could be successfully blamed on vice, then whatever institutional factors were contributing to them could continue to operate while the masses who provided cannon fodder or were driven to drink or to hedonistic abandonment took the blame on themselves. The checks would then become, in name and in fact, the ideological and political guardians of the established institutions. What can be more convenient than a natural or a self-inflicted method of removing a superfluous population, especially if such method is widely regarded as positive? Such are the guardians of "legitimacy."

The positive checks were of two types: misery and vice. Under the former Malthus included hard labor, overexposure, undernourishment, malnutrition, and other poverty-related factors, all of which tended to shorten life expectancy. Included here also were diseases, epidemics, famines, plagues, insalubrious urban dwellings, and bad infant care. Under vice Malthus included wars and excesses of all kinds.

Malthus advocated a view which measured the value of a commodity in terms of its cost to the purchaser. This cost included, over and above the cost of production, an amount required by the capitalist as a condition for continued production. This added cost was the capitalist profit, and profit—not use—was the purpose of capitalist production. Since commodities were exchanged for more money than was necessary to pay for the labor that went into making them, the exchange between capital and labor was unequal (Meek 1971: 145).

Malthus explained "gluts" (crises) in production in terms of this contradiction in the area of exchange: excessive accumulation of profits would bring a slowdown in consumption. Since he assumed that laborers were receiving all they were entitled to get, he recommended the creation of a class of unproductive consumers to prevent a glut. This class would be created by supporting the life-style of the landed aristocracy, their financial dependents, and servants. Hence unproductive consumption by wealthy elites, as Malthus saw the proposal, encouraged productivity and plenty by creating a demand for products and by thus keeping the profit motive in operation. Diversion of excessive profits from the capitalist would tend to encourage production by creating "effective demand." This logic changed abruptly on the matter of giving handouts to the poor: such unproductive consumption created scarcity, since it forced prices up by increasing demand. For this and other reasons Marx regarded Malthus as an apologist for the wealthier classes, and in particular for the landed aristocracy (Meek 1971:151–52).

The Malthusian proposition that appears to be least assailable is the view that population cannot increase indefinitely on a limited surface. However, the proposition that became the basis of natural selection theory (the view that overpopulation creates scarcity and thereby a struggle for existence) is controvertible and must be weighed against the view that exploitation is a selective factor in favor of fertility. Marx suggested as much when he took note of the inverse relationship between size of family and magnitude of wages (Marx 1906:706). Interestingly enough, Malthus viewed poverty as a condition unlikely to promote chastity, particularly when associated with idleness (Morris 1969:67), but this view did not represent the main drift of his thought. It should be sufficient to take note of the great transformation in the egg-laying capacity of hens under the selective impact of human exploitation, and over an interval of a century—from about 30 to about 280 eggs per year—to realize the full heuristic potential of this view for evolutionary theory. It should be noted also that Darwin made use of the selective impact of plant and animal husbandry as a heuristic guide in his search for the principle of natural selection.

What Marx did was to develop the idea that capitalist exploitation of labor creates a relative surplus population; though he did take note of the implications of Darwin's findings to Malthusian theory. When Darwin found that the geometric rate of increase applied to the whole plant and animal world he had, quite unwittingly, overturned Malthus's false assumption concerning the unequal operation of the ratios (Meek 1971:138).

4.

Karl Marx and Friedrich Engels:
On Capitalist Accumulation and Relative Surplus Population

If Malthus gave a plausible, almost axiomatic quality to the view that property and misery have their source in overpopulation, it was Marx and Engels who gave the most powerful expression to the view that poverty and misery have their source in exploitative institutions which are unsuited to human nature and which prevent normal development. Neither Marx nor Engels wrote a specifically anti-Malthus book, but their writings touch on Malthus's thought again and again, always with a critical eye, with Marx's criticisms being the more profound of the two. Their criticisms almost invariably end in disagreement with Malthus. Occasionally there is praise for an insight, but just as often the merit of that insight is declared null by a wrong turn of thought (Meek 1971:143). Marx expressed his contempt for Malthus quite openly; he saw him as a bought advocate for the powers that be (Meek 1971:133–36). Nevertheless, the Malthusian presence is there, a challenge to be dealt with. Close attention to the Marxian criticism of Malthus shows that it serves the very useful function of compacting the Marxian view, for Marx found in the Malthusian *Essay* both a libel on the human race and a great stimulus to clarify and develop his own view of the matters at issue (Marx and Engels 1962:1:391).

Is there a universal, abstract law of overpopulation which applies with equal force at all times and in all places? Marx's answer was that if any such law existed it applied only to plants and animals, and only to the extent that human beings had not interfered with them (Marx 1906:693). The validity of any laws of population growth was restricted to the historical limits of each specific mode of production (Marx 1906:692–93). Engels distinguished between eternal laws of nature and historical laws, and he classified economic laws under the category of historical laws. Whatever element of validity the Malthusian theory appeared to have retained throughout history was circumscribed within the conditions of class exploitation (Meek 1971:85).

Was there an eternal, iron law of wages which existed as a corollary to the law of overpopulation and which accounted for the trend of wages to fall to the level of the means of subsistence? Marx answered that the word "iron" was a watchword, a signal, which enabled the establishment's faithful to recognize one another (Marx and Engels 1962:2:29). The efforts of economists who wished to argue that socialism could not abolish poverty had been bolstered by postulation of the existence of such a law: since poverty was natural, it could not be abolished; it could only be spread around. But, Marx argued, if such a law existed, it would be impossible to abolish not only the wage-labor system but also any other social system, since all systems would be subject to eternal, iron laws (Marx and Engels 1962:2:29). Engels's answer was that whatever truth there appeared to have been to the operation of such a law throughout history was restricted to conditions where class rule existed; it certainly could not have operated under conditions such as ancient slavery or feudal serfdom, where labor was not performed for wages (Meek 1971:85).

Marx rejected the effort to use his account of the origins of capitalism in Western Europe as a lever for the construction and imposition of a similar movement upon people everywhere, regardless of specific historical conditions (Marx 1964:22), and he took pains to distinguish between a universal, natural law of struggle for existence which was premised on Malthusian assumptions about overpopulation, and the concrete struggles which take place between classes under varying and specific forms of society (Meek 1971:196). Marx's own use of the term "iron," in his reference to laws of capitalist production which work with iron necessity toward inevitable results, makes reference to the specific historical conditions in Germany and England. It might also be a polemical reversal of the ideological use of the term by bourgeois thinkers (Marx 1906:13).

To Marx and Engels poverty did not arise from overpopulation. A fundamental problem under capitalism was precisely that people starved in the midst of plenty. There was food around, but before it could be eaten, someone had to clear a profit (Meek 1971:61–62). People went jobless not because the plant and equipment needed to work with were absent, nor because there was an absence of work to be done; the problem was that profit stood like a ghost between the unemployed and the means of production (Marx and Engels 1962:2:146). The fundamental flaw in the system of capitalist production was that capital and its expansion—not human fulfillment, or the extension of the productive powers of labor as such—were the motive and end in production (Marx 1964:144). The system of capitalist production was like a sorcerer which had conjured whole populations of human beings out of the ground: it had placed the forces of nature under human control; it had revolutionized technology, transportation, and the like; but it had lost control over the productive forces thus unleashed (Marx and Engels 1962:1:39). The capitalist system had converted the forces of production into forms of private property for a few individuals, while the majority had been reduced to abstract individuals by having been robbed of all real substance of life (Marx 1964:174). The central contradiction of the capitalist system, and the reason for its inherent instability, was that the system of production and the system of appropriation were running at cross purposes: production was social and public, while appropriation was individual and private.

Private property over accumulated labor (in the form of plant, equipment, machinery, resources, etc.) converts it into a means for the exploitation of living labor, i.e., into capital. Because capitalist production is production for profit rather than for use, as labor revolutionizes its own productivity and efficiency through every improvement in the technology and scale of production, it also creates the means by which it becomes relatively superfluous itself; it creates an industrial reserve army of unemployed and under-employed workers. Thus what might otherwise be viewed as accumulated productive power becomes, because of the peculiar logic of capitalist production, accumulated destitution, want, poverty, and misery. Overpopulation becomes the cloak which hides the contradictory nature of capitalist production (Marx 1906:692–709).

Population growth does exert a pressure, but its pressure is not applied on the means of subsistence. It is applied rather on the means of employment. The means of subsistence increase whenever there is an increase in productive power, however minimal; the means of employment increase only when there is an increase in machine power and capital.

Total capital has two main components: constant capital and variable capital. Another term for constant capital is fixed capital. Constant capital consists of plant, equipment, machinery, etc. Variable capital is that portion which pays for the employment of living labor. Fixed capital is the means of production; variable capital is the means of employment. Marx refers to the ratio of fixed to variable capital as the "organic composition of capital." This ratio can be taken as an indicator of the scale and technical sophistication of industry; it is also an indicator of its productivity.

As the organic composition of capital increases with every step in the development of the technical sophistication and scale of the productive process, the two forms of capital do not change in the same direction in relative terms. Fixed capital increasingly accounts for a larger proportion of total capital, while decreasing shares are required to pay for the employment of labor—in *relative* terms. Thus if the productive process is conceived as beginning with half of the total capital taking a fixed form, and the other half taking a variable form, the successive ratios of fixed to total capital, and of variable to total capital, are as shown in Table 2.

In absolute terms both forms of capital might increase. But increasingly larger inversions of fixed capital are required to provide employment for equal contingents of laborers: fewer and fewer laborers are needed for equivalent increases in fixed capital. Hence as the organic composition of capital increases, a certain portion of the labor force is rendered relatively superfluous. It is displaced because of the greater productive power of a higher ratio of fixed to variable capital: by the increasing ability of fewer and fewer workers to produce more and more through more efficient technology, greater refinement in the specialization of labor, and through the economies of large scale production. Increased accumulation of capital does not automatically mean increased employment, nor does an increase in the working class automatically mean increased labor.

Overpopulation is not absolute; it is relative to increasing productive power and to increasing capital accumulation. The problem is not that the laboring masses overreproduce but that the population grows faster than the capitalist system of production can stand. The industrial reserve army of the unemployed and the under-

Table 2. **The Marxian Inverse Ratios**

Steps in the Organic Composition of Capital	Ratio of Fixed Capital to Total Capital	Ratio of Variable Capital to Total Capital
1/1	1/2	1/2
2/1	2/3	1/3
3/1	3/4	1/4
4/1	4/5	1/5
5/1	5/6	1/6
6/1	6/7	1/7
7/1	7/8	1/8
8/1	8/9	1/9

Source: Karl Marx, *Capital* (New York: Modern Library, 1906), p. 690.

employed is actually an essential part of the process of capitalist production. During the prosperity phase of the business cycle it provides a readily available pool of labor power which can be easily put to work. During the crisis or depression phase it serves to keep in check the aspirations of the employed sector of the labor force (Marx 1906:691–701). Moreover, the reproduction of each new generation of laborers is part and parcel of the process of capitalist production. The laborer's subsistence wages include both what is necessary to restore the worker's energies from day to day—food, clothing, shelter—and what is necessary to reproduce a new generation of laborers (Marx and Engels 1962:1:464).

Engels acknowledged the existence of an abstract possibility that the earth's population would one day reach a saturation point. He was also aware of the fact that the populations of France and of lower Austria had already, quite spontaneously, developed methods of regulating human reproduction, and he had no doubt that a communist society would be the most likely to develop effective programs to achieve those ends through planning (Meek 1971:120).

However, Engels regarded the concern with overpopulation current in his day as at best premature and at worst ridiculous. No one had yet proven that the productivity of the soil could increase only arithmetically, as Malthus claimed. Although the total land area was limited, labor power increased as the population increased. The advances made possible by the progress of science and technology were as limitless and as rapid as the rate of population growth (Meek 1971:63). The Valley of the Mississippi was as yet largely unsettled, and the whole population of Europe could be accommodated within its boundaries. Only about a third of the world's land area had been brought under cultivation, and the productivity of that third could be multiplied six-fold by methods already available. Mass production in industry and large scale agriculture were everyday showing a capacity to overwhelm the market with products, and their impacts were just beginning to be felt (Meek 1971: 63, 119).

No, the fundamental problem which lay at the source of poverty was not population growth but private control of the means of production. The emphasis placed on overpopulation was a diversion born out of the effort to avoid coming to terms with that fundamental issue. If poverty-related factors were bringing the lives of the poor to a premature end, it was not because private property was, as Malthus claimed, the most natural of positive laws, but because it was a most unnatural negation of the role of labor in the self-creation of humans and of the collective nature of that labor (Lewis 1965:47–48). If commodities went unsold and inventories accumulated during gluts in production, the reason was not a lack of effective demand, as Malthus claimed. Actually, demand rises just before a crisis. The problem was not one of relative underconsumption due to lack of purchasing power; it was rather one of relative overproduction due to the expropriation of surplus value in the form of profit. Profits are unpaid labor, not a value added to the process of production. They are secreted out of the process of production, not tagged onto the cost of production as a condition for exchange. What is produced could be consumed; the problem is that production is carried out for profit, not for use (Meek 1971: 32–34).

Malthus had actually advanced the best argument for carrying out a thoroughgoing reorganization of the productive process on an entirely different basis than production for the profit of the capitalist class. The system of capitalist production had degraded the producers of wealth to the level of commodities for sale in the market. Because of the peculiar conditions imposed by capitalist ownership of accumulated labor and by capitalist control of the productive process, work had been converted from the condition for human self-development and self-fulfillment into a means for the exploitation, domination, repression, mortification, agony, displacement, destitution, and neglect of living labor (Meek 1971:62).

To Marx, labor is but another word for value (Marx and Engels 1962:1:77), and labor is a creative force: it always produces more than it can consume, more than is necessary for mere survival. Now, the value of any commodity is the labor which would be necessary to replace it, and since under capitalism labor is reduced to a commodity, its value becomes mere subsistence. Thus alienated, labor under capitalism receives its full value in wages when it receives subsistence wages. When the capitalist hires a worker and pays a day's wages, he buys the worker's labor power for a day. The wages pay for that part òf the day's product which covers the cost of subsistence. The capitalist keeps the surplus over subsistence. Hence the struggle which is necessary in order to restore to labor control over its full creative potential is not and cannot be a mere struggle for existence, i.e., subsistence; it is rather a struggle for control of the means of production, the means of enjoyment, and the means of fulfillment. It is a struggle for control of the full creative powers of labor, for the sake of the full development and fulfillment of the creative powers of labor. The struggle for existence is a struggle which adapts to the conditions of capitalist exploitation; it divides the laboring masses and forces them to compete with one another. The class struggle is a struggle to abolish the status of labor as a commodity; it seeks control over the means of production in order to restore to labor control over its full power to create value. The struggle for existence ends in capitalism as usual; the class struggle ends in socialism, in man's freedom to be himself and to develop himself (Marx and Engels 1962:1:463–66; Meek 1971:208–12).

Marx regarded sex as the most natural relation between men and women; however, he rejected sexuality devoid of personality. The degree to which man and woman related to each other as persons and needed each other as persons was an index of the degree to which sexuality had developed into a self-consciously human activity. He rejected prostitution in all its forms, regardless of whether it was prostitution to private individuals or to a community of buyers

(Fromm 1969:126). Engels was later to argue that prostitution arose along with wage labor and slave labor, and that all of them emerged as correlates of widening property inequalities (Engels 1972:130).

In the *Manifesto*, both Marx and Engels argued that the bourgeois family is based on capital and private gain; that bourgeois husbands see their wives as instruments of production; that they take the greatest pleasure in seducing each other's wives, as well as the wives of the proletariat; that there is established in practice a system of community of wives involving both private and public prostitution; that such a system operates under the cover of hypocrisy, being open exclusively to the bourgeois; that modern industry tears up family ties among the proletariat, reducing their children to the status of instruments of labor and articles of commerce; hence that family life is in practice denied to the proletariat. With the abolition of private property, there would also be an abolition of the community of wives in its covert form and an openly legalized community of women would replace the hypocritically concealed form of that community. Since such a community was already in existence under concealment, Marx and Engels regarded the question of whether or not it was possible as a dead issue (Marx and Engels 1962:1:50–51).

In a later work, following Lewis Henry Morgan, Engels argued that monogamy is only the latest form that the marriage institution has taken. The purpose of this institution is to guarantee the reproduction of children of undisputed parentage. The necessity for such an undisputed identity became an issue with the emergence of inequalities based on private property under the control of males— usually in the form of cattle—who wanted to be certain that their wealth would be inherited by their offspring. Such an identification was neither possible nor necessary as long as both men and women had access to multiple mates. Women were the only identifiable parents under varying forms of multisided liaisons, and women could afford to remain uncertain about the father's identity as long as the requirements of child rearing were provided for by a primitive communism. Since the land and its products were owned by the women, and since inheritable valuables were passed down through the mother line, women were relatively secure. These conditions changed as natural selection led to a progressive broadening of the incest taboo (which tended to restrict the number of possible mates) and as the primitive economy gave way to a more complex specialization of labor, along with more highly developed means of production. As inequalities in property became more pronounced, multisided unions became more and more troublesome for the women.

Viewed historically, monogamy has tended to mean monogamy (exclusive cohabitation) for the female only, since it has coexisted with multisided unions on the male side. Engels spoke of modern individual sexual love as the greatest moral advance which was made possible by monogamy; however, he sounds less certain as to whether this advance is to be more fully realized within monogamy, parallel to it, or in opposition to it (Engels 1972:128–44).

Engels singled out two chief characteristics of what he called proletarian marriage: it was not monogamous in the historical sense of monogamy for the female only; it was free from "hetaerism" (the male consorting with unmarried females) and from adultery (Engels 1972:135).

Since the monogamous family is only the latest form taken by the family, the question arises as to whether or not this form of the family is permanent. Both Morgan and Engels recognize that full equality of the sexes has not been achieved under monogamy and that further improvement along these lines is possible. Both also recognize that the form of the family is subject to change if and when its present form fails to meet social requirements (Engels 1972:146).

5.

Contextual Analysis of Concepts:
"Scarcity," "Exploitation," and "Poverty"

To Malthus, "scarcity" means that there is a basic imbalance between the human capacity to reproduce and multiply its own wants and the corresponding capacity to produce the means and resources necessary for their satisfaction. Hence scarcity is relative to a tendency of human beings to reproduce beyond the means available for their support. Every step in human reproduction which results in population increase would thus tend to magnify scarcity. Therefore, scarcity comes down to the existence of a constant tendency of human beings to produce an oversupply of their own numbers, and the magnitude of this tendency is measured in terms of the means and resources available to supply the population with the necessities for subsistence. This scarcity, according to Malthus, is variously rooted in (1) the unequal operation of the laws of human nature with respect to the attraction between the sexes and the need for food, (2) the law of diminishing returns on additional increments in capital investments, and (3) the impossibility of indefinite population increase within a limited territory.

To Marx "exploitation" meant that within historically given social systems, such as feudalism and capitalism, the institutionalized method of appropriating the products of labor, namely, private ownership of the means of production, permitted the appropriation of the surplus produced over and above subsistence needs (in the forms of rents and profits) for purposes other than its use by the laboring classes. Exploitation is, then, an activity which conditions the process of production in such a way that the criterion for its continuation as an activity is not that it continue producing use values, but rather that it make available profits and rents for the owners of the means of production. Exploitation is an activity responsible for the starvation of human beings in the midst of plenty; it is responsible for unemployment where there is no lack of work that needs to be done or the means to do it with. Exploitation is a purpose added to and imposed upon the process of production: the utilization of labor and its products by the landowning class for the landowning class and by the capitalist class for the capitalist class. The existence of exploitation as an activity is contingent upon the existence of institutionalized class antagonisms and class rule.

Exploitation is the source of a redundant population of unemployed workers. The existence of this redundant population—the industrial reserve army—is not the result of an absolute and universal law of population increase, but is relative to the practice of class exploitation within historically specific social systems. The size of this surplus population is measured in terms of the size of the industrial reserve army of the unemployed and the underemployed.

Malthus conceived of poverty as a condition of life which involved real sufferings for those affected by it. The lives of the poor were influenced by a number of causes, all of which tended to shorten life expectancy: bad and insufficient food and clothing, bad nursing of children, excesses of all kinds, unwholesome occupations, exposure to the seasons, severe labor, large cities and industries, diseases, epidemics, infanticides, plagues, famines, and war.

Marx concurs with the view that poverty is a condition of life which involves distress, misery, agony of toil, mental degradation, ignorance, and he adds slavery, brutality, hunger, a lightless mortuary of a house (where the very air the worker breathes is the mephitic breath of plague given off by civilization) which, nevertheless, requires the payment of rent. A life lived in poverty is a life wherein neglect, insecurity, dirt, and putrefaction become the very elements of life. Poverty reduces a human being to the level of a laboring animal who finds tedium and mortification rather than fulfillment in work. For the poor, work becomes forced labor which denies their humanity rather than asserting it, and in exchange for such degradation only their barest needs—their subsistence needs—are met.

Marx and Malthus agree that poverty involves insufficient or low quality food and clothing and unsanitary living conditions. They agree that it involves severe and prolonged labor, unemployment, or underemployment, as well as unwholesome occupations; they agree that the poor have not been well informed, that redundancy is a state of life peculiar to the poor, and that poverty cannot be resolved through charity. They agree, finally, that poverty seriously affects life chances in terms of mortality rates and life expectancies. Fundamental disagreement arises on the matter of how to explain poverty. Malthus places the blame on nature and on vice; Marx points to a basic flaw in the institutional structure of society.

The most clearly identifiable level of living which is recognized in both theories as being indicative of poverty and which is, therefore, a means of comparison between them, would appear to be a standard of living which includes that part of the population living below the margin of subsistence. What this level of living amounts to under historically specific conditions remains to be seen.

6.

Cognitive Conclusions

The views of Malthus, on the one hand, and of Godwin, Marx, and Engels, on the other, do indeed constitute opposing perspectives from which it is possible to study the phenomenon of poverty. The characteristics of poverty which are common to both views are: insufficient and low quality food and clothing, overexposure, unsanitary living conditions, unwholesome occupations, severe and prolonged labor, unemployment and underemployment, diminished life chances, high mortality rates and low life expectancies, high reproductive rates, misinformation, and ignorance.

If poverty is viewed from the standpoint of scarcity theory, a few parameters are found to be of greater explanatory relevance with reference to the above list of subcategories. These parameters are: population growth (which in turn depends on fertility, mortality, and migration), the portion of the total population in the labor force, the ratio of that portion of the population which might be classified as dependent, the supply of food available and its rates of increase *vis-à-vis* the population, the amount and quality of housing available, the extent and level of education of the population, the character and structure of marriage and the family among the poor, the state of contraceptive practices, and the population policies implemented by the government.

If poverty is seen from the standpoint of exploitation theory, the following parameters are of greater explanatory relevance: trends in the organic composition of capital; trends in capital accumulation and in the concentration of ownership in agriculture, industry, and commerce; trends in finance; trends in productivity; trends in income distribution (in wages, profits, and rents); cyclical crises; and unemployment.

We now turn from a consideration of two known theoretical points of view to the available factual knowledge under the specific conditions of one selected society: Mexico. In this connection, the broadest questions we are concerned with answering are the following:

(1) What portion of the Mexican population lives below the margin of subsistence?

(2) What is the balance of forces (reproductive and productive) between population needs, on the one hand, and means of subsistence, on the other?

(3) What are their respective rates of growth, past, present, and predicted, and why?

(4) What specific form does private ownership of the means of production take in Mexico?

(5) What portion of the Mexican population is unemployed, or underemployed, and why?

(6) What are the trends in unemployment and underemployment, past, present, and predicted?

(7) What are the trends in land and capital concentration in Mexico?

(8) What are the trends in income derived from profits and rents?

(9) What relation is there between the latter trends and the incidence of business cycles?

(10) What relationship exists between business cycles and the size of the unemployed labor force?

(11) What is the relationship between the unemployed labor force and the population living below the level of subsistence?

These and other related questions will be the subject of our subsequent inquiries into Mexican society. As we pursue these inquiries, our efforts will be kept in a clearer perspective if we keep in mind the central thesis of this study: facts gathered under the guidance of concepts taken from antagonistic theories of poverty will not be neutral as regards the relative explanatory power of the theories in question.

PART TWO

Poverty in Mexico:
Its Extent and Depth

7.

Introduction

So much distance, so many roads,
So many different flags,
And the poverty is the same,
The men who wait are the same.

From the song "Milonga de Andar Lejos."

Two specific features of Mexican social structure make that society a strategic ground for testing the relative explanatory adequacy of Malthusian and Marxian perspectives on poverty. First, in 1970, Mexico's population grew at a rate of 3.4 per cent per year. This rate was on a par with the average for the region which shows the world's highest rates of population growth: Central America. Only two nations showed a rate of population growth higher than Mexico's in 1970; they were Costa Rica with 3.8 per cent and Kuwait with 8.2 per cent per year. India's rate of population growth during that same year was considerably smaller: 2.6 per cent per year (Population Reference Bureau 1971:1). Also, according to a study of income distribution carried out in 1950, the wealthiest 20 per cent of Mexico's families received 60 per cent of the income; while in India, 20 per cent of the families received 55 per cent of the income (Navarreté 1960:87–88). This finding was corroborated ten years later by the economist Reynolds (Reynolds 1970:75).

Despite its 1910 Revolution, Mexico has a distribution of income which is more unequal and more concentrated than is the case in several Latin American countries which have not had a comparable revolution. Considering first the 10 per cent of the population which

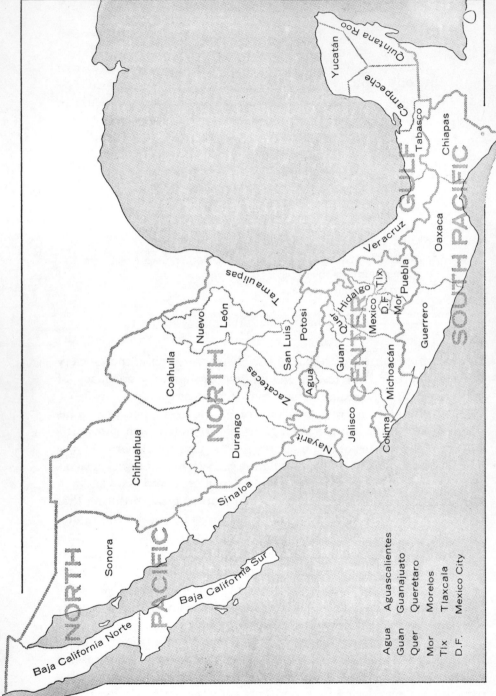

Map 1. **Statistical Zones of Mexico**

Agua Aguascalientes
Guan Guanajuato
Quer Querétaro
Mor   Morelos
Tlx   Tlaxcala
D.F. Mexico City

had the highest incomes in 1960, in a few selected Latin American nations, we find the shares of income to have been as follows: Mexico, 49.9 per cent; Argentina, 40.9 per cent; Brazil, 45.0 per cent; Colombia, 42.7 per cent; and Venezuela, 40.7 per cent. Considering now the 20 per cent of the population with the lowest incomes in 1960 we find the following distribution: Mexico, 4.2 per cent; Argentina, 5.2 per cent; Brazil, 4.2 per cent; Colombia, 5.9 per cent; and Venezuela, 4.0 per cent (Tello 1971:635).

If Mexico's population were to continue growing at the present rate, its numbers could be expected to double within approximately twenty-one years (Population Reference Bureau 1971:1). But these rates have not remained constant. During the last half century they have shown a fairly steady upward climb, having risen from slightly negative rates of growth during and immediately following the revolution to 1.6 in 1930 and to 2.8 in 1950 (Banco Nacional de Comercio 1970:31). The half-century since the revolution seems to have brought into existence conditions which permit Mexico's population to increase in a manner which seems to be unprecedented within Mexico's recorded history.

Students of the standard of living prevailing among Mexico's poorer classes appear to be in agreement that the lot of the majority of Mexico's population, that is, the lot of the poor and especially that of the rural poor, remains about the same as during colonial days, having changed little or not at all since Independence (Mendieta 1946:161–63). The traditional gulf between Mexico's richer and poorer classes led the naturalist Alexander von Humboldt to describe Mexico as "the country of inequality" at the turn of the nineteenth century. A contemporary student of the contrast between wealth and misery in Mexico admits that the Mexico of today is not what it was fifty or a hundred years ago; nonetheless, the changes which have taken place during the intervening years, he notes, have not altered the fact that Mexico is still "the country of inequality" (Aguilar 1967:82–83).

One study based on a comparison of the level of living index estimated that 51.2 per cent of the 1950 population were still living on about the same material plane as existed during colonial times. In population centers smaller than 10,000, the percentage of persons living at that same level was estimated at 63.2 per cent (Whetten 1950:18).

The preceding facts indicate that both the rate of population growth and the relative intensity of class polarization approach extreme levels in Mexico. If poverty is primarily the result of overpopulation, Mexican data should tend to support that position. If, on the other hand, poverty is predominantly the result of capitalist exploitation, Mexican data should tend to support that position.

> If there were an effective law
> that protected our children,
> there would not be a hundred thousand
> on the streets begging for bread,
> time and time again.
>
> From the song "Los Niños Trabajadores,"
> by Judith Reyes

8.

The Extent of Poverty in Mexico

This chapter is concerned with determining the degree to which poverty might be said to exist in Mexico. This assessment includes these dimensions of poverty: subsistence income level, food consumption patterns, medical services, housing characteristics, literacy, trends in the purchasing power of the minimum salary, and rural and urban poverty conditions.

Mexico's Ninth General Census of Population reports that in 1970, 26.8 per cent of its population 12 years old and over was economically active. The total reported population for that year was in the neighborhood of 48.4 million people, and of these, close to 13 million people were active economically. Of these latter, close to 8.4 million people received incomes of less than 1,000 pesos per month. In relative terms, then, close to 64.3 per cent of the economically active population had monthly incomes below this level. Those earning incomes below 500 pesos compose about 40.2 per cent of the economically active population—somewhat over 5.2 million people. These figures do not take into account an undetermined percentage of the more than 1.3 million people who declared no income because they had no income to report. Whatever the case, the reporting agency makes the point that about 15 million people altogether (including dependents) "do not share in the benefits derived from the present stage of development" (Banco Nacional de México 1971c:157).

This 15 million does not include the approximately 3.1 million with incomes between 500 and 999 pesos, nor does it include their dependents. The report mentioned above considers these people to have been in a "relatively improved situation."

It should be noted, however, that a study of salaries and fringe benefits based on 1960 census figures spoke of an income of 1,000 pesos as being insufficient to "satisfy the basic necessities of subsistence" given the cost of living prevailing at that time (Sosa 1964: 277). Yet of the 15 million people mentioned above, approximately 9 million have incomes between 200 and 499 pesos per month. The remaining 6 million have incomes between 1 and 199 pesos per month.

It should also be noted that many of these people were employed for only short periods during the year. Approximately 2 million landless peasants and agricultural wage laborers have work only during the growing season. Approximately 1.6 million other people have access to employment for about six months out of the year. An additional 839,706 are reported to have employment for 7 to 9 months. The remaining 10.5 million can count on having income for 10 to 12 months (Banco Nacional de México 1971c:163).

During the week prior to the Census, over a fifth (20.6 per cent) of the country's inhabitants did not include meat in their diet for a single day. More than a third of them (37.6 per cent) had meat one day only, and more than half (56 per cent) of them had meat for only two out of seven days. In absolute terms this means that roughly 27.1 million inhabitants either ate no meat at all or did so for two days or less during the week. As regards the consumption of eggs, 23.2 per cent of the population had no eggs at all, and 44.4 per cent had eggs for two days or less. Milk consumption was found to be nonexistent during the interval in question for 38.1 per cent of the population (18.5 million people). Over 45 per cent had milk on two days or less. The absence of wheat bread consumption indicates adherence to indigenous dietary practices based on corn consumption. Over 11.3 million people (23.4 per cent of the total population) ate no wheat bread during that interval. More than 70 per cent of the population ate no fish at all during that interval (Banco Nacional de México 1971c:163).

What these figures seem to indicate is that, at the very least, the diet of about a fifth of the Mexican population is protein poor. Closer examination of the problem will show the situation of the poor to be more serious than simply a protein deficient diet.

An indication of the availability of health services in the country can be obtained from the distribution of medical personnel. Nearly half (47.2 per cent) of the nation's physicians were located in the Federal District of Mexico, where the ratio of doctors to population was 1 to 540. The ratio in the rest of the country showed an average of 1 per 1,690 inhabitants, while in some of the poorer states such as Zacatecas, the ratio was 1 for every 6,530 inhabitants (Banco Nacional de México 1970c:310).

It is estimated that if the federal government were to spend 600 million pesos annually on medical services, it would take 22 years to meet the services requested. An average annual expenditure of 665.7 million pesos was authorized for medical-aid construction during the 1960-70 decade, but only 51 per cent of this appropriation was actually spent. The explanation given for this fiscal thriftiness actually amounts to a pseudoexplanation (Banco Nacional de México 1970c:310). It was that "the institutions which handle the budget are not enabled to carry out large scale programs." It is not clear whether they are authorized to carry out only small scale programs or why this is the case, although this question might become clearer later on. Whatever the case, somewhat less than two-thirds (30.6 million) of Mexico's inhabitants have no access to medical attention from either public or private sources and must resort to "welfare (charitable) institutions" for such attention, a fact which seems to mean that for most of them there is no attention at all (Banco Nacional de México 1970c:309).

As for housing, the available estimates for 1970 do not agree (Banco Nacional de México 1970c:310). Taking the more cautious of the two existing estimates for that year, we find that 40.1 per cent of the houses were one-room units and that 37.4 per cent of the population lived in such houses. Nearly seven-tenths of the housing units had two rooms or less, and 66.8 per cent of the population lived in such units. In absolute figures this means that over 18 million people lived in one-room houses and that about 32.2 million people lived in houses having two rooms or less (Banco Nacional de México 1971c:165). An over-all housing shortage of 4.5 million units was estimated for 1970. This estimate includes both the number of new homes which need to be built and the number which need to be remodeled (Banco Nacional de México 1971c:165). In a nation where the total number of houses in 1970 was roughly 8.4 million this shortage must be deemed serious (Banco Nacional de México 1971c: 165).

But the housing problem does not end here. Thirty-nine per cent of the houses were entirely without plumbing. In an additional 22.2

Graph 1. **Purchasing Power of the Minimum Salary as a Percentage of the Index of Retail Prices**

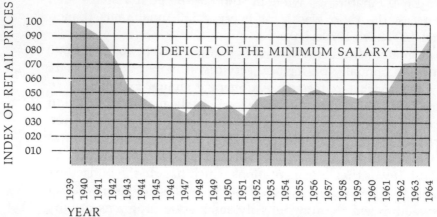

Source: González, "La Importancia Económica de Los Salarios Minimos," 10.

per cent of them water had to be obtained either outside the home but within the same building, or at a public faucet or hydrant. Both sewers and drainage were lacking in 58.5 per cent of the homes, and 41.1 per cent of the houses had earthen floors. Over two-thirds (68.2 per cent) of the houses lacked bathrooms. Despite the effort at electrification made by the government, 41.1 per cent of the houses still had no electricity. Thirty per cent of the houses had walls of adobe, and 5 per cent had walls of mud. In 44.2 per cent of the homes, meals were prepared with wood or charcoal for fuel. Finally, in 44.5 per cent of the houses, roofs were made of wood, palm-leaf thatching, or similar materials (Banco Nacional de México 1971c:165–66).

Despite the notable efforts being made to overcome illiteracy, 24 per cent of the population 10 years old and over was illiterate. In absolute terms Mexico had 7.7 million illiterates in 1970, and a total of 13.4 million inhabitants were lacking in any kind of formal schooling (Banco Nacional de México 1971c:155, 161). Indigenous populations which lack a knowledge of Spanish are largely "marginal" to the opportunities which modernization brings. Of necessity, such access is open to those with a knowledge of Spanish. In 1970 close to a million persons older than 5 years spoke only indigenous languages (Banco Nacional de México 1971c:156).

As early as 1934–35 the Mexican government began to fix minimum salaries in general terms for the country as a whole (Rodríguez 1966:10). In 1960, 39.6 per cent of the economically active population (4,491,702 workers) were subject to minimum salaries. This number comprised about 12.9 per cent of the total population of the country and 62.4 per cent of the population which declared incomes. These figures do not include people who, though self-employed, received lower incomes, nor do they include people who were unemployed through all but a few weeks of the year (Rodríguez 1966:9).

In 1960 the two-fifths of the workers (39.6 per cent) who were subject to minimum salaries received less than a fourth (24.1 per cent) of the total income paid to workers (Rodríguez 1966:9). Taking 1939 as the base period, when both the index of retail prices and the index of minimum salaries were equal to 100, it has been shown that the purchasing power of the minimum salary in 1960 was roughly half of what it was in 1939, while in 1964 a conservative estimate put it at close to nine-tenths of what it was during the base year (Rodríguez 1966:10). In fact, at no time following the base year did the purchasing power of the minimum salary again equal or exceed that of the base period, and in some years it showed a deficit below 100; for example, 61 and 65 per cent in 1947 and 1951 respectively (Rodríguez 1966:10). Also, during the period 1939-1964, a 10.6-fold increase in average minimum salaries was more than offset by a twelve-fold decrease in the purchasing power of the peso (Rodríguez 1966:10).

The Office of Technical Administration of the National Commission of Minimum Salaries has worked out family budgets which are considered to be representative (Camargo 1967:133). It is significant that this budget allocates three-fifths (60.1 per cent) of the total expenditures incurred by rural families in 1964 to food expenses. Rent takes up 9.5 per cent of the allocated expenses. The remaining 30.4 per cent of the expenses are allocated to clothing, shoes, school supplies, medical expenses, amusement, transportation, toiletries, and other items, with clothing and shoes accounting for about a third (10 per cent) of this last entry. In terms of pesos, the amounts allocated monthly to these items are as follows: food, 274.80; rent, 43.30; miscellaneous items above listed, including clothing and shoes, 138.99. The total amount of cash allowed for monthly expenditures amounts to 457.09 pesos (Camargo 1967:133–34).

An assessment of the purchasing power of minimum salaries in terms of the daily minimum family budget yielded interesting results. The analysis by rural areas showed the following (Rodríguez 1966: 12):

> . . . in 8 states minimum salaries cover the family budget . . . in ten it does not reach 90% and in 11 it covers from 90 to 99%. In Coahuila and Guanajuato there is an impressive deficit, because it barely covers 74% and 64% respectively. If we consider the price levels, the minimum salary probably barely covers 50% of the daily minimum family expenditures for 1965.

The analysis for urban areas indicated the following (Rodríguez 1966:12):

> . . . out of 29 entities considered, only Southern Baja California, Hidalgo, Mexico, Sinaloa, Sonora, Tamaulipas and Tlaxcala have a minimum salary superior to the minimum daily family budget. In nine entities the minimum salary does not quite reach 90% of the budget; and in Guanajuato it barely covers 76%.

It is evident that Mexico still has an "agrarian problem." It has been estimated that 50 per cent of the farming units included in the Census of 1960 qualify as infrasubsistence units. Their total production for that year was under 1,000 pesos per unit; taken together they accounted for only 4 per cent of the total agricultural production of the nation (González Salazar 1971:548). It has been estimated that the percentage of landless peasants in 1960 amounted to half of the total agricultural population and that their number already exceeded the total number of such peasants at the time of the Revolution of 1910, as well as the total for 1930. Over three-fourths (76 per cent) of the families headed by such field laborers are reported to have had, in 1960, average monthly per capita incomes of 59 pesos, while the per capita income for a third of such families was 43 pesos per month. Taken altogether, the agriculture wage workers are reported to have received only 8 per cent of the agricultural income in that same year (González Salazar 1971:548–49).

An article published in *El Trimestre Económico* in 1963 estimates that over 84 per cent (between 16 and 17 million) of the 19 million Mexican peasants produced for home consumption only and did not provide a market for industry (Navarreté 1963:584). One article

Table 3. **Annual Rates of Population Growth**

Decade	Urban* Population	Rural Population	Total Population
1930–40	2.22	1.49	1.73
1940–50	4.77	1.50	2.73
1950–60	4.89	1.51	3.08

*Localities with over 2,500 inhabitants.

Source: Raul Benítez Zenteno and Gustavo Cabrera Acevedo, *Proyecciones de la Población de Mexico, 1960–1980* (Mexico City: Banco Nacional de México, 1966), p. 57.

sums up the situation in rural Mexico as follows (Reyes 1969:146):

> The growing unemployment of the wage laborers and the fact that almost 80% of the farming units can be considered to be subsistence units, exhibits before us a landscape of poverty in the country which constitutes what *Licenciado* Gustavo Díaz Ordaz's government has defined as the Number One problem of Mexico.

With its agrarian problem still largely unresolved over sixty years after its 1910 Revolution, Mexico now has an urban problem which appears to be inextricably entangled with the rural one. An estimate of urban, rural, and total population growth rates for the three decades from 1930 to 1960 is shown in Table 3.

On the basis of the preceding figures it can be inferred that the population of both urban and rural areas tended to increase during the three decades from 1930 to 1960, with the rate of urban increase tending to be greater. In fact, the rate of urban increase was over three times faster during the 1940–60 interval. Moreover, the rural increase maintained itself at a fairly steady rate, while the rate of urban increase was relatively rapid, with a noticeable tendency of the rate of acceleration to slow down in the later years of the interval under consideration.

Had Mexico's urban centers continued growing during the decade of the sixties at the same rate as during the fifties, that is, at about 4.9 per cent per year, their population would have doubled in approximately 14 years (Population Reference Bureau 1971:1). What actually happened is that between 1960 and 1970 the number of inhabitants in Mexico's cities increased by 87 per cent, from a total of 10.5 million in the earlier year to 19.7 million in the latter year (Banco Nacional de México 1971a:23).

In 1970, 8.3 million Mexicans were reported to have been living in cities with populations between 100,000 and 500,000 (Banco Nacional de México 1971a:25). At the same time there were 11.5 million people living in cities with populations in excess of 500,000. Mexico had four such cities: Puebla, Monterrey, Guadalajara, and Mexico City (Banco Nacional de México 1971a:24–25).

Mexico City, with its large metropolitan area, is the most massive urban concentration center in the Mexican landscape. Its industrial, financial, commercial, political, and cultural centers give form to and set the pace for much of the daily life of the country. In relation to Mexican society, Mexico City is Chicago, New York, Washington, D.C., and Boston all wrapped into one. It is the repository of Mexico's achievements, problems, struggles, and dreams. Between 1960 and 1970 the total metropolitan population of Mexico's megalopolis increased from approximately 4,956,000 to 8,315,000 inhabitants (Banco Nacional de México 1971a:24).

One of the "cities" which forms part of this metropolitan complex is Netzahualcoyotl, a strip city which in 1970 was reported to have had, according to official census figures, a population of 571,035. Over and above this number, it has an estimated "floating" population of 200,000 people. Netzahualcoyotl stretches over a land area estimated at 70 square kilometers. Its population density appears to be in excess of 11,000 inhabitants per square kilometer (Banco Nacional de México 1970d:282). These people are living in housing units similar to those described earlier, i.e., one- to two-room units, built usually of adobe, thin partition materials, metal sheets, and wood. When bathrooms are available, and such cases are few, they are located outside. Water has to be obtained from taps which are available in all of the "colonies" (of which there are 47 containing 140,000 lots), but it is frequently contaminated with raw sewage. One study notes that "some areas receive potable water and have sewage disposal facilities, but with serious deficiencies: the two continually mix, raising the incidence of gastro-intestinal diseases, especially among children" (Banco Nacional de México 1970d:283–84).

There is a shortage of electricity but most areas of the town do get electricity, albeit from unauthorized sources: scores of unauthorized wires are reported to be attached to the cables of the electric company. Traffic in stolen goods is also reported to exist in some of these colonies (Banco Nacional de México 1970d:283). Also, the lack of classroom space is keeping a large number of school age children from attending school (Banco Nacional de México 1970d:283).

The outstanding characteristic of this town is said to be its living standards; it has been referred to as the residence of the underemployed (Banco Nacional de México 1970d:283):

> Most of the inhabitants lack any kind of training, for which reason they do marginal work in the Federal District, mostly services of all kinds, because the opportunities within the municipality are very limited. Some travelling salesmen and small artisans work here, and, on another level, the inhabitants work in the shops: pharmacies, tortilla shops, funeral homes and furniture shops (there are about 400 distributors).

Netzahualcoyotl has other problems. Among them are: (1) overcrowding—there are ten or more inhabitants per housing unit, (2) insufficient transportation facilities, (3) provisional marketing facilities lacking the minimum of services, where the goods sold are of the lowest quality, and where the traffic proceeds under highly unsanitary conditions (Banco Nacional de México 1970d:283–84).

The absence of census data for Netzahualcoyotl for 1960 may or may not be due to its mushroomlike emergence over a period of a few years (Banco Nacional de México 1971a:24; 1970d:282). Whatever the case, its 1970 population was large enough for some observers to view it as Mexico's fourth largest city.

Netzahualcoyotl was built on land which was originally at the bottom of the ancient Lake Texcoco (Banco Nacional de México 1970d:282). Up until about 1903, this lake stood in the way of Mexico City's expansion in an easterly direction, and drainage operations began at that time (Hayner 1968:169). During the rainy seasons these lands are still subject to flooding, and the available collectors of these brackish waters are reported to be insufficient to prevent flood damage (Banco Nacional de México 1970d:283).

Settlement of these lands is reported to have begun in the mid 1940's by migrants who settled there in search of employment. The land seems to have been held under several forms of tenure, having passed from *ejidal* and communal property to federal property to privately held land which came then to be used for speculative purposes (Banco Nacional de México 1970d:282). The land was then subdivided into lots, but it is not now clear who owns the several lots. Consequently, necessary urban services have not been provided, and the people are insecure and on the defensive. The situation is fraught with tension and is potentially very explosive (Banco Nacional de México 1970d:283–84).

Netzahualcoyotl is not unique. As many as three hundred proletarian colonies are reported to have been in existence at the periphery of Mexico City in 1955: "They covered 30% of the land area of the city. These neighborhoods make an almost complete circle around the outer part of the city with a two mile break on the west and another two mile break on the south" (Hayner 1968:176).

Oscar Lewis estimated that in 1956 nearly half of Mexico City's population lived in slums known as *vecindades.* He noted also that a number of beautification programs were being carried out in Mexico City, such as installing fountains, planting flowers along the principal streets, building more hygienic markets, and driving the beggars and vendors off the streets, all with a view to making the city more attractive for U.S. tourists. Lewis noted also that Mexico could not produce jobs for all its people; that about one million *braceros* had migrated to the U.S. seeking work between 1942 and 1955; that this figure did not include "wetbacks" who entered the U.S. illegally; and that chronic inflation, which accounted for a five-fold increase in the cost of living since 1939, was continuously squeezing the real income of the poor. Lewis also estimated that in 1956 about two-thirds of Mexico's population was inadequately fed, clothed, and housed (Lewis 1959:22–23).

On the basis of these facts it seems safe to conclude that an income of 1,000 pesos per month was not adequate for subsistence in Mexico in 1970, since by 1960 this figure was already considered to be insufficient, and its purchasing power can only have decreased considerably in the intervening decade. Yet in excess of half of Mexico's 1970 population were living below this income level.

It can be safely assumed that, at the very least, the diet of 20 per cent of Mexico's 1970 population is seriously lacking in animal proteins. It seems safe to assume also that the diet of nearly half of Mexico's population shows some degree of protein deficiency.

Nearly two-thirds of Mexico's population has no access to medical services. Roughly two-fifths of Mexico's 1970 population were living in one-room houses which had earthen floors and roofs made of wood or of palm leaves, and where meals were cooked with wood or charcoal. These houses were wholly lacking in plumbing. Roughly three-fifths of the housing units were lacking in bathrooms and drainage. In 1970, Mexico is estimated to have had a housing shortage amounting to 4.5 million housing units. Nearly a fourth of Mexico's population 10 years old and over was illiterate in 1970.

Nearly two-fifths of Mexico's economically active population was on minimum salaries in 1960. If the purchasing power of the minimum salary is set at 100 for 1939, it can be concluded that at no time during the interval 1939-1964 did the purchasing power of the minimum salary again rise to 100. In fact, in 1960 it was at roughly half the 1939 level. By official estimates approximately three-fifths of the rural family budget was spent on food in 1960. In most areas of Mexico the minimum salary is not sufficient to cover the family budget. In areas such as Coahuila and Guanajuato the situation of the workers on minimum salaries must be regarded as extremely desperate.

Approximately half of Mexico's farm units were classified as infra-subsistence in 1960, and over four-fifths of the farm units produce only for home consumption. Moreover, approximately half of Mexico's rural dwellers were landless in 1960.

As late as 1963 Mexico's official circles acknowledged rural poverty to be Mexico's number one problem and, at the same time, Mexico has a growing urban problem. From 1950 to 1960 Mexico's urban population grew three times faster than the rural. The urban population nearly doubled during the 1960-1970 decade. Proletarian "colonies" are mushrooming at the periphery of large cities, especially around the Federal District. On the basis of the available facts it must be concluded that living conditions in those colonies must be extremely trying.

The conclusion is therefore warranted that poverty does in fact exist in Mexico and that approximately half of Mexico's 1970 population was living under conditions which were either below or perilously close to a bare subsistence level. For the majority of these people life can be no more than a struggle for a subsistence which remains constantly beyond reach—a struggle which continuously saps human vitality.

> Passionate heart
> Disguise your sadness
> Disguise your sadness
> Passionate heart
>
> One who is born to misfortune
> From the cradle on begins
> From the cradle on begins
> To live a martyr's life

> From the Huastecan song
> "Soy soldado de Levita."

9.

The Depth of Poverty in Mexico:
A Case Study

This chapter seeks insight into the experience-world of a life lived under conditions of poverty in Mexico. The subject, Guadalupe Vélez, lived most of her adult life in one of the poorest slum neighborhoods in Mexico City (the Panaderos *vecindad*) and was the poorest resident in that *vecindad* in terms of every measure considered except religious images, where her collection stood out as one of the largest. One of the methodological peculiarities of the study of the life history is that in-depth understanding requires in-depth research, usually by a single observer. The materials for this chapter are drawn exclusively from the book *A Death in the Sánchez Family*, by Oscar Lewis.

The life of Guadalupe Vélez shows the influence of all of those destructive forces which bear most heavily on the lives of the poor: hunger, exposure, ignorance, illiteracy, lack of medical attention, disease, vice, demoralization, cruelty, violence, and high infant mortality rates. Her life also shows the influence of high reproductive rates and of redundancy arising from industrial concentration. Saddest of all is the fact that her culture found time in her life for daily church attendance at 4:00 a.m. in her early childhood years but no time or disposition to prepare her for the most elemental facts of her biology. The worship of God was all important, the understanding of elemental facts of her human nature not in the least. Hence the outstanding characteristics of her sexual life experience are ignorance, violence, and the double standard. These and other features of her biography are the subject of the following pages.

49

When Guadalupe recalled her childhood she did so with a sense of martyrdom: trauma, victimization, and privation were the dominant experiences of her life. She was one of eighteen children born to a family of Guanajuato; only seven had survived past the first year of life. Her parents were religious and had been married in church; they eked out a living by selling sweets in the plaza. At three in the morning the children were awakened to haul water for the garden; at four there was mass to attend. Never had she been allowed to attend school or to play with other children. Instead, she did the marketing and the cooking, babysat her younger brothers, and did other household chores. In fact, she had no childhood. To make matters worse, she grew up illiterate like her parents.

When menstruation began at age 12 she was in such darkness about her biology that it shocked and frightened her into hiding in a deep hole. She was afraid that when her parents found out she would be punished. When her mother learned what happened, she told Guadalupe not to worry, for it happened to everyone.

At age 13, a thirty-year-old neighbor man (Fidencio) abducted her at knife point, took her to a cave, and raped her. She bled profusely and was taken to his mother's house. She stayed in bed for fifteen days, until the bleeding stopped, without medical attention. Her father found her there, and being a man who believed that a girl was worth nothing after she lost her virginity, he gave Guadalupe a merciless beating which required another fifteen-day recovery period. Guadalupe was then forced to marry Fidencio in a church wedding.

Guadalupe's mother-in-law did not like her and forced her to grind corn at a rate of six *cuartillos* a day and then to make large piles of tortillas to sell in the plaza. She became pregnant but did not know that this was what had happened. Instead she thought an animal must have gotten into her. Realizing her condition, Fidencio, off on a pass from the army, took her back from an aunt's house — where she had been taken on account of his mother's rejection of her — to his mother's house.

Fidencio himself beat her, and his mother kept her half starved on a diet of greens without salt. One day word came that Fidencio had been killed fighting with the army of the revolution, and at that time Guadalupe was told she had to return to Guanajuato. This expulsion was followed by a number of further hardships and tragedies, including a lonely walk to Guanajuato carrying her child during the rainy season—at which time they came close to dying from hunger and drowning in a flooded river. She also learned that her older brother had been killed while defending a friend, that her father had died from grief and anger, and that the whole family had moved to Mexico City.

Guadalupe followed her family to Mexico City. When she arrived she was so emaciated and ragged that her mother did not recognize her. When she finally did recognize her, she could not hold back her tears.

While the family was rooming with an aunt in Mexico City, Guadalupe and her sister Lenore helped the family income by selling spiked coffee at a corner stand. This was against the law, and Guadalupe ended up in jail three times. Subsequently Guadalupe changed jobs. She and a friend were then tricked into going to a brothel. At first she did not understand what kind of a place it was. She had been accustomed to sleeping on a mat on the floor all her life; since this place had beds she could not see how it could be bad.

When her son was five years old, her mother-in-law asked to be allowed to borrow him to see whether her remaining son would stop drinking with the child around. Instead the child was turned against his mother and would slam the door on her. He himself became a drunkard and later died in a drunken binge.

By this time Guadalupe had suffered so much from her previous marriage that she vowed never to marry again. She then met Alfredo and fell in love with him, and he left his wife and child for her. He then became a lieutenant in the revolutionary army, and she followed him to Matamoros. Alfredo turned out to be a jealous man. He chased other women but would not allow Guadalupe to as much as look at other men; when she spied on him he beat her. He left Guadalupe when she became pregnant. To ward off starvation Guadalupe took in washing. After this experience she found herself unable to believe in anybody.

When Salvador, her second son, was born she found it difficult to support herself and her child. For a while she cooked for the army. When the army was disbanded she first tried a job in Veracruz, which paid her nothing. There she fell ill with malaria; swollen and shaking with chills she returned to Mexico City.

Her family had been forced to move out of the room they had shared earlier with a relative. They then found a room they could occupy for four pesos per month plus janitorial services. It was covered by a half roof, and they got wet when it rained.

In the process of recovering her health Guadalupe acquired a taste for alcoholic beverages. She later found a job making tortillas. At this point the family began to share a room with her brother Pedro and his common-law wife.

At about age thirty Guadalupe met Ignacio. He sold newspapers and saw her every day. They became sweethearts and set up house-keeping as man and wife. Since she had vowed not to marry again, she refused to marry Ignacio. Together they got into the habit of drinking pulque every night, and Salvador grew into his teens with a taste for it. Salvador was later killed by a man who ran off with his common-law wife.

With Ignacio she suffered hunger on rainy days, since on such days he could not sell newspapers. At one time he left her for two years to go with another woman. In fact, Guadalupe was convinced he had seven women besides her but felt she was the only one who could stand him. When Ignacio died, she accepted Gaspar as her common-law husband.

All of Guadalupe's brothers—with the exception of one who died from typhus—died from drink. Even her father was drunk when he died. Her sister Lenore died while pregnant with her sixth child, and drink is suspected to have contributed to her early end at twenty-eight. Guadalupe's mother died of cancer, and Guadalupe herself died of intestinal cancer.

Commenting on her death in particular and about death among the poor in general, one of Guadalupe's nieces (Consuelo Sánchez) says (Lewis 1969:35):

I have never been able to accept death the way it comes to people in my class. We are all going to die, yes, but why in such inhuman miserable conditions? I've always thought there was no need for the poor to die like that. Their struggle is so tremendous . . . so titanic . . . no, no, it isn't fair. They can be saved. I refuse to resign myself to death in that tragic form.

She died on the Day of the Dead, and as was her custom, she had prepared for the visit of the souls of her dead relatives with an offering of candles, water, and flowers.

According to her common-law husband's account (Gaspar) she had risen early to sweep the *vecindad's* courtyard and to help a friend of hers sell *chinchol*, following which, being ill, she went to bed. Thereupon her husband got up and told her to get up— even if it were to do no more than to sew a button on his jacket for him. To this her reply was, "Soon, I'll do it soon" (Lewis 1969:78). He then left for the market and upon his return a friend of his came running to tell him, "Lupita is dead" (Lewis 1969:78). In conversation with Consuelo, crying, he said (Lewis 1969:78):

> She's gone and left us, Señorita Consuelo . . . . Do you know how much I had in my pocket when I found her stretched out on the floor? Twenty *centavos*. That was all I had. . . . God, not even enough for a bus . . . nothing for a doctor, or anything.

Gaspar then walked to the police station (for an hour and a half) where he was told that his case was not one for the police. This was followed by several trips back and forth to the same places, for he did not know his way around the various offices.

Consuelo asked Gaspar why Guadalupe had not been admitted to the hospital on a pass she was to receive from her physician. His reply was that either there were no beds available or none would be given them on account of their not having money. Straining to control his grief Gaspar added (Lewis 1969:79):

> Where was I going to get the money from, *Senorita* Consuelo? I was without work. There is a lot of competition now, and my trade has been made cheap [Gaspar was a shoe repairman]. Wherever you go downtown you can see the boxes of cheap shoes. They offered me fifty *centavos* a pair for nailing shoes and I am better off selling alcohol here. Doña Ana pays me two *pesos* a day for selling little bottles of her stuff out in the street and that's what my old lady and me were living on. But even so we had everything pawned . . . everything we ever bought: the

Table 4. **Funeral Expenses (in pesos) of
            Guadalupe Sánchez**

Casket	400.00
Hearse	75.00
Flowers and candles	20.40
Food and liquor	Unspecified
High Mass	30.00
Total funeral expenses	525.40+

iron, my *viejita's* dress, even my working tools. We had nothing at all. And in the hospital they wanted five *pesos*, then ten *pesos!* There we would go, my little old woman and I, step by step . . . she could hardly walk, but we kept on. When the pain took hold of her she would just lean against the wall and say to me, "Look, man, I can't walk any more, I can't make it." And I would say to her, "Come on, don't give up. Aren't you a strong woman? Am I not here, or what?" And on we would go again, step by step.

Guadalupe was sixty-two when she died. Funeral arrangements were left in the hands of Gaspar, Manuel, Roberto, and Consuelo Sánchez. Gaspar sold his possessions to help defray the costs of the funeral, which according to Manuel "was the very poorest there is. She went second class right to the end" (Lewis 1969:92). The funeral expenses are shown in Table 4.

It is not entirely clear how the money was raised, because some of it was used for other purposes, and there was no close accounting of it. It is clear though that Roberto's godmother lent 250.00 pesos for the purpose. Manuel picked up 100.00 pesos by taking up a collection among friends with the help of two close friends. Roberto collected an unspecified amount during the wake. Gaspar got drunk on one peso Roberto gave him to buy cigarettes for the wake. He also emptied the bottle of alcohol so that none was available when he fell and cut his head at the wake.

Soon after Guadalupe's death the presence of each of two priests was successively requested to administer last rites. Both declined on account of the distance. One of them lived only four blocks away. At the cemetery the officiating priest in charge of the chapel gave them a choice between a high mass, a funeral mass, and a plain mass at (according to Roberto and Consuelo) 35.00, 25.00, and 15.00 pesos, respectively. Manuel says he was asked to pay 30.00 pesos for this purpose and that he did so.

Consuelo notes that Guadalupe had purchased the right to a permanent grave but that, through some unspecified bungling on the part of Roberto, she ended up in a transient, reusable grave. In connection with funeral costs a point made by Consuelo stands out (Lewis 1969:77):

> There wasn't a family in that *vecindad* that could bury anyone without taking up a collection. One family had kept the body in the courtyard for several days while they went around begging for money. The body had begun to smell already. Roberto and I happened to go there and when we heard about it we went to Casa Grande to beg for money ourselves.

According to Consuelo, her Aunt Guadalupe's character had the qualities of gentleness, kindness, meekness, and absolute inability to rebel against the will of her masters. A readiness to serve and to obey were her outstanding qualities. With reference to Guadalupe's religious devotion Consuelo notes (Lewis 1969:37):

> She revered the designs of God, unquestioningly following His commandments. Saints become saints because of their suffering. Well, she suffered martyrdom from the time they named her Guadalupe.

Consuelo resented the neglect through which Guadalupe died and saw Mexico City's steel structures rising admist corpses—the corpses of peasants and poverty-stricken city dwellers who were being weakened and killed by starvation and by other means. Consuelo had little regard for official claims that Mexico was now a prosperous, economically solid, and politically strong country.

Consuelo summed up her aunt's life by saying (Lewis 1969: 36–37; emphasis mine) that Guadalupe

> had lived in a humble little nest full of lice, rats, filth, and garbage, hidden among the folds of the formal gown of that elegant lady, Mexico

City. In that 'solid foundation' my aunt ate, slept, loved, and suffered. She gave shelter there for a *peso* or two to any brother in misery, so she could pay her extravagant month's rent of thirty *pesos*. She swept the yard every day at six in the morning for fifteen *pesos* a month, unplugged the drains of the *vecindad* for two *pesos* more, and washed a dozen pieces of laundry for three. For three times eight cents, North American, she knelt at the wash tub from seven in the morning until six at night. Besides all this, to be sure of something to eat, she would go from neighbor to neighbor minding the children for a mother who had just given birth, washing dishes and diapers, or scraping floors with steel wood and sandpaper, in return for which she might receive a *taco* which she would share with her *compañero*, Gaspar, or with some other hungry person. *She even managed to find something to feed her dog.*

Oscar Lewis himself summed up this study by saying that Guadalupe's death illumined her life. Quoting from a Danish author, Lewis says, "Poor people don't belong in heaven, they have to be thankful if they can get into the earth" (Lewis 1969:x).

Guadalupe's life history provides the following insights:

Poverty reduced her life to depths of misery and darkness which defy belief. The poverty which constrained and constricted her life within narrow, subhuman limits shows dimensions which involve both a poverty of material means and a poverty of ideas and character.

Guadalupe suffered hunger throughout her life. The hunger of her earlier years was due, at least in part, to marital irresponsibility. That of her latter years was due mostly to other factors, including economic insecurity, occupational obsolescence, and exploitation through rents. Guadalupe did not receive medical attention when her needs for such attention were most pressing.

Guadalupe and her family experienced repeated evictions from crowded and rudimentary quarters, one of which lacked sufficient roofing to keep the family dry in rainy weather.

Guadalupe, like her parents before her, grew up illiterate. Although she was required to attend mass daily at 4:00 A.M. during her childhood years, she was allowed to grow up in total ignorance of the most elementary facts of her human biology. She was introduced to sex at age thirteen through forcible rape. After a brutal beating, in punishment for her role as a victim of rape, she was forced to marry the man who raped her. When she became pregnant she was unaware of her pregnancy as a pregnancy. Following her husband's death as a soldier of the revolutionary army Guadalupe resolved never to marry again. Her "marriage" to her first husband was decidedly not a marriage of love, free from economic considerations. It was, rather, as Godwin puts it, "an affair of property," a ritually solemnized and dignified sacrifice of her human capacity for love to force and to economic interests.

Guadalupe's second "lover," for whom she felt love, had affairs with other women but would not permit Guadalupe to even look at other men, and he beat her when she pried into his affairs. When Guadalupe became pregnant he abandoned her.

Guadalupe's second, third, and fourth unions were common-law arrangements. At one point her third husband left her for two years; at that time Guadalupe suspected him of having as many as seven women, and regarded herself as the only one who could stand him. This union lasted through most of her adult life.

Guadalupe's fourth husband was a shoe repairman out of work. His occupation had become redundant with the growing efficiency of shoe factories. Indications are he chose Guadalupe partly because, at her age, there was no danger of pregnancy.

Guadalupe was jailed three times for selling spiked coffee and she came close to a life of prostitution. Murder took the life of one of her brothers and of her second son. All but one of her adult brothers died from the effects of alcohol addiction, as did her first son.

Guadalupe's parents had eighteen children, eleven of whom (61 per cent) died during their first year of life.

Guadalupe's husbands subsisted through a number of activities, ranging from revolutionary activities to selling newspapers and peddling *chinchol*.

She herself worked up to the last moments of her harassed existence; her activities ranged from washing clothes and sweeping to baby sitting and selling *chinchol*, all of them in exchange for a bare and miserable subsistence. Her life span was long in comparison to that of her brothers and sisters, since she outlived all of them.

She died in such poverty that a collection had to be taken in order to bury her, and although she had made arrangements for a permanent grave, she ended up buried in a reusable one. A mass held at the cemetery "for the well being of her soul" required the payment of thirty pesos.

The poor are indeed lucky if they can stay in the grave.

PART THREE
Historically Specific Theories and Related Trends

10.

Scarcity and Poverty in Mexico:

Malthusian Theories

Existence is a circle, and we err when
from a desire to measure it we assign
the cradle and the grave to its extremes.

From the poem "In the Face of Death,"
by Manuel Acuña.

A January, 1970 article published by the Banco de México bears the title "Fifty Million Mexicans: Do We Face Overpopulation?" The article begins by noting that Malthusian theory has been the subject of much criticism and controversy because developed countries have shown a tremendous capacity to increase production. Since the end of the Second World War, however, Malthusian theories have acquired new currency, and the reason for this resurgence lies in the growing disparity in wealth between developed and underdeveloped parts of the world, coupled with more rapid rates of population growth in underdeveloped countries (Banco Nacional de México 1970b:10).

The position taken by this article is that Mexico is an overpopulated country, since nearly half of its population exists at the fringes of society and is surrounded by a "culture of poverty" which closes any opportunities for progress by creating a vicious circle of hunger, lack of education, sickness, and other hardships (Banco Nacional de México 1970b:11–12). The article further asserts that Mexico's current situation is serious. Although Mexico has consistently shown one of the highest rates of development among underdeveloped nations, further development is becoming more and more difficult, since every year for the next ten years 2 million new people will swell the population and 800,000 new jobs will have to be provided every year (Banco Nacional de México 1970b:13). The addition of each newborn child makes for a decrease in resources per capita and makes it increasingly less possible to give each child the help it needs. Also, population growth forces investments in what is called social "infrastructure," where returns on investments are either "negligible or nonexistent" for a long time and diverts capital from more productive investment channels (Banco Nacional de México 1970b: 12). Clearly, the position taken by the bank is that Mexico's problem of poverty stems from a scarcity of means to care for the population.

This argument turns out to be circular: There is poverty because there is scarcity, there is scarcity because there is overpopulation, there is overpopulation because there is poverty, there is poverty because there is scarcity . . . and so on. This perspective also tends to be one-sided, or at most, mention is made of a disproportionate distribution of income, while the institutional conditions and limitations on that distribution are left unexamined. This article, put out by what appears to be the most powerful bank in Mexico, represents in essence a contemporary restatement of the Malthusian point of view within the specific setting of Mexican society.

The vicious circle just mentioned has been presented in another form (Blanco 1965:105–107). Namely, the population explosion results in poverty, and the poor tend to show the highest population growth rates; hence, it is said, there is a danger that existing population growth trends might be fostering "genetic decay" and "racial erosion." The assumption here clearly is that the poor are either genetically or racially inferior, or at the very least, that current trends will lead in that direction.

This second article attacks the policy of *laissez faire; laissez passer!* in regard to what it calls the "primitive fertility" of the underdeveloped world, including Mexico, and urges adoption of a policy of demographic planning for the years 1965–70 that appeared in the March 1965 edition of *Revista de Economia*. As if to emphasize the recurring relevance and specific applicability to Mexican conditions of Malthusian population (read "scarcity") theory, the article begins with the condescending caption from André Gide, "Everything has been said, but since no one listens, it is necessary to say it again" (Blanco 1965:105).

Mexico, Blanco notes, contributes 1.5 million of the 40 million new dinner guests that the undeveloped world adds yearly to the already "scant and crowded dinner table of the world" (Blanco 1965:105). As the author states the point, "Mexico is contributing to the annual increment—always in geometric proportion as Malthus predicted—with nearly 1.5 million new dinner guests, even though this figure will continue increasing with each passing year" (Blanco 1965:105). It is emphasized that this rate of population growth is greater than that of India. The need on the part of the government to choose between quantity and quality of population is underlined, and the specter of the checks in the form of pitiless hunger, malnutrition, and sickness in the absence of such choice is raised.

Overpopulation, it is noted, has other consequences besides poverty, among them, environmental damage, unemployment, and criminality. This view derides the expectation that population problems can be solved through technological development, attacks the absurdity of national planning without population planning, and stresses the point that such planning would only, at best, spread the misery around.

Yet another study, which appears to be the most detailed and comprehensive to date on the relations between demographic growth and economic development and which is the product of collective effort under the auspices of El Colegio de México, offers a more balanced presentation of the evidence while providing plenty of grist for the Malthusian mills (Centro de Estudios Económicos y Demográficos 1970). This study emphasizes that population growth tends to retard economic development by absorbing capital formation and that such growth reduces the relative importance of the advances already made (Centro 1970:227). That is, population growth brings about a relative shrinkage of capital, whether in the form of goods, services, resources, or infrastructure (Centro 1970:227):

> The rate of growth of the population represents already a little more than half of the growth of the Gross Internal Product, and this amounts to saying that, in general terms, somewhat more than half of the gross capital formation must go to do no more than maintain the same income *per capita*.

The existence of a "surplus population" in Mexico is also defined in terms of the existence of population sectors that require goods and services without providing equivalent returns. The existence of widespread underemployment in all sectors of the economy is also emphasized in this connection (Centro 1970:231). The study grudgingly recognizes that such populations are entitled to goods and services, though not on an equal basis. This indicates that the term "surplus population" is used to mean exactly what it says (Centro 1970:232).

An important specific feature of Mexico's population growth is reported to be that, contrary to expectation on the basis of studies of the more developed countries, savings have shown a tendency to increase as the population growth rates accelerated, a fact which points to the influence of the existing pattern of ownership in industry and the related pattern of income distribution as well as to the wide disparities in saving potential which are related to those patterns. Certain consequences of population growth (namely, the availability of a wider market and of cheap labor that is employed at low, or even decreasing, real salaries), which are regarded by this study as positive contributions of such growth to industrial development, constitute conflicting claims on the market potential and on the purchasing power of the population (Centro 1970:228).

The simplest statement of the relation between population growth and poverty is that when the population increases in unequal proportion to the resources, services, and institutions available, the lot of the population will progressively deteriorate (Population Reference Bureau 1963:134). One fact that is inescapably driven home when one attempts to study scarcity theory within the specific context of Mexican society is that Mexican society is not an entirely self-contained and isolated context. It is rather a context that is intricately interwoven with commercial, industrial, financial, technological, and intellectual cross-currents at an international level. Within this international context the most overwhelmingly salient component for Mexico is "the colossus of the North," that is, the United States. A speech by Robert McNamara, former United States secretary of defense during the Viet Nam War, indicates an important strand in that contextual web. McNamara spoke on "Dynamic Misery" in his capacity as president of the World Bank. A central point in his talk was that population growth presented the greatest obstacle to economic progress and to social welfare among the world's poor nations, particularly in Latin America (Banco Nacional de México 1970b:10). The expression "dynamic misery" was intended to convey the view that population growth was widening and deepening at accelerating rates the vast inequality of wealth between the developed and under-developed nations of the world, in particular in Latin America, where population growth rates are typically high. A number of population-related myths came under attack. Among them: "cheap labor" is not really cheap but expensive; an untrained, unskilled population cannot be a source of strength; virgin lands cannot be made productive without capital investments (García 1969:155–56).

Besides creating poverty, population growth has been said to create land and job hunger and to threaten social stability (Corwin 1964:477). The reluctance of Mexico's planners to accept population control has been explained both in terms of a Mexican ethos that favors population growth and in terms of apprehension concerning the possible consequences of admitting that land reform and social welfare have failed to solve Mexico's problems (Corwin 1964:477–80).

A clear and unequivocal accusation has been made by Corwin to the effect that the Marxian explanation of poverty in terms of exploi-tation has been used to relieve Mexico's proliferating poor from responsibility for the consequences of their actions and to justify Mexico's compulsive need to grow—an urge said to have grown out of historic trauma (Corwin 1964:479). Also, Mexico's planners and intellectuals have been chided (Larkin 1970:319) for a one-sided emphasis on solving Mexico's problem of poverty through measures (such as irrigation, fertilization, industrial growth, and social justice) which systematically exclude effective efforts to limit population growth.

The Population Reference Bureau has published an article entitled "Mexico: The Problem of People." This article stresses the view that "liberal plans" in Mexico, must come to terms with a "reac-tionary" geography, since Mexico is regarded as being "a beautiful place in which to live but a hard place in which to make a living" (Fisher 1964:182–83). Only eight per cent of the country consists of level terrain. Overpopulation is said to be a consequence of the very effort to improve the living standards of the population, its inevitable result being social instability and inevitable doom through soil deple-

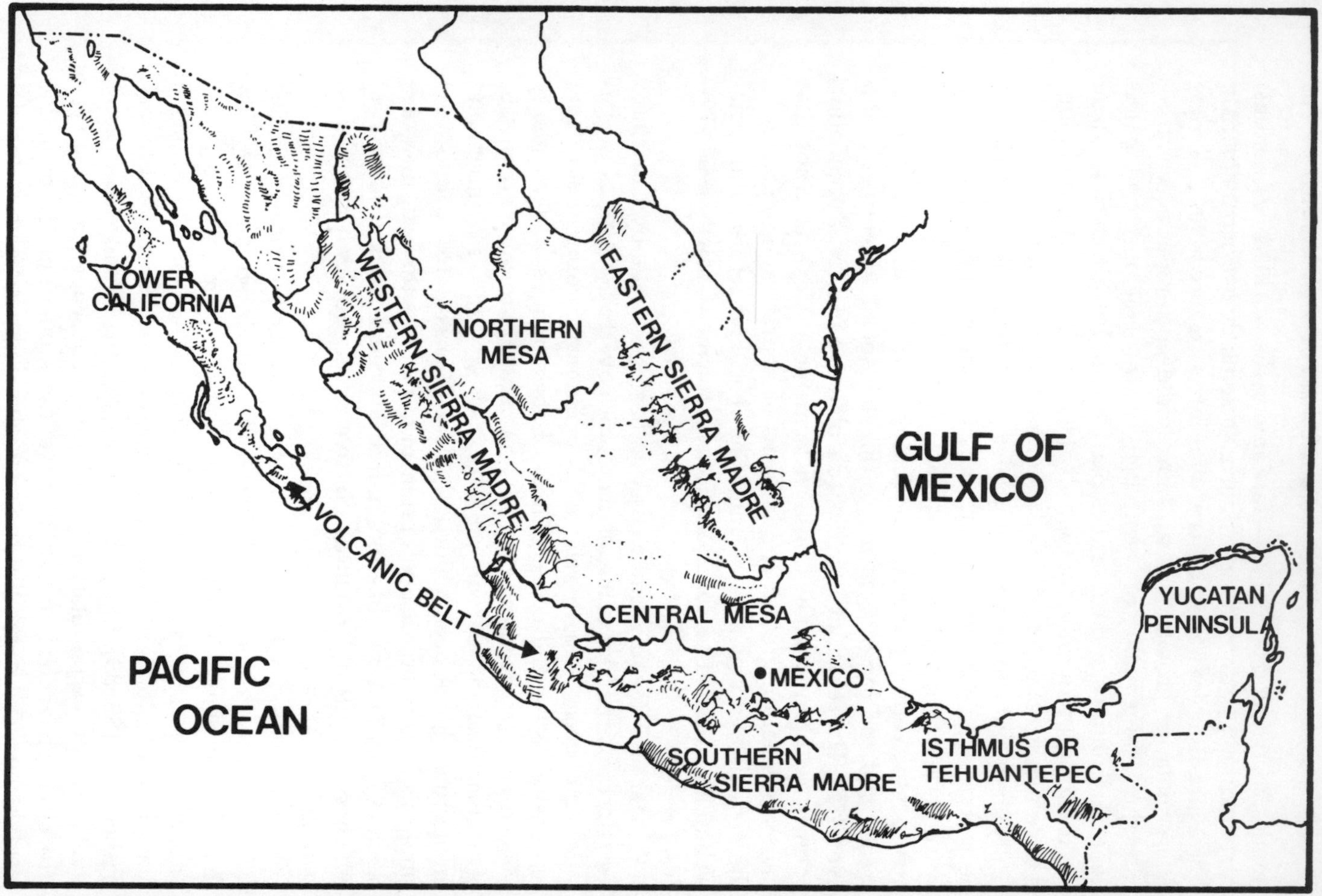

Map 2. Relief Map of Mexico

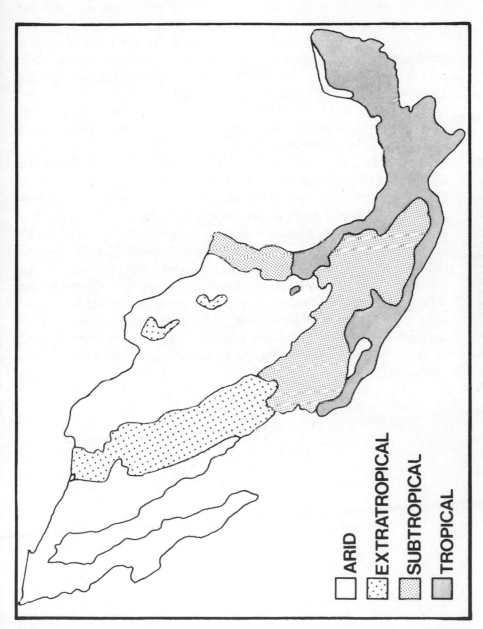

Map 3. Temperature and Humidity Zones of Mexico

ARID

EXTRATROPICAL

SUBTROPICAL

TROPICAL

tion. Emphasis is placed also on the need for a fourth "R," for reproduction, in Mexico's educational system (Fisher 1964:200–201).

The demographer Jaffe has argued that the coexistence of low productivity and underemployment in Mexico is of such magnitude that the production levels of 1955 could have been achieved by the 1940 population provided that a shift in population had occurred away from the less productive sectors and toward the more productive sectors. On this basis Jaffe concluded that Mexico did not need more people (Jaffe 1959:269–70).

Some adherents of exploitation theory nevertheless recognize the importance of population growth in creating scarcity (Alvarez 1966:168). They note also that the problem of overcoming poverty becomes cumulatively more difficult as population grows and as rates of growth accelerate. Alvarez y Lezama has estimated that if Mexico's government continues to use the ineffective methods it has used to improve the people's living standards in the past, in excess of one hundred years of effort will be required to solve problems whose solutions would be needed in the next five years. Moreover, he indicates that the problems created by population growth are of such magnitude that a collapse of major proportions is predictable unless steps are taken to solve the accompanying problems (Alvarez 1966:168).

11.

Trends Related to Scarcity
and Poverty in Mexico

Population. It took Mexico's population three centuries of colonial life and half a century of independent life to recover from the devastating impact of the conquest and to return to its pre-conquest population of nine million inhabitants (Fisher 1964:174; Pozas 1962: 249). Over sixty-five additional years (1870 to the late 1930's) were needed for Mexico's population to reach eighteen million inhabitants. In the thirty years between 1940 and 1970 Mexico added thirty million people to its population (Banco Nacional de México 1971b:229). It is evident that Mexico has entered upon an unprecedented phase of population growth, a phenomenon which cannot but have vast implications for the Mexican habitat, for the social structure, and for the quality of life of individual Mexicans.

In 1910 Mexico's population was growing at a rate of 1.1 per cent per year. In 1921 the growth rate was a negative 0.5 per cent. In 1930 and 1940 the growth rate was 1.6 and 1.7 per year respectively. After 1940 growth rates show a tendency to accelerate to average annual rates of 2.8 in 1950, 3.1 in 1960, and 3.4 in 1970. (Banco Nacional de Comercio 1970:31). If Mexico's population continues to grow at the same rate as in the 1960's it will reach a total population of 82 million inhabitants by 1985. It will then be the eighth most populous country in the world (Banco Nacional de México 1970b:13).

According to one estimate made in 1960, 62 per cent of Mexico's population was concentrated in the central region, 27 per cent in the north, and the remaining 11 per cent in the southern region. The central region has also been called one of the poorest in agricultural resources (Delegación Mexicana 1960:349).

69

How are Mexico's rates of population growth to be explained? Since populations can only grow by an excess of births over deaths or by migration, it is necessary that we examine each of these three variables as well as the possible factors which have made for variation in each of them.

Immigration cannot be regarded as a noticeable factor in Mexico's population growth. For a number of structural reasons (among them an abundant supply of manual labor, low salaries, and class inequalities), Mexico does not attract immigrants in any considerable number (Loyo 1963:10). For a number of other reasons (including the proliferation of a landless proletariat, underemployment and unemployment, and differential living standards in Mexico and the U.S.), Mexico's migration figures show a net out-migration northward. The bulk of these migrants is made up of braceros and wetbacks.

A recent study reports that nearly one million Mexicans emigrated to the United States between 1900 and 1950 (Hernández 1967:18). Another study reports 5.7 million persons of Mexican birth living in the United States in 1960, while the number of United States citizens living in Mexico was estimated at 48,500 in 1956 (Whetten 1964:79–80). There is a difference of 4.7 million persons in the migration figures given by these two studies. The wide disparity may be related to the differential enumeration of (1) braceros, whose flow is regulated by law and whose stay in the United States is temporary, (2) wetbacks, who enter the United States surreptitiously, and (3) persons who have a more or less permanent immigrant status.

Oscar Lewis summed up the nature of the primary migratory currents as related to Mexico, along with their significance to Mexican life (Lewis 1959:23).

> Were the United States suddenly to close its borders to the *braceros* a major crisis would probably follow in Mexico. Mexico has also become increasingly dependent upon the U.S. tourist trade to stabilize its economy. In 1957 over 700,000 tourists from the United States spent almost 600 million dollars in Mexico to make tourism the single largest industry in the country. The income from the tourist trade is about equal to the total Mexican federal budget.

Part of Mexico's dollar holdings also appear to come from remissions made by braceros to their families from the United States.

In sum, while migratory movements from, to, and within Mexico do appear to have much economic importance, migration cannot be a factor in explaining Mexico's population growth. If anything, the relationship would appear to be the other way around. Hence, the explanation for Mexico's population growth must be sought in the balance between births and deaths (Benítez and Cabrera 1966: 163; Whetten 1964:80).

According to figures corrected for underregistration and for under-enumeration which were released by El Colegio de México, Mexico's birth rate during the interval 1895–1910 varied somewhere between 47.3 and 50.5 births per thousand population. During this same interval the mortality rate varied somewhere between 32.6 and 35.5 deaths per thousand population. This left a rate of natural increase varying somewhere between 11.8 persons per thousand to 17.9 persons per thousand, and a rate of population growth varying somewhere between 1.2 per cent and 1.8 per cent per year. By contrast, in 1965 the birth rate stood at 44.3 per thousand, while the death rate averaged 9.4 per thousand during the interval 1965–1967. This shows an approximate rate of natural increase of 34.9 for 1965 and a population growth rate of about 3.5 per cent per year (Centro 1970:8). In 1970 birth and death rates were 42 and 9 per thousand respectively (Population Reference Bureau 1971:1).

The most recent years for which data are available indicate a possible slowing of Mexico's population growth rates. A Population Council estimate for 1973 places Mexico's rate of natural increase somewhere between 3.2 and 3.5 per cent per year (Berelson 1974:28). This same report estimates that Mexico's total population for that year was 55 million inhabitants, with a crude birth rate of 43 to 45 per thousand and a crude death rate of 10 to 12 per thousand. A United Nations map dated May, 1974, estimates Mexico's annual population growth rate for the interval 1970–1975 at 3.25 per cent per year, with a total population of 54,302,792 and an expected doubling time of 21 years (United Nations 1974:Map No. 2753).

It is clear that Mexico's birth rates have remained essentially stable at a high level during the present century, showing a slight tendency to decline. Mexico's increasing population cannot, therefore, be explained in terms of increasing birth rates. On the other hand, Mexico's death rates have declined sharply during this century.

The number of deaths per thousand population has been reduced to only a small fraction of what it was at the turn of the twentieth century. The explanation for Mexico's rapidly increasing population, therefore, lies in the fact that more Mexicans are living longer lives. Hence, to understand Mexico's population explosion it is necessary to delve into the factors which control the average life-expectancy in Mexico, a figure which more than doubled in less than a century.

Close examination of death rates by causes of death shows that by far the most important decline in death rates was in deaths occasioned by parasitic and infectious diseases which affect primarily the population under five years old, deaths closely related to malnutrition, hunger, epidemics, plagues, and wars, and deaths subject to a degree of control through relatively inexpensive medicines and vaccines. Mexico's infant mortality rate (defined as deaths per thousand live births) declined from 324.2 in 1896–1898 to 62.7 in 1964–1966. These declines are largely a result of increased control over infectious diseases such as gastroenteritis, pneumonia, and the common cold (Centro 1970:25). The reduction of these deaths is also in part the result of more productive agricultural and industrial technology, of increasing literacy and greater familiarity with modern hygiene, of improved sanitation and water purification, and of social reforms which followed the revolution of 1910–1917 (Alba y Alvarado 1971:150–51).

It is significant that the trend shown by Mexico's statistics of deaths by causes is not unique to Mexico but follows a pattern which has been manifested on a world-wide basis as a part of the process of modernization. It is significant too that despite its sharp decline, Mexico's rate of deaths from infectious and parasitic diseases is still relatively high by comparison to rates experienced by industrialized nations such as Holland (Alba y Alvarado 1971:153).

Mexico's rapid population growth in the face of stable to slowly declining birth rates must, then, be regarded as the result of a complex of factors, chief among which are science, technology, education, and social reforms. However, the statistics of death from "unknown causes" disguise the extent to which deaths from famine and starvation still occur in Mexico (Alba y Alvarado 1971:162).

Graph 2. **Trends in the Births and Deaths per Thousand Inhabitants in Mexico, 1895–1965**

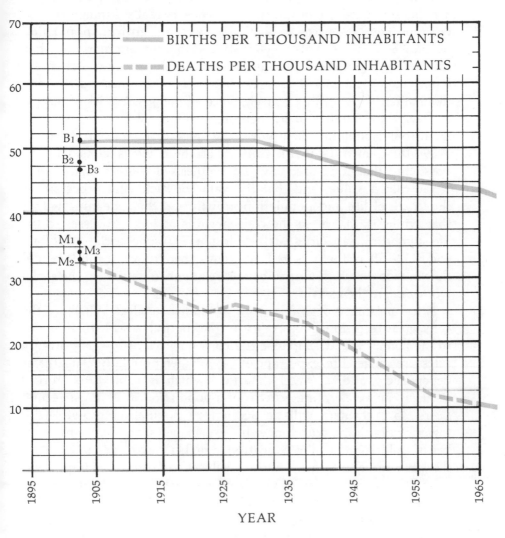

YEAR

Source: *Centro de Estudios Económicos y Demográficos, Dinámica de la Población de México*, 8.

Note: Points B1, B2, B3, and M1, M2, M3 are different estimates of births and deaths for the same year, provided by the same source. B1 and M2 were selected because of a reported tendency to underestimate growth rates for that period.

The value of lower mortality and a longer life expectancy has been judged from two opposing perspectives. One view denies that a policy designed to promote these ends is really humane unless equipment and resources are available to use the growing population which would result. This view abstracts capital from man and then assesses the significance, in human terms, of lower mortality and a longer life expectancy (Fisher 1964:181–82). The other view asserts that human life is a value in itself, since all the possibilities of human creativity are implicit in it, including capital. This view abstracts man from capital and then judges the value of human life (Urquidi 1969:118; Centro 1970:12). Neither of these views considers the possibility that it is precisely the synthesis of nature-man-human world that *is* value, and that the value of such vital processes as the length of life and population growth find their meaning within that synthesis, that is, in the consequences of such processes to the life-supporting capacities of the biosphere, to the social structure, and to the life of the person. Both views, then, reflect a fundamental flaw in thought about human beings' relations to nature, to the social world, and to themselves.

Is less mortality desirable from all human angles? What are the consequences of lower mortality to the natural world, to humans, to the human world? Suppose the consequences of lower mortality rates are longer life expectancies, a younger population, a greater dependency ratio, a larger "market" which is subject to "forced savings," an accelerating growth of a population in its most fecund years, so that there will be accelerated population growth with lowering mortality, with longer life expectancies, an increasing number of children in need of education, a higher rate of dependency on the labor force, a larger "market" subject to "forced savings," and an increasing proportion of young people in their most fecund years, and so on *ad infinitum*. There is, then, a real question as to what these processes (carried far enough) will do to the carrying capacity of the biosphere, to the capacity of human beings to bear the strain, and to the kind of social system that will result. The historical consequences could be disastrous. But are all of these really the consequences of decreasing mortality? Can a human being opt for higher mortality without pushing the species man out of the synthesis of nature-man-human world and without forfeiting any claim

Table 5. **Economically Active Population of Mexico by Sectors and Activities, 1950, 1960, 1970***

Sectors and Activities	1950 Absolute	Per Cent	1960 Absolute	Per Cent	1970 Absolute	Per Cent
Total	8.345,240	100.0	11.332,016	100.0	15.891,139	100.0
Primary sector	4.964,559	59.49	6.285,070	55.46	7.986,072	50.26
Agriculture, livestock, forestry, game and fishing	4.866,557	58.32	6.143,540	54.21	7.778,290	48.95
Mining	98,002	1.17	141,530	1.25	207,782	1.31
Secondary sector	1.232,826	14.77	2.005,813	17.70	3.428,479	21.57
Manufacturing	981,142	11.76	1.556,091	13.73	2.590,181	16.30
Construction	226,497	2.71	408,279	3.60	773,354	4.86
Electricity, gas, etc.	25,187	0.30	41,443	0.37	64,944	0.41
Tertiary sector	2.147,855	25.74	3.041,133	26.84	4.476,588	28.17
Commerce	690,141	8.27	1.075,174	9.49	1.717,549	10.81
Transportation	212,454	2.55	356,939	3.15	621,041	3.91
Services	1.245,260	14.92	1.609,020	14.20	2.137,998	13.45

*Data for 1950 and 1960 are from the respective censuses; data for 1970 are projected.

Source: Banco Nacional de México, "General Panorama," *Review of the Economic Situation* 46:306.

to status as human? If not, what alternatives are there, if any?

We shall return to these questions in due course. In the meantime it will be sufficient to point out that something appears to be wrong with a conception of value which sees low life expectancy as an index of poverty and which cannot see a high life expectancy as an index of wealth. Something seems to be wrong with a conception of value which denies value to a longer life by a wider population unless it can be used by resources and equipment or unless it can become a market from which forced savings can be extracted.

Employment. Mexico's growing population requires growing sources sources of productive employment. The annual contingent of new job seekers increased from 300,000 in the 1950's (Fisher 1964:195) to a figure somewhere between 700,000 and 800,000 in the 1970's (Banco Nacional de México 1971b:231; Banco Nacional de México 1970b:13).

One source estimated the relative size of Mexico's labor force at 33.4 per cent in 1900 and 32.4 per cent in 1950. The base population for this study appears to have been the population 10 years old and over (Centro 1970:151). Another estimate for the same years places the percentages at 35 and 32 respectively. It is not clear what base population was used for these estimates (Reynolds 1970:18). The latest (1970) estimate for the size of the labor force places it at 26.8 per cent. The base population here was "twelve years old and over" (Banco Nacional de México 1971c:156). About all that can be inferred from these data is that Mexico's labor force, depending on definition, varies somewhere between a third and a fourth of the base population and that there seems to have been a moderate decline in the relative size of the labor force from 1900 to 1970.

Between 1950 and 1970 there were some noticeable changes in the composition of the labor force by sectors. Agriculture, livestock farming, forestry, hunting, and fishing accounted for 58.3 per cent of the economically active population in 1950 and for about 48.9 per cent in 1970. What is called the "secondary sector," which includes manufacturing, construction, electricity, and other activities, accounted for 14.8 per cent of the economically active population in 1950 and for 21.6 per cent in 1970. The "tertiary sector," which includes commerce, transportation, and services, accounted for 25.7 per cent of the economically active population in 1950 and 28.2 per cent in 1970. In relative terms the secondary sector showed the largest increases; the tertiary sector increased to a lesser degree while agriculture lost in relative size. In absolute terms the economically active agricultural population increased from approximately 4.9 million to approximately 7.8 million persons. The secondary sector nearly trebled in size, increasing from 1.2 million in 1950 to 3.4 million in 1970. The tertiary sector somewhat more than doubled in size from 2.1 million in 1950 to 4.5 million in 1970. The largest relative share under the secondary sector in 1970 was taken up by manufacturing, with 16.3 per cent of the total economically active population; second in line was construction with 4.9 per cent. The largest share under the tertiary sector in this same year was taken up by services, with 13.4 per cent; next in line was commerce, with 10.8 per cent (Banco Nacional de México 1970c:306).

In sum, the importance of the primary sector as a source of employment in the Mexican economy has been declining, while that of the secondary and tertiary sectors has been increasing. As late as 1970 nearly half of Mexico's economically active population was still occupied within the primary sector, i.e., in rural-type activities.

The apparent shrinkage in the relative size of the labor force has a correlate in the increasing magnitude of the dependency ratio. Trends in Mexico's dependency ratio are increasingly converting Mexico into a nation where children (and, to a markedly lesser extent, the aged) predominate. Taking the dependency ratio as the sum of those under 15 plus those over 65, divided by the number of those aged 15 to 65, Mexico had a dependency ratio of 824 in 1950, 958 in 1960, and a projected dependency of 1010 by 1980 (Banco Nacional de Comercio 1970:32). An estimate of the dependency ratio for 1970 places it roughly at 990 (Benítez y Cabrera 1966:166–67). These trends can only increase the burden of responsibility on the productive age groups, especially if population growth rates continue indefinitely at high levels. The weight of responsibility would decrease in the long run if birth rates were to drop.

As was pointed out earlier, the situation wherein the younger age groups tend to increasingly predominate results in a lowering of the median age and tends to increase the need for schools, the number of persons who will be looking for work, and the number of women in their most fecund years. One author estimates an average of 3.55 dependents per head of family in 1960 (Rodríguez 1966:9).

Food and Nutrition. The food supply required to maintain Mexico's growing population has shown a tendency to increase at rates faster than the rates of population growth since the early 1930's. Food production taken by itself was growing at a rate of 5.6 per cent per year during 1940–60; that is, it was doubling at approximately 13-year intervals, *slightly less than twice* the rate of population growth. Worth noting also is the fact that agricultural production for industrial and export uses was increasing at a rate of 8.7 per cent per year, that is, doubling at an approximate rate of once in 8.5 years (Editorial 1963:346).

From these growth-rate figures it would appear that Mexico has succeeded in attaining a long-term rate of growth in agricultural production which advances faster than the rate of population growth. This statement holds even for a longer interval than the 1940–60 decades. Agricultural production rates for 1932–67 have been estimated at 4.8 per cent per year (Reyes 1967:201). This rate exceeds by 0.9 per cent the population growth rate for 1965, which was, if not the highest, then one of the highest rates ever experienced by Mexico within recorded times.

In terms of the principal food items consumed by Mexico, between 1925 and 1961 corn production trebled and bean production increased somewhat less than fourfold. During 1939–61 wheat production trebled, and increases of the same order were reported for a number of other products such as rice, potatoes, tomatoes, and other food staples. Also, the index of cattle production is reported to have doubled between 1921 and 1934 and doubled again by 1956 (Centro 1970:218).

The weight of the evidence for the years of Mexico's development, therefore, is heavily on the side of a reversal of the Malthusian view. This trend stands in sharp contrast to the tendency for the population to increase faster than crop production during the years of Porfirio Díaz's dictatorship. The political nature of these shortages becomes apparent when the rapid rate of growth in export crop production is considered. An overall estimate of growth rates during the years 1877 to 1910 (years of the dictatorship of Porfirio Díaz) indicates that per capita crop production *declined* at a rate of 0.8 per cent per year. During this interval the rate of growth of crop production, then, failed to keep up with population growth rates, for although the growth of the total real crop production was 0.6 per cent per year, the population is estimated to have grown at a rate of 1.4 per cent per year during this interval. Moreover, the full reality of the trend toward a politically created scarcity of food does not become evident until notice is taken of the fact that the production of export crops was increasing at the rapid rate of 6 per cent

Table 6.   **Growth of Crop Production During the Major Periods of Mexican Economic Development**
(Compound annual rates of growth)

	Porfiriato 1877–1907	Revolution and Reform 1910–1940	Development 1940–1960
Total real crop production (1)	0.6	1.1	6.3
Total population (2)	1.4	0.9	2.9
Per capita crop production (1 minus 2)	−0.8	0.2	3.4

Source: Clark Winston Reynolds, *The Mexican Economy: Twentieth Century Structure and Growth* (New Haven, Conn.: Yale University Press, 1970), p. 96.

per year (Reynolds 1970:96). During the years of revolution, reform, and recovery (1919–40) the rate of growth of crop production per capita increased to 0.2 per cent per year. The population was now increasing at 0.9 per cent per year, while the total real crop production was growing at the rate of 1.1 per cent per year. Finally, during the interval 1940–60 per capita crop production grew at a rate of 3.4 per cent per year. Total crop production during this score of years was growing at a rate of 6.3 per cent—more than twice as fast as the rate of population growth (2.9 per cent) (Reynolds 1970: 96). An estimate from another source of rates of total agricultural growth for the same 20-year interval reads 5.9 per cent (Editorial 1963:346). Since the figures given are compound rates of growth, what they indicate is that while total agricultural production was doubling at intervals of approximately 11 or 12 years, the population was doubling at an approximate rate of once every 24 years. Hence, the population was growing at a rate *half as fast* as the rate of agricultural crop production. These figures, however, do not refer solely to food production; they are more inclusive than that.

One study has argued that per capita food production has tended to stagnate during the interval 1958–68 because of rapid population growth (Banco de México 1970a). This study draws a comparison

Table 7. **Agricultural Production and Food Indices in Mexico**
(Average 1952–56 = 100)

	Agricultural Production		Food Production	
Year	Total	Per Person	Total	Per Person
1955	113	110	109	105
1956	115	108	116	109
1957	131	119	132	120
1958	141	124	142	125
1959	133	113	140	119
1960	141	116	145	119
1961	148	117	154	123
1962	153	118	158	122
1963	161	119	161	123
1964	170	122	175	126
1965	175	121	182	126
1966	180	121	186	125
1967	186	121	195	127
1968	189	119	199	125

Source: Banco Nacional de México, "Feeding the Mexicans: Levels are Still Very Low," *Review of the Economic Situation* 46:168.

of indexes of total food production with indexes of food production per person during the interval 1955–68. Using the interval 1952–56 as the base period (100), the figures show that the index of total food production increased by 90 percentage points (from 109 to 199), while the index of food production per person increased by only 20 percentage points (from 105 to 125) (Banco de México 1970a: 168). The study says:

> Improvements in agricultural methods and increases in the amount of land cultivated have almost doubled Mexico's agricultural output during the last fifteen years. But the rapid population growth has kept the *per capita* product at the same level as eleven years ago, and at a level only slightly higher than that of fifteen years ago.

Table 8. **Growth of Agricultural Production in Mexico**
(Compound annual rates of growth)

	1877– 1900	1900– 1907	1907– 25	1925– 40	1940– 50	1950– 60
Total physical crop production	0.0	2.8	0.0	2.7	8.2	4.3
Total population	1.5	1.1	0.1	1.6	2.8	3.1
Agricultural production, per capita	−1.5	1.7	−0.1	1.1	5.4	1.2
GDP per capita (1950 pesos)	0.6	3.1	2.3	−0.1	3.8	2.9

Source: Clark Winston Reynolds, *The Mexican Economy: Twentieth-Century Structure and Growth* (New Haven, Conn.: Yale University Press, 1970), p. 104.

The last per capita figure (125) had been reached in 1958, and the index fluctuated erratically after that. This fact seems to indicate that in the decade 1958–68 per capita food production figures tended to stagnate. Hence, growth rates from 1940 to 1968 cannot have been uniformly high. In fact, a breakdown of total and per capita growth rates for the interval 1940–60 shows that total physical crop production growth rates declined from 8.2 per cent per year in 1940–50 to 4.3 per cent per year in 1950–60, while per capita agricultural production growth rates declined from 5.4 to 1.2 respectively. However, the rate of population growth accounts for only 0.3 per cent of the difference in the latter figures, since population growth rates increased only from 2.8 to 3.1 during the same intervals (Reynolds 1970:104). The bulk of the decrease in the per capita growth rate (a total of 3.9 percentage points) will probably have to be sought in other political and economic factors such as changes in the rates of public and private investments, the availability of credit, and perhaps other factors.

It is evident that relative shrinkage of production per capita is a predictable consequence of population growth. However, the importance of population growth as a factor in limiting the supply of the per capita product available has been exaggerated by a one-sided emphasis on population growth which fails to consider the importance of the broader conditions of production in determining the growth rate and the size of the total supply.

But the figures we have been dealing with are *per capita production* figures. They do not tell us what percentage of the population actually has *access* to what amounts and types of foods. The fact that per capita production and per capita consumption are not the same is of crucial importance. One estimate is that at least 80 per cent of the Mexican population (Suárez 1962:380) suffers from malnutrition. Another (1958) study estimated that the average consumption of calories in Mexico was 515 calories below the recommended 2,500 minimum daily intake and that 15 per cent of the population suffered from hunger owing to a diet restricted to beans, *tortillas*, and *chile* (Rodríguez 1966:12).

More recent studies show that the minimum dietary standards set by the United Nations' Food and Agriculture Organization as regards the average daily supply of calories available per person had only just been reached in 1967. The FAO's recommended minimum daily dietary requirement per person for underdeveloped countries is as follows: calories, 2600; proteins, 75 grams; animal proteins, 25 grams. The figures of what is actually available in Mexico are the following: calories, 2625 per day; proteins, 76 grams per day; animal proteins, 22.9 per day. The same study noted that it is doubtful whether these levels could be maintained in the future. A contrast is then drawn in food consumption patterns found in rural and urban areas (Banco Nacional de México 1970a:165–69).

Through its technical studies and investigations, the National Nutritional Institute:

> has proved that the traditional food of people in rural areas consists of maize, beans, and chile, containing 2,000 calories and 54 grams of proteins, 9 grams of which are of animal origin, per day, a level which is among the lowest in the world. The nourishment of the most vulnerable group—preschool children—is particularly striking. They receive a daily average of 940 calories and 26 grams of protein, of which only 7.8 are of animal origin. These levels are well below the acceptable minimum, and the consumption of animal protein is barely half the recommended minimum.

le 9. Calorie and Protein Contents of the Food Supply per Person: Mexico and the U.S.A.

	Mexico			FAO's Minimum Recommended for an Underdeveloped Country	U.S.A.	
	1961–62	1966	1967		1960–62	1966–67
ories (per day)	2,500	2,550	2,625	2,600	3,120	3,160
tein (grams per ay)	65.0	65.7	76.0	75.0	92.4	93.8
mal protein grams per day)	15.5	15.2	22.9	25.0	64.3	65.1

urce: Banco Nacional de México, "Feeding the Mexicans: Levels Are Still Very Low," *Review* ie *Economic Situation* 46:165.

With 17.7 per cent of the country's population, the Federal District was reported to consume one-third of all the meat consumed in the country. The daily average consumption of beef per person in this metropolis was 66 grams per day, while in the country as a whole it was 33 grams per day (Banco Nacional de México 1970a:169).

Despite the apparent shortage of animal proteins in the country, 678,000 head of cattle are reported to have exported in 1968–69. The FAO study says (Banco Nacional de México 1970a:170):

> Since meat is the item most lacking in domestic consumption it is incongruous from the point of view of nourishment that 678,000 head of cattle on the hoof and 30 million kilos of boned meat were sold abroad during 1968–69. Even more paradoxical are the official authorizations allowing for the exportation of another 780,000 cattle on the hoof and about 250,000 head in boned meat during 1969–70.

Seen from the point of view of the nutritional standards of the Mexican masses, what these facts indicate has been aptly summarized by a recent article on the "Balance of food in Mexico in

Table 10.   **Mexican Food Exports**
             (Millions of pesos)

	1960	1968	Per Cent growth 1960–68
Live animals	234.8	326.4	39.0
Dead animals for food, meat, and meat products	129.3	450.7	248.6
Dairy products, eggs, honey, fish, and seafood	484.7	762.3	57.3
Cereals, grains, starch, and flour	285.8	780.7	173.2
Fruits and vegetables	406.5	918.8	126.0
Sugar, honey, and their products	726.2	1,202.5	65.6
Cacao, coffee, tea, spices, and their products	831.1	1,011.6	21.7
Other foods	50.6	27.5	45.7
Total	3,177.9	5,553.4	74.8

Source: Banco Nacional de México, "Feeding the Mexicans: Levels Are Still Very Low," *Review of the Economic Situation*, 46:170.

1967." The progress which has been made, this article notes, "has tended more to satisfy hunger than to balance the diet and nutrition of the population" (Ramírez y Chávez 1969:80–81). This same article notes that the available Mexican diet is poor in vitamins A and C and in riboflavin. To the extent that it does reflect the actual diet, then, the actual supply of food does not provide a balanced diet (Ramírez y Chávez 1969:78).

A third study dealing with nutritional problems in Mexico points out that over half of the proteins consumed by the Mexican people have their source in corn, a cereal whose protein content is low and of low conversion value. This study estimates that in order for a child weighing 20 kilograms (44 pounds) to obtain his daily supply of proteins from corn, he would have to ingest nearly 3 kilograms (6.6 pounds) of corn per day—an amount which would kill him (Suárez 1962:378). A consequence of this diet (Suárez assumes a recommended level of 3,000 calories consumed per day), which the author

Table 11. **Supply of Food for Human Consumption, per Capita, Mexico and U.S.A.**
(Grams per day)

Type of Food	Mexico				U.S.A.
	1954–56	1961–62	1966	1967	1967
Cereals	346	354	356	417	177
Potatoes and other starches	45	27	24	21	133
Sugar and sugar products	88	99	109	97	133
Legumes, nuts, and seeds	53	63	67	70	23
Vegetables	n.a.	38	25	33	269
Fruit	135	174	187	126	239
Meat	54	53	53	43[*]	295
Eggs	12	12	11	15	51
Fish	6	6	9	. . .	17
Milk	190	172	156	308	665
Fats and oils	26	28	26	18	61

*Includes fish.

Source: Banco Nacional de México, "Feeding the Mexicans: Levels Are Still Very Low," *Review of the Economic Situation,* 46:167.

considered low in calories (by 219), fats (by 70 grams), and proteins—a diet based heavily on the consumption of tortillas, beans, chile, and an occasional piece of meat—is a pattern of growth which is described as follows (Suárez 1962:373):

> We would have grown somewhat short, after having been a bit pot-bellied in childhood, we would have been the victims of frequent infectious diseases; during working hours we would have felt a bit tired too early; and our output, economic, social and personal will be less than we would have wanted; a decrepit old age would have arrived prematurely and death decidedly so, along with the individual, family and social loss which this means. . . .

The reliance of Mexicans on corn as their basic food source has been called "the biological tragedy under which the Mexican people live"

(Suárez 1962:373). Among the consequences of this situation has been a chronic protein deficiency which appears to be more intense in the southern regions of the country. One of the reported consequences of this regional difference is the contrast in stature between Mexicans of northern and southern origin. Northerners are reported to be generally taller than southerners, and the average adult height of successive generations of southerners is reported to have been decreasing (Suárez 1962:374). But hunger and malnutrition slow down both physical and mental development, and besides reducing productivity and resistance to disease, they tend to be goads to criminal behavior (Banco Nacional de México 1970a:170). In her work on *The Magnitude of Hunger in Mexico*, Ana María Flores observed (Lajous 1968:63):

> Hungry and undernourished human beings are individuals lacking in determination and tend to be lazy, scarcely capable of doing mental work and little able to do physical work. It can be asserted that their output is almost zero. . . .

This brings us to a question raised in an inaugural speech of the new President of the National Institute of Agricultural Economics in May, 1969. The author asks; "How is it possible that with such important achievements from the point of view of production and an agrarian process of more than half a century we should still have such low levels of living in the rural areas?" (Reyes 1969:145). His answer is double-edged: (1) the agrarian ideal that each peasant should have a parcel of land has been exceeded by demographic growth, and (2) an absurd situation exists, wherein agricultural surpluses exist in the midst of a sea of necessities (Reyes 1969:147). The first answer, as we have seen, is an answer Malthus gives; while the second is a point emphasized by Engels. The latter will be touched again in due course, under exploitation theory. For the moment we shall follow out the first one.

As of 1964 a total of 54 million hectares had been redistributed under Mexico's Agrarian Reform laws. (One hectare equals 2.471 acres.) Between 1960 and 1969 alone, 22 million hectares were redistributed. This latter sum was taken from 12,000 landed estates which, as of that same date according to a study conducted by the

Table 12.   Nutrients: Availability and Recommended Levels
in Mexico

Nutrients	Availability per Inhabitant	Recommended Levels
Calories	2625	2600*
Total proteins (gr)	76.0	75*
Animal proteins (gr)	22.9	25*
Calcium (mg)	1043	600†
Iron (mg)	20.77	18*
Vitamin A (mg)	0.797	1.800†
Thiamin (mg)	2.41	1.30†
Riboflavin (mg)	1.03	1.90†
Niacin (mg)	27.8	21.5†
Vitamin C (mg)	65	85

*Minimum recommendations of the FAO for underdeveloped countries.

†National Nutrition Institute, with recommendations for availability.

Source: Juan Ramírez Hernández y Adolfo Chávez, "Balance de los Alimentos en Mexico Durante el Año 1967," *Revista Mexicana de Sociologia* 31:78.

Center for Agrarian Investigations, still contained 40 million hectares which could be redistributed under the law. However, when the end of that redistribution process is reached, although 3 million peasants will have benefited from it, a larger number of peasants will be in existence who will have no opportunity to receive land. Hence, although much remains to be done by way of agrarian reform, a total solution of the problems in the countryside cannot be expected from land distribution (Reyes 1969:146).

This idea that it is no longer realistic to attempt to secure a parcel of land for each peasant appears to be taking hold. For instance Gilberto Loyo, a demographer who has long been an advocate for the priority of reform in Mexico's institutional structures, recognizes that much of what went by the name of agrarian reform was no more than political expediency designed to relieve the pressures of the moment. He goes on to say (Loyo 1965:141):

> Agrarian Reform seeks to raise the regional level of living and not to create conditions which will tend to keep the *ejidatario* in poverty with small parcels, in regions of unreliable rainfall, or even worse, where crops resistant to drought can frequently not be harvested. Hence, the Institutional Revolutionary Party asserts that Mexico must formulate an agrarian policy which is free from illusions and from the grave inconveniences of the *minifundio*, a policy which is not set in motion by the unrealizable urge that all peasants should have an *ejidal* parcel, no matter what kind of place it is. In a region where the Agrarian Reform is directed toward raising the levels of living with seriousness and honesty, it might turn out that not all peasants will have a parcel of land, but it will also allow that all of those who were unable to obtain one can hope to live better dedicated to other activities which will develop through the general progress of the region.

Are we to conclude, then, that the limits of agricultural expansion have been reached, given the relatively fixed extensions of land available? That is to say, aside from the questions of how much more land might be available for redistribution and what basic changes in the institutional structure of Mexico's agriculture might provide more effective alternatives to the problems of hunger and malnutrition, we want to know whether continental Mexico has reached the saturation point for agricultural expansion.

Assuming the high United Nations estimate for 1970, Mexico's 52.5 million inhabitants were spread over a territory of 763,944 square miles, with a density of 69.1 inhabitants per square mile. Cross-country comparisons are useless for the purpose of determining saturation, for if we compare this density, as one article does (Fisher 1964:175), to Canada's (5.7 per square mile) it appears to be over-populated. But if we compare it with Spain or India (Lajous 1968: 59), Mexico appears to be underpopulated (Spain: 176.8, and India: 438.1 per square mile).

Estimates are that only 15 to 18 per cent of Mexico's territory is open to cultivation and that about 44 per cent is grazing land (Banco

Nacional de Comercio 1970:23; Fisher 1964:183; Lajous 1968:61). Between 18 and 34 per cent is believed to be forest land (Fisher 1964:183; Banco Nacional de Comercio 1970:22). Also, between 7 and 23 per cent of the territory is believed to be worthless for agriculture (Fisher 1964:183). It seems that some of the land classified as worthless by the latter estimate is considered forest land by the other. There is agreement that only 6.4 to 7 per cent of the 15 to 18 per cent of the land area which is tillable is actually under cultivation. This means that a minimum of one-third and a maximum of one-half of the land which is tillable is actually under cultivation. Can the land not under cultivation be brought under cultivation? One answer is that bringing new untilled lands under cultivation "is not a very probable solution because the supply of suitable land is shrinking" (Fisher 1964:184). Another answer is that only about half of the tillable land (9 per cent of the total) can be brought under cultivation "without prior improvement" (Lajous 1968:61) such as irrigation, drainage, and the like.

The first of the two answers begs the question, since the supply of suitable land is shrinking *because* more of it is being brought under cultivation, yet the probability of bringing more land under cultivation is precisely what is denied (Fisher 1964:184). It can be assumed, then, that an amount of land equal to one-half to two-thirds of the area classified as tillable can be brought under cultivation through improvement of some kind. Since the corresponding estimates of the total amount of tillable land amount to approximately 30 and 36 million hectares respectively, we can venture an estimate that a minimum of 15 to 20 million hectares and a maximum of 18 to 24 million hectares could be brought under cultivation, probably on condition of a prior improvement.

On the basis of the data available, then, there is no reason to suppose that Mexico has reached the limits of agricultural expansion possible to it. On the contrary, the data at hand indicate that there is sizable room for future expansion, provided a method is found to muster the resources needed to bring about the necessary improvements.

Indeed, the total land area which could be brought into production through various methods of irrigation is estimated at 9,035,000 hectares. By 1969, 3.9 million of these had already been brought under cultivation (Banco Nacional de Comercio 1970:24–25). Also, 2 per cent of the total area could be made productive through drainage (Lajous 1968:61). If this were accomplished, the total surface reported to be potentially productive by these methods would amount to approximately 12.9 million acres.

Still more land could probably be opened up for cultivation if the difficulties in Mexican transportation could be overcome. One problem is the mountainous nature of the terrain, with its consequent isolation of areas due to difficulties in road building. Another is the fact that Mexico's roads tend to be heavily oriented in a north-south direction and to concentrate toward Mexico City, leaving wide areas relatively undeveloped due to isolation (Lajous 1968:61).

It is evident that Mexico still has room for agricultural expansion. However, a question should be raised as to the advisability of allowing population to expand as an end in itself, not subject to control, while every nook and cranny of available, usable space is brought under the plow or put to grazing. An even more fundamental question can be raised as to the types, intensity, and scope of land use which are most conducive to maintaining the life-supporting capacity of the biosphere.

The available data concerning diminishing returns on added units of capital are ambiguous, though nevertheless interesting. A study which does not include public investments in infrastructure within its definition of capital (Reynolds 1970:114–26) has shown that the highest increase in productivity which remains unexplained by inputs of land, labor, and capital took place in Mexico's poorest and least developed region. The lowest such unexplained increase took place in Mexico's wealthiest and most highly developed region. It is quite possible that the opening up of new roads under government auspices, the opening up of new lands, and increased opportunities for applying available labor have all been factors in producing such results. A possibility also exists that the low initial levels of productivity in the least developed region would tend to show even low absolute increases as high percentage increases in productivity. Notable also is the fact that the wealthiest and most developed region experienced productivity losses in 1930 and 1940 and productivity increases during 1950 and 1960—increases which were insufficient to offset the former losses.

The question of whether or not returns on additional units of capital input actually decrease is, of course, important for any effort to determine the optimum level of development, leaving aside the question of environmental impact. However, even if a redesigned study (one which took off from a more inclusive conception of capital) were to show clearly and unambiguously that such a tendency is actually in operation, a question would still remain as to how to account for the fact that the increases which do take place are distributed unequally.

The Mexican federal government's expenditures for agricultural development are reported to have declined from 21.9 per cent of the budget in 1940 to 13.0 per cent in 1968, while its expenditures for social welfare increased from 10.2 per cent of the federal public investments in 1940 to 24.3 per cent in 1969 (Centro 1970:225). Social welfare expenditures include outlays on health and assistance programs, educative and cultural services, social insurance, urban works, and welfare (Centro 1970:233). The above-mentioned trends in the allocation of federal funds have been explained in terms of the needs created by Mexico's high rates of population growth. Mexico's federal budget amounts to only 10 to 15 per cent of the GNP (Centro 1970:232; La Cascia 1969:28).

Housing. Since the bulk of the efforts of the Mexican masses is expended to keep their families supplied with food, little is left to tackle the housing problem. Families who spend from 60 to 85 per cent of their incomes on food cannot, of course, begin to deal with the problem (O'Farril 1966:39). They must consider themselves fortunate if they can stay out of debt, let alone save anything. The cost of building a house in Mexico which provides sanitation, livability, and security has been estimated at 9.5 times the Gross National Product per capita (Bugarín 1968:19). Assuming a figure of 530 dollars per capita for that year (at 12.50 pesos per dollar), the cost of one such housing unit may be estimated at 62,937.50 pesos. Assuming that these were all the costs involved, for the 64.3 per cent of Mexico's (1970) economically active population whose incomes fall below 1,000 pesos per month, the very least such a house would cost in terms of years working full time, and putting all their income to pay for the house, would be five years, three months. For the overwhelming majority of them, then, to build a house would be chimerical.

The evidence indicates that private enterprise found it unprofitable to build houses for people whose incomes were below one thousand pesos per month in 1960, a figure which included nearly four-fifths of the population at the time (Carrera 1968:215, 217–18).

One estimate (1967) is that 45.9 per cent of Mexico's houses were renter-occupied (Camargo 1967:134). These houses are reported to be located mostly in urban areas. Rural houses are reported to be predominantly owner-occupied, but conditions there are worse. People who live in *ejidal* lands, in rural areas, find the problem complicated by the fact that private finance will not risk long-term loans for building on lands which are not alienable, since such lands cannot be used as collateral on loans.

The scarcity of housing in Mexico, as an editorial article in *Revista de Economia* put it "is more than just a recognizable phenomenon. It is also something one can breathe and touch" (Editorial 1966:36). The Center of Economic and Demographic studies has placed the shortage at 46.1 per cent of the units already available (Centro 1970:225). Projections are that 4.7 million new houses will be needed by 1980 due to demographic growth alone. Four million others will be needed just to cover the deficit carried over from 1969, and 4.3 million further housing units will be needed to make up for deterioration. In other words, a total of 13 million new housing units will be needed by 1980 (Centro 1970:225), or close to half again as many housing units as Mexico had in 1969.

What makes the shortage so palpable and suffocating is crowding. In rural areas there are 3.4 persons per room. In urban areas the average is 2.6. For the nation as a whole the crowding index is 2.9 per room (Centro 1970:225).

One writer who clearly itemizes the efforts of both government and private industry to meet Mexico's housing needs despairs of the possibility of bringing the problem to a solution within a generation. He says (O'Farril 1966:40):

We are, today, to such an extent pressed to improve the infra-human conditions in which so many of our countrymen live, that it has become necessary to channel all the available resources to this type of program,

Table 13. **Housing Units in Mexico**

Fixture	Per Cent of Urban Units Lacking	Per Cent of Rural Units Lacking
Windows	32	68
Drainage	23	77
Water	15	85
Electric lights	15	85
Sanitation	2	98

Source: Sergio Camargo Piñuela, "Vivienda y Población," *Revista de Economía* 30:134.

even though it can be seen quite clearly that it will not be possible to meet the deficit within a generation.

A solution to the housing problem appears out of reach within a generation.

Education. Mexico's expenditures on education increased in relative terms from 0.9 per cent of its Gross Internal Product in 1950 to 2.1 per cent of that sum in 1965. Even though this represents more than a doubling in 15 years, this figure must be regarded as low by comparison to other Latin-American countries such as Argentina, Chile, and Cuba, which in 1965 spent 3.3, 3.6, and 5.6 per cent respectively of their GIP's in education (Centro 1970:220).

Federal programs designed to reduce the illiteracy rate have had considerable success since the revolution. The percentage of illiterates was reduced from nearly three-fourths of the base population (eleven years old and over) in 1910 to nearly one-fourth of the base population (ten and over) in 1970. Also, more Mexicans are attending school longer. There can be little doubt that intensive efforts have been made to raise the level of schooling of the population. Between 1950 and 1967 the percentage of primary school-age children (5 to 14) attending school increased from 39.8 to 58.6. During the same interval the percentage of secondary school-age children (13 to 18) attending school increased from 3.8 to 15.1. The corresponding figure for college-age youth (19 to 24) increased from 1.1 to 3.1 per cent (Centro 1970:221). However, the rate of growth in the extent of schooling open to the population has shown signs of slowing down and was expected to have reached stagnation by 1970 (Centro 1970: 234). Furthermore Mexico's schools show a low retention rate, i.e., in 1965 only a fourth of the students were retained through the sixth grade. In rural areas, slightly over one-fourth are retained through the third grade (Centro 1970:222).

While the younger generation has experienced such high attrition rates in the classroom, the elder generation in the labor force has been handicapped by a low level of education. Fully one-fourth (25.4 per cent)of the economically active population in 1964–65 had never attended school. Those who had fewer than three years of elementary school training made up 60.5 per cent of the economically active population. Only 15.25 per cent had managed to make it through the sixth grade. Those whose education included six grades or less made up fully 88 per cent of the economically active population (Tello 1971:651). Low educational levels, of course, create obstacles to modernizing Mexico's power to produce. Higher education in Mexico remains a privilege of the very few. One survey conducted by the Banco de México (1970) showed that only 1.2 per cent of Mexico's university students came from the 40 per cent of the population with the lowest income levels (Tello 1971:651).

Family Planning and the Catholic Church. Lewis's data suggest that poverty discourages marriage and encourages common-law unions (Lewis 1959:27, 29; Lewis 1969:xxviii). Among the typical characteristics manifested by families living in poverty Lewis lists the following (Lewis 1963:xxvi–xxvii):

> . . . living in crowded quarters, a lack of privacy, gregariousness, a high incidence of alcoholism, frequent resort to violence in the settlement of quarrels, frequent use of physical violence in the training of children, wife beating, early initiation into sex, free unions or consensual marriages, a relative high incidence of the abandonment of mothers and children, a trend toward mother centered families and a much greater knowledge of maternal relatives, the predominance of the nuclear family, a strong predisposition to authoritarianism, and a great emphasis upon

family solidarity—an ideal only rarely achieved. Other traits include a strong present time orientation with relatively little ability to defer gratification and plan for the future, a sense of resignation and fatalism based upon the realities of their difficult life situation, a belief in male superiority which reaches its crystallization in *machismo* or the cult of masculinity, a corresponding martyr complex among women, and finally, a high tolerance for psychological pathology of all sorts.

The "cult of masculinity" and the female "martyrdom complex" are rooted in, and find expression through, inequality of power and status between the sexes. The one poor family studied by Lewis which comes closest to having equality in both senses is the Gutierrez family (Lewis 1959:135–36, 29–30).

Inequality between the sexes takes its more glaring form on the matter of standards of sexual conduct. A double standard can be seen running strongly through the main characters of two of Lewis's major books: Pedro Martínez and Jesús Sánchez. During a quarrel over the neighbor woman Eulalia, Pedro says to Esperanza Martínez (his wife), "I am a man and I can do as I like. You have to watch yourself because you are a woman" (Lewis 1967:357). Eulalia was just one of Pedro's extramarital affairs. Before her there had been Gloria and Rutilda, and when his affairs with them were over "[he] had lots of other women. [He] even had one in Mexico City, the merchant to whom [he] sent hog plums" (Lewis 1967:338). There had also been an orphan girl whom he "conquered" on the empty promise that he would marry her, and there were others (Lewis 1967:171). Jesús Sánchez, after recounting the tense evenings with Lenora Sánchez (his first wife) over the latter's jealousy and the family's shortage of money, recounts his having visited a whorehouse, where he got an infection, following which he had an affair with Lupita. He then congratulates himself on his good luck, "in spite of [his] bad conduct" on never having heard "that any of the women who had lived with [him] weren't true to [him]" (Lewis 1963:12). After Lupita there were Elena, Delila, and others. Lenora and Elena died prematurely. All of Jesús's liaisons were common-law unions. Pedro married Esperanza.

Pedro and Esperanza had twelve children in wedlock. Pedro acknowledges at least one other child out of wedlock. Six of the children born in wedlock died before reaching maturity, all of them before or during the revolution (Lewis 1967:xli, 34). Jesús had six children by Lenora, two by Lupita, and two by Delila. He is also reported to have had a child by Lupita's niece, a girl who later married a man who accepted her child. Only four of Jesús's children by Lenora reached maturity (Lewis 1963:xxxii, iii, 492, 140).

Among the typical experiences which poverty holds for the poor, Lewis lists the following (Lewis 1963:26):

> . . . the constant struggle for survival, unemployment and underemployment, low wages, a miscellany of unskilled occupations, child labor, the absence of savings, a chronic shortage of cash, the absence of food reserves in the home, the pattern of frequent buying of small quantities of food many times a day as the need arises, the pawning of personal goods, borrowing from local money lenders at usurious rates of interest, spontaneous credit devices *(tandas)* organized by neighbors, and the use of second hand clothing and furniture.

Pedro's wife and children often went hungry. Felipe, one of Pedro's sons, recounts that his mother was often reduced to cooking decomposing corn and meat for the children and herself. However, there were times when she could not find food of any kind (Lewis 1967: 218–19).

> When we had nothing to eat my *mamá* would get up very early to see where she could buy corn, if she had money, or if she didn't, to see where she might borrow corn. If she came back without corn because no one would lend her any, she said, "Well, I will go somewhere else." By then it was almost eleven o'clock and we still had no breakfast, not even coffee or a piece of bread, and my poor little mother came back, almost crying, if she was unable to get either money or corn.

Jesús was food purchaser for a restaurant and raised some animals on the side. He managed to provide enough food for several households, including at times the children of his son Manuel and of his daughter Marta. Speaking of his father as a provider Manuel says (Lewis 1963:345):

> I never understood how my father managed, and frankly I don't want to. He had always provided us with enough food. . .he took care of so many people on so little money. I cross myself when I think about it,

not that I believe my father did anything wrong . . . he has absolutely no use for a crook. . .but since he bought all the food for the restaurant, he probably charged them a little more and kept fifty *centavos* or a *peso* on every purchase.

Because of his position as a food purchaser and his strong sense of responsibility as a provider, Lewis regarded Jesús as being "unusual among lower class Mexican men" (Lewis 1959:28).

The possibility of using contraceptive methods to reduce Mexico's population growth rates has become a topic of considerable interest in Mexico. The reaction has been a mixture of distrust for the ulterior motives, actual or imagined, thought to lie behind family planning agencies and genuine concern with the consequences of continued high birth rates. The point has been made that the need for family planning is manifested in the number of abortions actually taking place. As García-Peña has written, "It is absurd to think that family planning programs are sinister and coercive intrigues, intended to obligate the poor to do something that they really do not wish to do. The high number of illicit abortions should be sufficient to bring an end to this fiction" (García-Peña 1969:157).

The point has also been made that, given the extent of wealth concentration in Mexico, there would be malnutrition even if the number of children were cut down to only one per family, and that therefore the concern shown by U.S. agencies with Mexico's birth rates appears to arise from a desire to divert attention from real issues (Lajous 1968:59).

> The campaign in favor of birth control as a panacea against multiple social ills, managed from Washington, is in full swing. It has the altruistic motive of making the lives of millions of poor Latin Americans more grateful if not more satisfying. For they will no longer be anguished at the sight of five to eight children dying of hunger, since wealth is accumulated in a few hands, instead they will suffer only from the undernourishment of their one and only child—such is the ideal of "birth control."

The attitude in favor of further population growth is at times defended on grounds that further population growth will stimulate further development of agriculture, industry, etc. The claim is that, in the long run, population growth widens demand. Holders of this view oppose contraception because they view contraception as an unnatural practice (Lajous 1968:59).

The pro-natalist policy implemented by the Soviet Union has fostered a widely held but incorrect view that Marx and Engels were opponents of policies designed to limit population growth. Marx and Engels regarded the development of methods to limit the population as consistent with the judgment of an intelligent population and had no doubt that such methods could be developed when the need to limit the population arose, but they saw no such widespread need in their time. Also, they were aware of the early efforts to develop and apply contraceptive methods (Urlanis 1970:144).

The position taken by the Mexican demographer Loyo may mark the beginning of a wider acknowledgment of the need to achieve a reduction in the birth rate similar to that in the mortality rate. Loyo's warning is clear. He says that ". . . the efforts of our people and governments to accelerate economic and social development might turn out to be useless if no effort is made to eliminate within ten or fifteen years. . .the contradiction between high fecundity rates which are typical of backward countries and low mortality rates which tend to decrease even more, and which are typical of highly developed countries (Loyo 1966:256).

However, Loyo insists that such an aim should not detract attention from the need for reforms of an economic and social nature. Mr. Loyo attended the First Panamerican Assembly on Population (1965) as a member of the Mexican delegation. He was instrumental in having adopted by the assembly as its seventh recommendation this resolution: "The re-examination of conscience concerning the dangers which arise from rapid demographic growth and the policies which in that respect can be formulated and applied, should not distract attention from the need for basic reform of an economic and social nature" (Primera Asamblea 1965:276). Among other things, the assembly also recognized that an excessively rapid rate of population growth forms an obstacle to economic development. It recommended that the participating governments establish family planning services and recognize a continuous obligation to help church leaders in the task of obtaining the most complete scientific information available regarding the biological, social, and economic aspects of problems related to population (Primera Asamblea 1965: 277–79).

Three years later (1968) there took place in Caracas, Venezuela, a Meeting Concerning Population Policy in Relation to Development in Latin America. With the exception of Cuba, all countries of the hemisphere are reported to have sent delegates. The very fact that this meeting took place has been interpreted to have been "a fundamental step in Latin America's re-examination of conscience on the human problem *par excellence:* that of consciously determining the size of the human family" (Eliecer 1968:196).

There is growing recognition among bishops and other members of the Catholic church hierarchy in Latin America in general, and in Mexico in particular, that the church's role in the problems created by population growth has been mainly negative (La Iglesia 1968:285).

> The demographic problem has not had an adequate answer, either at the level of the society or at the level of the family. It would be more correct to say that the Church has been absent. True, it has come forth in defense of human values; and has required respect for the freedom of parents. But, with a few rare exceptions it has done so in a negative way, showing a lack of understanding of that anguishing problem.

If the previous society might be said to have been "Christian," this same document notes, "then a process of de-Christianization might be said to have been going on." (La Iglesia 1968:287). This document notes further (La Iglesia 1968:291):

> The Marxist vision is making itself increasingly more acceptable among young university students and workers, who do not see in the Church a bold solution. There is a growing indifference among the young to religious values. They are even less interested in God.

Has the church's traditional position toward contraception had any effect on Mexico's birth rates? In Weberian terms, is the church's traditional opposition to artificial methods of contraception "economically relevant"? The *Centro de Estudios Económicos y Demográficos* in Mexico City attempted to relate the degree of religiosity (in terms of frequency of church attendance) shown by women over twenty who had ever been pregnant to the number of live births per woman. There were a total of 1,913 Mexico City women in the sample. Of those women, 57.2 per cent were found to attend church once a week. The average number of children born alive to these women was 3.98. For the 21.5 per cent of the women who attended church once or twice a month, the average number of live births was 4.13. The number of women who attended church only once a month made up only 17.1 per cent of the total and they averaged 4.11 live births each. Only 2.8 per cent of the women in the sample never did attend church, and they averaged 3.3 births each (Centro 1970:81). The study concludes that women who attend church with greater frequency have a smaller number of children, on the average, but that the differences are small. Those who do not attend church at all have a smaller number of children than those who attend, but the importance of the difference is limited due to the small relative number of the women in this group—a total of 56 women (Centro 1970:80).

An effort to relate number of children to per capita consumption in pesos (again for Mexico City only) appears to yield more definitive results. Women whose consumption levels in 1964 were between 21 and 323 pesos averaged 5.27 live births. Women whose consumption levels were between 2,142 and 3,050 pesos averaged 2.21 live births (Centro 1970:79). Similar differences are reported for different educational levels, with women lacking any schooling whatever averaging 4.06 live births and women trained at the university level averaging only 1.82. These last figures are also restricted to Mexico City (Centro 1970:77).

Confronted with the question whether the high percentage of Catholics (96.5 per cent) in the population accounts for the high Mexican birth rates, one article notes (Whetten 1964:350):

> This must undoubtedly be an important factor in the problem, although France and Ireland are also Catholic nations, and in spite of that they have consistently maintained low birth rates, above all in comparison with other European countries, after 1890. Argentina has a birth rate of 22 per thousand in comparison to 45.5 for Mexico.

Pilot family planning projects in Mexico City have found that the poor, wives as well as husbands, are receptive to contraceptive methods. Despite bans on publicity, the number of clients seeking information and aid has increased at very rapid rates. Leaders of these projects note that there is a gap of misunderstanding between what Mexico's intellectuals think the popular reaction to contraception would be and what that reaction actually is, since it is often assumed that the people would oppose contraceptive measures and yet the people, are, in fact, receptive.

The Mexican government has not followed an unwavering population policy line during the last fifty years, although the trend of that policy has been weighed on the side of favoring population growth. The classic statement of the Mexican government's pro-natalist policy was formulated during the Cárdenas administration. The key point in this statement is that a larger population is needed to improve Mexico's living standards. It is interesting to note that Mexico's most reformist administration was also the most committed to population growth. A spokesman for the National Revolutionary Party during that administration's tenure in office took note of "'the neo-malthusianism of the militarist and imperialist countries:' [stating also that] the standards of living in underpopulated countries (including Mexico) could not be raised without decided increases in population" (Jaffe 1959:252–53). This policy is reported to have been reaffirmed in 1947, through the enactment of the General Population Act. This act states that "the purpose of the government is to encourage population growth through natural increase, aided by health measures to lower infant and child mortality, and through immigration (Jaffe 1959:253).

The available facts concerning Mexico's population policy suggest that U.S. expansionism has had a hand—aside from any influence church teaching on contraception might have had—in creating a motive for the promotion of population growth in Mexico. Mexican leaders could not but have been keenly aware of the fact that Mexico lost half of its territory to the United States during the so-called "Mexican War." The facts suggest also that such family planning programs as have been established up until the very recent past have tended to be stopgap measures intended to relieve current strains rather than to lead the way into a more consciously planned pattern of population growth. Perhaps Mexico has now begun to move in the direction of implementing such a policy. One thing is certain: Mexico's pattern of population growth during the twentieth century is of such magnitude that those leaders who are in a position to influence it can either approve or disapprove of it, but they can no longer ignore it.

It should be noted before passing on to the next subject that the strongest pro-natalist statement quoted above was made in 1935 during the administration which (1) carried forward the most intensive program of land reform, unmatched by that of any other post-revolutionary administration before or since; (2) nationalized Mexico's oil industries; (3) Mexicanized insurance companies; and, among other things, (4) established new governmental institutions of credit; i.e., Nacional Financiera (LaCascia 1969:16–17). Through its various programs the Cárdenas administration set the basis for Mexico's most impressive decade of economic growth—the 1940's.

After some initial hesitation the recent Echeverría administration seemed to have come around to a position in favor of limiting population growth. This policy was continued by the Lopez Portillo administration and by 1979 had had a noticeable impact on the birth rate.

12.

Exploitation and Poverty in Mexico:
Marxian Theories

To protect the land holdings
of the great hacienda owners,
the government made a treaty
with those imperialists.

Now we export farmworkers
for the Texas foreman,
and we remove from his land
the Mexican farmworker!

From the song "Corrido de Santo Domingo,"
by Judith Reyes.

Explanations of poverty in terms of exploitation are by no means found only among intellectuals in Mexico; they are also found among relatively uneducated people whose notions of socialism and communism are vague or indefinite (Lewis 1967:127–28; Lewis 1963:497). Among the poor there is a sense that the revolution has miscarried and that it succeeded only in substituting one set of exploiters for another. In the past "it was the hacienda owners who exploited us," said Pedro Martínez, an aged peasant who had fought with the Zapatista forces. "Now it's the government and bankers. It's all the same" (Lewis 1959:42).

Pedro no longer believed in all the talk he heard about the revolution. In fact so far as he was concerned, the revolution had been a failure. The whole situation added up to this: Zapata had lost and Carranza had won. When people talked about the revolution, they meant Carranza's not Zapata's. In many ways Mexicans were freer, but many were not free to eat. The more peace prevailed, the more hunger there was. Freedom there was, he thought, a lot of freedom, but people were not free to eat. For the rich, the situation was heavenly. The rich would come in and build houses with swimming pools in lots where poor people, who had previously lived there in little huts, could not find enough well water to drink. Scarcity was scarcity for the poor. What the farmer produced, what the poor man produced, sold cheap. What the man of science produced sold dear. The people no longer counted for anything. People in his village did not really understand what was going on. To Pedro they were all blindfolded. Their lack of culture, their disunity, and their poverty kept them from seeing through things (Lewis 1967:456–57).

Jesús Sánchez, a denizen of Mexico City's urban slums who had migrated from Veracruz at an early age, saw little chance of an improvement in the working man's lot. Though he recognized that Mexico had made some progress, he saw little hope of doing away with exploitation. The manner in which exploitation took place had changed, but not the fact of exploitation. Price increases were always more than enough to reverse any improvement in the worker's living standards through wage increases (Lewis 1963:497).

Both of these men apparently came face to face with a set of facts within the structure of Mexican life for which the concept of exploitation provides a more or less distinctive cognitive category. The historically specific theoretical effort which most closely addresses itself to the questions concerning poverty raised by Marx and Engels is that of Alonso Aguilar Monteverde. Aguilar has noted that the degree of inequality found in Mexico is seldom matched elsewhere in the world. Mexico's elite is small and immensely rich, and the large masses of the people have nothing, and work only to eat badly (Aguilar 1967:83). The contrast between these classes is a constant feature of Mexico's social landscape. On the one hand there are prosperous businessmen living in expensive and impressive residential colonies bearing such names as Paseo de la Reforma or Lomas de Chapultepec. On the other side are miserable peasants and proletarian slums bearing such names as Mixteca Oaxaqueña and Valle de la Muerte. Well-being on one side has its counterpart in neglect on the other. Mexico is a backward and contradictory country where "justice is no more than a theme for demagogic speeches and un-delivered promises" (Aguilar 1967:83).

Aguilar recognizes that one of the distinctive features of Mexico's investment policy since the revolution has been a degree of participation by the public sector which is larger than usual for underdeveloped nations. Nonetheless, this policy is administered in such a way that the private sector ends up being the chief beneficiary of the government's financial ventures. Typical is a situation where if federal government investments account for 40 per cent of the total, and private investments account for 60 per cent, the return on public investments will account for 20 per cent of the product obtained, while the return on private investments will account for 80 per cent. The situation amounts to this: the state invests to benefit private enterprise. Also, public investments are made in such a way that they tend to cover deficiencies in private investments (Aguilar 1967:56–57). The federal government's fiscal intakes absorb only 8 per cent of the National Product. In other nations this figure is as high as 20 to 30 per cent (Aguilar 1967:64).

What capital accumulation has been possible during the last century has taken place through a massive exploitation of labor (Aguilar 1967:71). Typically, less than a third of the total product is paid in the form of wages and salaries in Mexico. By contrast, Mexico's capitalists receive between 40 and 50 per cent of the total product. The rate of profit on capital investments frequently exceeds 20 per cent, and even 25 and 30 per cent, of the annual invested capital (Aguilar 1967:73–74). For approximately 8 out of every 10 economically active persons, real income either stayed the same or declined during the early 1960's. Many people receive wages below the minimum, and wages are almost always lagging behind prices. Real relative salaries, with reference to the productivity levels of those who receive them, show a clear tendency to decline (Aguilar 1967:73).

Both unemployment and underemployment have been typical of Mexico's economic development. One estimate is that together they account for more than 6.3 million inhabitants, or 18 per cent of the population of the country. By another estimate 30 per cent of the country's rural population is underemployed, working only from three to six months of the year (Aguilar 1967:72).

Table 14.   **Rate of Exploitation of Work in Selected Industries in Mexico**

Industry	Rate %
Average	120.5
Flour milling, wheat	1023.2
Milk, condensed, evaporated and dried	502.4
Cigarettes	191.2
Synthetic fibers	177.6
Fertilizers	149.1
Automobile assembly	141.4
Cement	140.0
Soaps and detergents	98.2
Smelting and sheet metal	88.0
Paper and cellulose	77.8

Source: Alonso Aguilar Monteverde y Fernando Carmona, *Mexico: Riqueza y Miseria* (Mexico City: Editorial Nuestro Tiempo, 1967), p. 77.

In agriculture the average income of entrepreneurs is about thirty to fifty times larger than the average income of laborers. The average rate of exploitation for a sample of 877 industries is 120.5 per cent, with a 50 per cent rate of exploitation indicating that three hours out of a nine-hour working day are appropriated in the form of profits and that six hours are paid in the form of wages and salaries. Low salaries are not due to low productivity, since Mexico's industries showed a relatively high (6.4 to 1) organic composition of capital in 1964, a fact which expresses the growing productivity of labor. This ratio means that only about 13 per cent of the total capital available in 1964 was paid in the form of salaries. Assuming an earlier ratio of constant to variable capital of 1 to 1, the 1964 ratio of 6.4 to 1 would indicate an increase in productivity and a relative decrease in the need for labor (Aguilar 1967:78).

The rate of exploitation in commerce is reported to be even higher than in industry, i.e., 240 per cent. These rates of exploitation are seen as indicating that a large savings potential exists in Mexico— a potential which, if invested, could help promote rapid economic growth. Workers' incomes have not kept up with increases in productivity. It is doubtful that Mexico's bourgeois will translate the surplus appropriated into a means for promoting accelerated economic development. Instead, a progressive slowing down of Mexico's economic growth rates is predicted. Aguilar Monteverde concludes that fundamental changes in the structure of Mexico's political economy would be necessary in order to reverse these trends.

Fernando Carmona has taken on the task of coming to terms with official claims about an ongoing "Mexican Miracle" (Carmona 1970). The so-called Mexican Miracle takes the form of high economic growth rates despite Mexico's rapidly expanding population (Carmona 1970:7). Mexico has achieved—or such is the official claim— one of the most rapid rates of economic growth in the world within a framework of peace and political stability. This growth has been steady and has been accompanied by advances on many fronts, including education, social services, social security, urban splendor, and modernization in agriculture (Carmona 1970:14). Mexico's agricultural production not only has been able to keep ahead of its population growth (one of the most rapid in the world) in the midst of a population explosion; it also has assured food for rapidly growing urban centers, provided raw materials for a growing number of Mexican industries, and permitted an increase in exports (Carmona 1970:23–24).

In view of Mexico's high rates of exploitation (172.0 in 1966) the miracle is, Carmona notes, that the millions of Mexico's poor have been able to survive at all (Carmona 1970:90, 95). Actually, Mexico's GNP growth rates are small by comparison to a number of other countries and yield paltry results when translated to absolute increase figures. During the interval 1960–65, the rate of growth of Mexico's real GNP per capita was 2.5 per cent per year. The corresponding figure for France was 3.7 and for Japan 10.2 (Carmona 1970:37). The Mexican Miracle is, to a large extent, a "statistical development," i.e., illusory (Carmona 1970:87). A per capita growth rate of 1.6 per cent per year in the United States (1950–63) yields

93.77 dollars in absolute terms. A per capita growth rate of 2.8 per cent per year in Mexico yields 5.74 dollars per year in absolute terms (Carmona 1970:39). The degree to which misery is actually present in the country can be seen in the fact that the income of three-fourths of the inhabitants of the Federal District was below the average GNP per capita (566 dollars per year) and in the fact that the average monthly income per capita in rural communities was approximately 10 dollars in 1963 (Carmona 1970:50, 94).

Carmona makes reference to the existence of a gigantic and growing mass of underemployed and pariahs whose living conditions are worse than those of the proletariat in general (Carmona 1970:91–92). He also identifies three fundamental structural problems in Mexico's growth, i.e., external dependence, internal and external monopolistic concentration of wealth and income, and the state capitalism which keeps the system going (Carmona 1970:99). Sixty per cent of Mexico's trade takes place with the United States. He also takes note of the flow of braceros and tourists and concludes that Mexico's one-sided dependence on the United States is an indicator of the failure of the revolution. There is hardly an important United States firm, Carmona notes, which does not have a subsidiary in Mexico. Mexico's post-revolution establishment is described as a form of capitalism of underdevelopment, with a dominant class which is itself dominated. He also presents a detailed analysis of some of the reforms of Mexico's political economy following the revolution, beginning with a rejection of *laissez-faire* capitalism and Porfirismo and ending with the re-emergence of a powerful oligarchic stratum coupled with neo-Porfirismo in politics during the presidency of Miguel Alemán (Carmona 1970:57–81).

Carmona notes also that a sizable number of foreign investigators, in particular some of United States origin (such as Tannenbaum, Mosk, Brandenburg, and Vernon), tend to study Mexico with a focus on political economy and from conservative and reactionary positions—positions which are not merely economic in nature. More often than not, Carmona notes, their work alerts private interests, foundations, monopolies (real or imagined), the CIA, the State Department, and universities concerning developments in Mexico (Carmona 1970:29–30).

Pablo González Casanova views Mexico as an exploitation colony where the exploited form two distinct sectors, one of which partici-pates in Mexico's development while the other is marginal. In his view, this duality is the most distinctive feature of Mexico's develop-ment (González 1970:116; González 1966:218–19). Four-fifths of Mexico's population in 1961 and 1962 received incomes which were insufficient (less than 1,000 pesos per month) to provide a "modest standard of living" (González 1970:109). Sixty per cent of Mexico's population is estimated to be marginal (González 1970:119). Partly because of a variety of indexes of "marginality" used, all of which yield different population sizes, and partly also from lack of con-ceptual clarity and a tendency to shift in focus from the indigenous problem to the rural problem, the relative figure just given is not consistent with an absolute figure of 10.6 million marginal inhabi-tants given elsewhere concerning the size of this marginal population (González 1968:66).

A situation exists in Mexico whereby in 1949 only 24 per cent of the national income went to the working sector, while in 1960 only 31.4 per cent trickled down to them. By comparison the working class income in other countries in 1950, taken as a percentage of national income figures, was as follows: France, 49 per cent; Canada, 59 per cent; Switzerland, 59 per cent; the United States, 65 per cent; England, 67 per cent. The 1960 figures for Mexico were still lower than those of any other developed country (González 1970:105).

Although Mexico is admitted to be an exploitation colony, Gon-zález Casanova takes exception with the view that Mexican history can be interpreted in terms of the class struggle. In his view what is important is the duality of the exploited population and "the national struggle" (González 1968:79–80). Whether or not one sees Mexico as a profoundly dissatisfied nation which is ripe for revolu-tion depends on whether or not the observer takes a short- or long-term view of Mexican history after the revolution (González 1970: 109). A short-term focus reveals that profound inequalities are still to be found a half century after the revolution. These inequalities are in life expectancy (the poor experience a death rate twice as high as that of the rich), diet, education, clothing, shelter, and income (González 1968:65–73; González 1970:108). However, a longer-term focus reveals that there have been sharp reductions in the degree of inequality in some areas and moderate reductions in others (González 1966:224). It is also noted that in the quarter century between 1940 and 1965, the GNP quadrupled and the GNP per capita doubled. Moreover, land reform redistributed a vast amount of land to a sizable sector of the peasantry (González 1970:109–10).

González Casanova mentions two studies which deal with changes in Mexico's class structure since the turn of the century. He agrees with the one which estimates the least amount of change (González 1968:77). Nonetheless, he maintains that the trend of Mexico's development as regards wealth redistribution has tended toward integration of all inhabitants into full citizenship (González 1968:78). In his view the rate of growth of the participating population is more rapid than that of the general population and far more rapid than that of the marginal population (González 1966:225). Hence, although he admits that there are really two Mexicos, one of which is rural, poor, uneducated, and partly marginal, while the other is urban, developing, and "mainly participant," he denies that Mexico is ripe for revolution; that is, he denies that the class of the poor in Mexico are ready to pass from the status of a class in itself to the status of a class for itself (González 1968:73, 64–65). A number of factors tend to foster a psychology of individual salvation, among them nationalization of some industries, rural-urban migration, and the international flow of braceros and wetbacks, all of which are seen as powerful palliatives to inequality (González 1968:76; González 1970:114). Other factors besides those which foster a psychology of individual salvation contribute to a relative absence of class consciousness in Mexico. Among them are one party rule which receives electoral support, a political rhetoric which identifies class consciousness with revolutionary ideals, and union activities cued from above (González 1968:73–75, 79).

All of the above factors tend to make reformists and conformists out of the masses of Mexico's poor. Lower class fatalism, upper class paternalism, reformism, and nationalism all combine to hold back class action (González 1968:80). González Casanova notes that the lack of class consciousness is not due to the alienation of the working class, as some Marxists argue, but rather to the priority of the national over the class struggle in Mexico and to structural differences between the marginal sector and the participating sector (González 1968:80). The problem of the marginal population does not receive organized expression from below; it rests only in the political and moral consciousness of Mexico's ruling class, its civil servants, and its intellectuals. The marginal sector finds itself isolated when the government responds to pressures applied by the participating sector, since such responses tend to favor the latter (González 1968:79–80). González Casanova concludes that the existing system has a good chance of surviving as long as its economy continues to grow at a rapid pace and as long as a policy of "balanced mobilization" continues. He also acknowledges that post-war economic growth rates became stagnant after declining and that even the most optimistic are worried on that account (González 1968:80: González 1970:115, 118–19).

José Rangel Contla has made the point that Mexican history has not followed classical Marxist lines of historical change on the matter of growing proletarianization of the middle class (Rangel 1970:413). On the basis of statistical data he shows that the relative size of the proletariat decreased sharply between 1921 and 1950 and again increased moderately to sharply between 1950 and 1960. The absolute size of the proletariat increased only slightly between 1921 and 1950 and very sharply between 1950 and 1960. By contrast, the relative size of the *petite bourgeoisie* showed a marked increase between 1921 and 1950 and a sharp but less abrupt decrease between 1950 and 1960. The absolute size of the *petite bourgeoisie* trebled between 1921 and 1950 and registered a slight decrease between 1950 and 1960 (Rangel 1970:403–405, 414).

Two main factors are responsible for these trends according to Rangel: the modification of Mexico's legal system of land tenure under the terms of Article 27 of the Constitution of 1917, and the federal government's recent efforts to promote Mexico's industrialization. The program of land reform tended to sidetrack the tendency toward growing proletarianization, widened the *petit-bourgeois* sector, and sought to silence the agrarian demands of the Zapatista forces. On the other hand, the federal government's efforts to promote industrialization have once more set in motion the process of property concentration and the tendency toward growing proletarianization (Rangel 1970:413).

Francisco Alvarez y Lezama has made the point that what appears to be overpopulation in Mexico is really the result of turning the increasing productivity of labor away from its end of supplying the necessities of labor and toward maintaining the living standards of the dominant bourgeois. Hence what appears as relative overproduction from the point of view of labor's inability to buy what it produces takes the form of capital concentration on the side of the few who are rich. Hence, although the masses of the people were the source of the revolution, they have not been its chief beneficiaries (Alvarez 1966:164).

13.

Trends Related to
Exploitation and Poverty
in Mexico

The concentration of land ownership in the hands of a relatively small number of privileged families, coupled with the growing destitution of the peasantry, had reached such proportions prior to the 1910–1917 Revolution that the word "extreme" fails to convey a full sense of the situation. A 1910 estimate indicates that 90 per cent of the rural villagers in the Central Mesa owned no land beyond the lots their huts were built on (Whetten 1950:11). Another estimate, which appears to err on the conservative side, is that 70 per cent of the tillable land in the country was controlled by 1 per cent of the population (Dozer 1953:122). Three companies owned 78 per cent of the land in Baja California, accounting thus for 93,798 square kilometers (Brinsmade 1916:12–13). An interview with Don Luis Terrazas produced a classic anecdote which sums up a period in Mexican history. "Es Usted de Chihuahua? [Are you from Chihuahua?]" a reporter asked him. Don Luis quipped, "Chihuahua es de mi! [Chihuahua is mine!]." His pun was a play on the Spanish use of the word *of* instead of from. Don Luis was lord and master of 60,000 square kilometers of land, very nearly a fourth of the total land area (245,000 square kilometers) of the state of Chihuahua (Mendieta 1946:164).

The situation just described was the culmination of a long historical struggle between two forms of land tenure which had been present throughout the history of Mexico. One of those viewed ownership as inseparable from labor performed. The other conceived ownership as an abstract right of a possessor over the land and its products, irrespective of any productive relationship to the land. Both of these forms were present in Mexico before and after the Spanish conquest, although the earlier form prevailed before the conquest and during the early years of the colonial interval (Simpson 1937:6). The Spanish conquest gave impetus to the latter and set in motion a process of expansion of the large, privately owned, hacienda-type holdings at the expense of the small, communal, non-alienable type of holdings (Beals 1952–53:327; Mendieta 1946:90). The Revolution of 1910–17 rose out of the final collapse of village community-type holdings under the pressure of laws and policies designed to promote the expansion of the large haciendas.

The impact of the conquest began with the transfer of privately owned lands from the control of the Aztec nobility and warlords to the conquerors. This process was facilitated because the natives were at first allowed to sell their lands (Mendieta 1946:90). The *encomienda* system placed under the control of each colonist an amount of land equal to more than half as much as the total land area which the so-called legal fund allowed to each town (Mendieta 1946:90). The privileged position of the conquerors, in particular their military and economic dominance, coupled with their advantageous position in matters of legal interpretation and manipulation, made possible the expansion of the large haciendas by a simple process of expulsion of the natives from their lands until they were confined within the limits of the "legal" fund (Mendieta 1946:89). Once the large haciendas were established, their size tended to be maintained through the practice known as *mayorazgo* (primogeniture): a legal requirement to retain the land within the family and to transfer it to the owner's elder son upon the death of the owner (Mendieta 1946:89). Early efforts to limit the transferability of Indian lands to cases where the transfer was shown to be absolutely necessary and convenient failed to stem the tide toward dispossession of the natives (Mendieta 1946:66, 77).

During the War of Independence, José María Morelos recognized the depth of the agrarian problem when he decreed that all haciendas larger than two leagues should be put to use. Agriculture, he argued, would yield greater benefits if many people dedicated themselves to the improvement of a small piece of land than if one man held large tracts of land which had to be worked by the forced labor of thousands of slaves (Ramos 1936:94–95). Following Independence, the Mexican government (headed by Royalist Creoles) sought to focus attention on population redistribution as a method of solving the agrarian problem. Efforts of this type ended in failure, and the loss of 50 per cent of Mexico's territory to the United States in 1848 tended to preclude any remaining possibilities in that direction (Ramos 1936:98, 101; Mendieta 1946:105–106).

Subsequent reform movements tended to follow the path of least resistance and established the legal basis that set the stage for the final collapse. According to one estimate the church controlled "at least half of the real property and capital of the country" at the end of the Colonial interval (Mendieta 1946:12). Through royal grants, *encomiendas*, deeds, and so on the church had acquired control of vast landed estates, which it administered for the benefit of the cult and for the increment of its wealth. Control over these vast estates gave the church immense economic and political power and interests to protect (Whetten 1950:12). As its wealth increased, the church's role as protector and uplifter of the native populations, such as it was, lost more and more ground to its role as protector of the status quo. More and more it became the supporter of governments which would support its interests (Cabrera 1916:10).

Efforts to find an internal solution to Mexico's problems then focused attention on church lands. Under the terms of the Juarez Law of 1855 the privileges of the military and clerical classes were abolished, and church properties were placed under the administrative control of the civil authorities. The Lerdo Law of 1856 sought to abolish all properties held by religious corporations which were not actually being used by them. All church lands being leased by tenants were now open to purchase by the tenant at prices to be determined by rental charges (Robertson 1930:487–88). Article 27 of the Constitution of 1857 provided that "no civil or ecclesiastical corporation of whatever character should have the legal capacity to acquire or administer real estate, except such buildings as might be necessary for the service of the respective corporations" (Robertson 1930:488). Since the term "corporation" also applied to native communities, this law had consequences that went beyond its impact on the church. The law was interpreted to mean that native communities had been stripped of their juridical personality and that they no longer existed as communities. Thereafter native communities found themselves legally unable to defend their territories. Thus the over-all thrust of this law was that it favored the growth of the large haciendas at the expense of native lands (Mendieta 1946:132). The over-all intent of the law had been to solve the agrarian problem by individualizing the communal holdings of the natives; its actual impact was to legalize the sale of once communal lands (Mendieta 1946:159).

The blow that completed the despoliation of the peasantry came in the form of a series of laws promulgated during the thirty-year dictatorship of Porfirio Díaz. These laws were passed between 1883 and 1894 and were known as the *Leyes de Deslindes* (surveying laws). By virtue of these laws, the original natural demarcations of *ejidal* lands that were described in the royal grants of 1573 and later were declared null and void (Brinsmade 1916:12). The *ejido*, along with the legal fund and the *propio*, had been one of the three types of landholdings which were ceded "to the moral entity of the people" and which were reinstituted during the colony to protect native communities against further encroachment (Mendieta 1946:64, 77). The *ejidatario* had the right of usufruct and could transfer the land to his heirs but could not sell the land. All the lands of the *ejido* which were in excess of one square league were declared *demasias* (surplus lands) of the national territory and were left open for denunciation. These laws left the way open for the establishment of surveying companies, which sought government permission to survey lands. In exchange for this service they received two-thirds of the lands found—accurately or not—to be surplus lands. They also had a legal option to buy the remaining third (Brinsmade 1916:12). Under the provision of these laws approximately thirty million hectares had been "surveyed" by 1885 (Mendieta 1946:138–39). The expropriation of such "surplus" lands left peasant communities encircled and shut in by haciendas and ranchos. The peasants were now reduced to having to work for wages in the surrounding *latifundios*, most of which had been formed out of lands that previously belonged to the villages (Mendieta 1946:160–61).

These events set the stage for the revolutionary upheavals of 1910 to 1917. The peasant revolt was led by Emiliano Zapata in the south and by Pancho Villa in the north. Concerning Zapata, his biographer Womack said, "Anenecuilcans recalled a story of his childhood— that once as a child he had seen his father break down and cry in frustration at a local hacienda's enclosure of a village orchard, and that he had promised his father he would get the land back" (Womack 1968:6).

Pancho Villa's initiation into revolutionary politics has a similar source, though it adds an extra twist (Beals 1971:57):

> His father died when he was ten. At sixteen he was a sharecropper on the Gogojita Hacienda in Cantalan, where he lived with his mother, two brothers, and two younger sisters. Coming home from the fields on September 22, 1904, Villa killed *hacendado* Agustín López Negrete for violating his fifteen-year-old sister Marcella. He then fled into the nearby Sierra de la Silla in the Gamón range.

It is a commonplace assumption that the 1910–17 Revolution abolished the *latifundio* system through reforms carried out to implement the provisions of the 1917 Constitution. Actually, today there is talk about the emergence of a new type of *latifundismo* which is controlled by "nylon-shirt farmers" (Delgado 1962:76).

In order to have an idea of what has happened to land distribution since the revolution, we must first investigate the types of landholdings which were intended by the Constitution of 1917 and then examine the pattern of land distribution prevailing at a later date (1960). The Constitution of 1917 had defined "property" as "the right of a man to the product of his personal work" (Mendieta 1946:200). By thus defining property the constitution had rejected the view that property is an abstract right of a possessor over a thing irrespective of function performed; it also acknowledged the view that the legal right to dispose of the products of work had its source in work itself. Despite these changes in legal outlook, however, over half a century following these changes there were still land owners in Mexico who could, were they willing to take their chances on the possible public reactions, paraphrase Don Luis' boast with a measure of truth.

Article 27 of the Constitution of 1917 states (Mendieta 1946:197–98):

> The nation has the right to impose on private property the modalities dictated by the public interest; it also has the right to regulate the use of natural resources which are susceptible to appropriation, in order to

work out an equitable distribution of the public wealth and to care for its conservation.

This article provided the legal basis for what in Mexico is known as the *política impositiva*, whose implementation in the agrarian sector led to the program of land redistribution and in the industrial sector led to (among other things) the nationalization of the oil industries. This same article provided that two forms of landholding were to co-exist in Mexico thereafter: the *ejido* and the small property.

Depending on the supply and reliability of water and rainfall, the size of each *ejidal* unit was to vary from 3 to 8 hectares. The size of the small property, following the same criteria, was to vary between 150 and 300 hectares. Middle-sized properties could continue to exist only as long as holdings in excess of the above limits were not indispensable for the endowment of population centers in need of land (Mendieta 1946:203, 258).

There are, therefore, two distinctive systems of land tenure in Mexico, each of which shows differentiation within.

Figures dealing with the concentration of landholdings for 1970 are lacking. The available figures are for 1960, and the situation they reveal must be interpreted in light of the fact that between 1960 and 1969 alone 22 million hectares of land were reported to have been taken from 12,000 landed estates and redistributed under the program of agrarian reform. Also, a total of 54 million hectares (1 hectare equals 2.471 acres) had been redistributed by 1964 under Mexico's agrarian reform laws (LaCascia 1969:111).

Approximately 61 per cent of Mexico's farm acreage was still held under private forms of ownership in 1960. In that same year *ejidal* lands accounted for approximately 26 per cent of the total acreage which, together with the acreage held under communal forms of ownership, accounted for only about 31 per cent of the total (Tello 1971:638).

In 1960 the total land area under *ejidal* control was 44.5 million hectares and the total number of persons living in those *ejidal* lands *(ejidatarios)* was approximately 1.5 million, gathered in 18,301 *ejidal* settlements. *Ejidal* parcels ranged in size from one-tenth of a hectare to 10.1 hectares and over, while the modal size was between one-tenth of a hectare and one hectare. The average parcel size appears to have been somewhere under four hectares (Gómez 1970:698).

Considering now the distribution of lands held privately in 1960, we find that 4,000 estates with sizes in excess of 5,000 hectares, which accounted for only 0.3 per cent of the total number of private units, encompassed 56.6 per cent of the total land area held in private hands. If we consider all estates with sizes in excess of 1,000 hectares, we find that 13,000 such units, comprising only 1 per cent of the total number of haciendas, accounted for nearly three-fourths of the total area held privately (Tello 1971:639).

At the other extreme of the private sector, 899,000 estates smaller than 5 hectares each *(minifundios)* and accounting for 66.8 per cent of the total number of private holdings encompassed only 1.1 per cent of the total land area held under private control (Tello 1971: 639). It is clear that the range of variation of the *ejidal*-sized holdings and of the small properties which were to serve as guidelines for land reform, have been implemented in such a way as to minimize the modal size of the *ejido* and to maximize the size of the modified private holdings.

The pattern of land ownership still in existence led one observer to note that such a degree of concentration placed Mexico's land reform program under quotation marks (Reyes 1969:146). This same situation led another observer to speak of the Constitution of 1917 as the best work of political fiction written in Mexico (Carmona 1970:9). One author reports that 500 to 600 families control a large portion of the best irrigated lands and that cattle production is under the control of 100 to 150 families. Such family estates are reported to be in the northwest, north, central, and Gulf regions, with a scattering in other parts of the country. Along with land they control cattle, water, plant, equipment, and the best cattle breeds (Aguilar 1967:31).

Hence there is talk about the emergence of a new type of *latifundista*, within which are included politicians, bankers, industrialists, and others whose life-style is such that the luxury of the *Porfirista* land owners pales by comparison (Gómez 1970:693; Aguilar 1967: 76). Aguilar Monteverde has estimated that the income of capitalists in agriculture must be between thirty and fifty times greater than the income of peasants and wage workers. He also estimated the joint income paid to labor at 30 to 33 per cent of the aggregate income, which suggests that a relatively small number of capitalists in agriculture receive most of the value produced by labor while labor receives only a third or less of the total product (Aguilar 1967:75). Hence a wide contrast exists between the extravagance and luxurious life conditions of the wealthy landowners and the precarious and sordid life conditions of the agricultural laborers and peasants.

In 1910, 42 per cent of Mexico's wealth was reported to have been under foreign control. At the time Mexico was spoken of as the mother of foreigners and the stepmother of Mexicans. An estimate of the extent of United States control in some key sectors can only be hazarded from the following figures: railways, 64 per cent; minerals, 75 per cent; petroleum, 58 per cent (Singer 1969:51). Another estimate is that nearly half of Mexico's natural resources were owned by United States citizens before the 1910 revolution. Two-thirds of the total investments in the decade preceding the revolution were estimated to have originated in the activities of foreign financiers (Himes 1965:157). Foreign capital is reported to have had a "considerable" share in the early development of banking, commerce, hydroelectric power, textiles, chicle, and coffee, in addition to the three industries mentioned above. Only in the production of henequen, cane sugar, hides, and cattle did Mexicans hold a controlling share (Singer 1969:51).

Porfirio Díaz ruled through a select circle of men who, admiringly at first and derisively later, were known as *científicos*. A coalition of the *científicos* and foreign interests obtained concessions in banking, mining, petroleum, and other industries. Intellectually the *científicos* were under the influence of Comtean positivism and Social Darwinism. Some of them feared the ravenous and "marvelous collective animal" (Woodward 1971:74–92) on the north which had already deprived Mexico of half of its territory during the war known in the United States as the Mexican War. They viewed the "collective animal" as being equipped with "an enormous intestine" for which not enough food existed. It was also "armed and ready to devour" Mexico. They saw peace and industrial progress as essential for national survival. When they spoke of freedom, it was mostly the freedom to enrich themselves (Woodward 1971:74–92).

Under the rule of Don Porfirio and his *científicos* there was a spectacular growth in the production of export crops such as cotton, sugar, and henequen, as well as in the production of cattle. Correlatively, there was a decrease in the production of such food crops as corn, wheat, and beans (Himes 1965:155). During the three Díaz decades, the rate of increase in the growth of export crops per capita was approximately 4.6 per cent per year (Reynolds 1970:96). The per capita production of corn, a food staple, was cut almost in half, from 282 to 144 kilograms per person (Reyes 1967:196). Mexican production was oriented toward international markets, and the country's railways were built toward the sea.

Article 27 of the Constitution of 1917 contained a number of restrictions on foreign ownership of land, as well as a number of antimonopoly provisions. The latter, however, did not prevent a continuation of the trends toward capital concentration after the revolution (LaCascia 1969:7; Camargo 1964:266). A list of the firms that control Mexican industries, from automobiles to food packaging, reads much like a *Who's Who* among international corporations (Aguilar 1967:32–33): DuPont, Monsanto, Imperial Chemical, Allied Chemical, Union Carbide, Cyanamid, General Motors, Ford, Chrysler, Volkswagen, Parke Davis, Merck and Co., The Sydney Ross Co., Squibb, Anderson Clayton, Lieber Brothers, Nestle, Heinz, Kraft, Del Monte, and Celanese. These industries and others dominate the production of chemicals, automobiles, pharmaceuticals, artificial fibers, cooking oil, cotton, and tires and fruit, vegetable, and other food packaging. The production of iron works, cement, sugar, wheat flour, beer, and tobacco products is under the control of companies bearing Spanish names. The names, however, are misleading in the cases of the cement and the tobacco industries since foreign capital predominates in the former and controls the latter. Among those listed, this leaves only iron works, sugar, wheat flour, and beer production under Mexican control—that is, under the control of a few Mexican families. In a number of fields from one to three firms either control or predominate; cotton production, glass, iron, synthetic fibers, cooking oil, tobacco, and beer are cases in point.

The extent of capital concentration in Mexico's industries is such that in 1965, 1.5 per cent of the total number of establishments controlled approximately 77 per cent of the total capital and accounted for 75 per cent of the total value of production (Rangel 1970: 415). Also in 1965 this same 1.5 per cent of the total number of establishments employed approximately 45 per cent of the total number of persons employed in industry (González Salazar 1971: 549–50; Tello 1971:634–35).

By contrast, at the bottom of the distribution of capital holdings by size of establishment we find that in 1965, 85 per cent of the total number of establishments employed only 16.2 per cent of the personnel and accounted for 1.8 per cent of the invested capital. These same establishments accounted for 3.9 per cent of the total production. This appears to be an area where some of Mexico's hidden unemployment is to be sought (González Salazar 1971:549–50). The extent of capital concentration in Mexico is also reflected in the fact that the Federal District, with approximately one-sixth of the country's population, accounted for twice the amount of capital reserves available in the rest of the country (Carmona 1970: 42).

What does the concentration of capital, of production, and, to a lesser degree, of labor power mean? We have seen, while considering the structure of Mexico's labor force, that somewhat over a fifth (21.6 per cent) of Mexico's economically active population was employed in the "secondary," or industrial, sector. We saw also that approximately half (48.9 per cent) of the same population was employed in the primary, or rural-type, sector. Hence estimates of the population rendered superfluous by industrial concentration are not likely to account for as large a portion of the industrial reserve army as concentration of ownership in the rural sector would. Nonetheless, the population rendered jobless between 1960 and 1965 by changes in the intensity of use of capital resources has been estimated at 378,289. This figure is reported to account for 19 per cent of the total number of persons (2,008,545) employed in industry in 1960. In the same article it is estimated that 200,144 jobs were eliminated between 1950 and 1960 as a result of increases in productivity and that an additional 36,325 jobs were done away with by increases of the same type between 1960 and 1965 (Trejo 1970:114–18).

Economists who are familiar with trends toward capital concentration in Mexico emphasize different facets of the impact of such concentration on Mexican life (Carmona 1970:89; González Salazar 1971:547; Tello 1971:637–38). They point to: (1) a necessary correlation between, on the one hand, capital concentration and, on the other, exploitation of labor, forced savings, and the division of the labor force into an employed and an unemployed sector, with the unemployed sector exerting a depressing effect on the employed sector; (2) dependence abroad coupled with imbalances within and between the various sectors of Mexico's economy, concentration of income and incapacity of the industrial sector to provide employment for the growing population, plus high rates of exploitation of labor; and finally (3) the fact that such trends are not unique to Mexico and the likelihood that they will become more pronounced in the future.

Mexico nationalized its petroleum industries under the terms of a presidential decree issued on March 18, 1938. Before expropriation practically all of the oil extracted was exported. Foreign investments in oil were so profitable that companies could recover their original investments in six years. After nationalization oil production was oriented toward the internal needs of the economy (Camargo 1964: 267–68). Mexico's mines are still privately owned, and the production of gold and silver has shown a sustained downward trend, which seems to indicate that the available supply of these minerals is beginning to approach exhaustion. Most of Mexico's mines are owned by Mexicans, but the most powerful companies—the ones which account for practically "all of the production of the fields" —are subsidiaries of international concerns (Camargo 1964:270–71).

Mexico's commerce before the revolution centered primarily on the *tiendas de raya* which formed part of every hacienda along with the chapel and the jail (Ortega 1966:50). These *tiendas* have been described as permanent agencies of robbery and as slave factories that kept the laborers of the hacienda under conditions of debt peonage (Mendieta 1946:166–67). The unequal exchange between the hacienda *tiendas* and the laborers of the field is reflected in the fact that, during the presidency of Porfirio Díaz, wage increases failed to keep up with increases in the price of food. The state of Puebla registered a 50 per cent increase in wages during that interval, while the price of corn increased by 200 per cent and that of *chile* increased by 800 per cent. This situation was shown to be widely prevalent by a study conducted by the Federal Department of Development (Brinsmade 1916:15).

The over-all pattern of development of Mexico's commerce in the years following the revolution is one of regional imbalance, and this unbalanced pattern is both a consequence of an unbalanced economy and a factor in maintaining that imbalance. A recent study dealing with the unbalanced growth of Mexico's economy has identified three clearly distinguishable regional functions in Mexico's economy. The first region, consisting of the North Pacific, the North, and the Gulf Coast zones, produces articles for export and obtains foreign exchange; a second region, the Federal District, absorbs the foreign exchange, invests in new industry, attracts commercial enterprises, and keeps consumer articles at low prices; the remainder of the country produces consumer's goods at low prices.

The three zones that make up the first region accounted for 62.5 per cent of Mexico's exports in 1964. Only about a fourth of the total exports originate in the Federal District. By contrast, over three-fourths (78.2 per cent) of the imports brought to the country are destined for the Federal District (de la Peña 1966:307). The same study shows that while per capita income in the Federal District increased at a rate of 6 per cent per year between 1956 and 1964, the three above-mentioned heaviest contributors to the country's exports experienced declining real per capita incomes during the same interval. The declines were as follows: North Pacific Zone, −0.8 per cent; Gulf of Mexico, −1.0 per cent; North, −0.5 per cent (de la Peña 1966:306). Assuming these rates to be constant, the Federal District's real per capita income would double every twelve years while that of the North Pacific would be cut in half in approximately eighty-eight years.

Chapter 8 showed that during the interval 1939 to 1964, there was a 10.6-fold increase in average minimum salaries and a twelve-fold decrease in the purchasing power of the peso. It showed also that for the great masses of those receiving minimum salaries, these salaries were not enough to cover the minimum family budget; in addition, at no time up to 1964 did these salaries return to the 1939 base level, where the index of the purchasing power of the minimum salary was 100. Therefore the question is, assuming the correctness of both sets of figures, if the rate of increase of food prices is not keeping up with minimum salaries, and if the purchasing power of the peso is, nevertheless, decreasing faster than the rate of increase in minimum salaries—what accounts for the rate of inflation? Perhaps another look at some of the items listed under the family budget might give us a clue. We are restricted by the fact that the listing at hand is for the rural rather than the urban family. Nonetheless, another look may be fruitful.

The rural family budget for 1964 allocated 60.1 per cent of the family expenses to food costs. A total of 9.5 per cent went to pay rent. One-tenth of these remaining costs paid for clothing and shoes. The inflationary pressures that render the increases in minimum salaries worthless must then have their source in increased costs in some or all of these other factors; and perhaps in some not included here.

The fact that food prices have been kept relatively low and that food expenses, nevertheless, account for such a high proportion of the rural family budget suggests that the rates of inflation are to be sought in the secondary and tertiary sectors of Mexico's economy, in particular in the tertiary, or commercial, sector, where rates of exploitation show every indication of being higher than in the secondary, or industrial, sector. Part of the inflation must be stimulated by inflationary trends that are transmitted to Mexico from the United States and other nations via the import market. Mexico's inflationary trends are often viewed as a method of forcibly extracting "savings" from the population; so the investment potential available is viewed as arising at the expense of the growing impoverishment of the masses.

The preceding information suggests that Mexico's rural areas still bear a disproportionate share of the burden of "forced savings" which are extracted from the laboring population. Since as late as 1970 nearly half (48.9 per cent) of Mexico's economically active population was employed in rural-related primary occupations, the likelihood is that a substantial portion of the burden of exploitation is still on the shoulders of Mexico's peasantry. However, there can be little doubt that this burden has increasingly shifted toward the the urban masses, since Mexico's population has been predominantly urban since the early sixties (González Aparicio 1963:93). Quite apart from the question of where the heavier burden lies, it is ultimately at the expense of the living standards of Mexico's poor that Mexico's industrialization is advancing. In this connection Lewis says (Lewis 1963:xxx–xxxi):

> . . . with all of their inglorious defects and weaknesses, it is the poor who emerge as the true heroes of contemporary Mexico, for they are paying the cost of the industrial progress of the nation. Indeed, the political stability of Mexico is grim testimony to the great capacity for misery and suffering of the ordinary Mexican. But even the Mexican capacity for suffering has its limits, and unless ways are found to achieve a more equitable distribution of the growing national wealth and a greater equality of sacrifice during the difficult period of industrialization, we may expect social upheavals, sooner or later.

The relative importance of both imports and exports with reference to Mexico's GNP has been declining in recent years. Also, since the end of World War II, with the exception of a single year (1949), Mexico's imports have exceeded her exports (Padilla 1969:26–27).

The international and intranational imbalances that are built into the structure of the Mexican economy cannot but be reflected in a differential distribution of purchasing power by regions. The population endowed with purchasing power has been defined as the population having incomes above 1,500, above 1,000, and above 750 pesos per month in 1964, depending on whether the level-of-living index for the region was above 100, between 77.5 and 100, or below 77.5. On the basis of this classification, it has been found ". . . that the Federal District is the only zone which has a population which can be considered as having purchasing power up to the level of 38.2%" (de la Peña 1966:309–10). The percentage of the population with purchasing power in the remaining regions is as follows: North Pacific, 28.0; Gulf, 13.0; North, 14.0; Center, 12.8; and South, 9.5. Also, it is the Federal District's purchasing power that makes it an attractive market for investors (de la Peña 1966:310):

> This market of the Federal District acts like a vicious circle in the economic development of Mexico, on the one hand it is the zone which has the highest rate of economic development, on the other it is the one which has managed to achieve purchasing power. This situation determines that the major portion of investments takes place in that region

and in nearby points, accentuating thus the regional disequilibrium in the process of development.

Mexico's commerce has shown a high degree of capital concentration in recent years, with 1.3 per cent of the largest establishments accounting for 60.4 per cent of the total capital and for 21.7 per cent of the personnel in 1965, while approximately 96 per cent of the smallest enterprises at the other extreme accounted for only about a fifth of the total capital and for about two-thirds of the total number of employees. The large contingent of small establishments in commerce is even more likely than that in industry to be a reservoir of hidden unemployment and underemployment.

The category of "services" includes two sectors. One of them is classified as "modern," and it includes such activities as transportation, organized commerce, and banks. The other is classified as "traditional," and it includes small street vendors, domestics, and other personal services. The category of "services" is at best an ambiguous concept and at worst a wastebasket concept that hides a great deal of underemployment (Centro 1970:238). The available figures on concentration in services show that in 1965, 1.0 per cent of the largest establishments accounted for 63.6 per cent of the invested capital and for 53.6 per cent of the total income (González Salazar 1971:550). At the other extreme we find that 57.9 per cent of the establishments were lacking in personnel receiving wages and salaries. These establishments (taken together with those having five or fewer employees receiving wages or salaries) accounted for 77.7 per cent of the total number of establishments, for 12.9 per cent of the invested capital, and for 17.5 per cent of the total income. The small establishments also included about a third of the labor force engaged in services (González Salazar 1971:549–50).

The Mexican Revolution brought about changes in the structure of investments: in the relative contribution of private, public, domestic, and foreign sources of investment funds and in the nation's banking system. A total of 94 million pesos are reported to have been available for investment from all sources in 1902–1903. Over half (51.2 per cent) of those investment funds came from abroad. Over three-fourths (77.7 per cent) came from private sources. The percentage of investable public funds available to the government was

22.3 per cent of the total (7.4 per cent of these borrowed from abroad). Only 5.3 per cent of these public funds—less than a fourth of what was available—were actually invested by the government (Rostro 1965:293).

Following the revolution certain limitations were placed on ownership in such activities as communication, transportation, petrochemicals, forestry, and fishing, as well as in the production of selected minerals and nonalcoholic beverages. In all of these it was required that the major portion should be Mexican-owned. New mining ventures were required to include Mexicans in the ownership of 51 per cent of the stock (LaCascia 1969:61). However, disguised foreign control of industrial and commercial establishments is a common occurrence (Zamora 1960:358).

Mexico's credit-granting institutions underwent considerable overhauling during the 1930's. Two key institutions that emerged out of these changes and are concerned with Mexico's development are the Banco de México and Nacional Financiera. Both are active in formulating new undertakings, investing in them, and selling them to domestic and foreign interests. Once purchased, such ventures can always be resold to those institutions (LaCascia 1969:33–41). This repurchase policy often becomes an easy method of extracting financial success out of bankrupt and poorly administered private ventures (Carmona 1970:69).

The early 1940's were years of rapid economic development for Mexico. The reforms of the Cárdenas administration, the greater degree of state participation in investments, the decline in the egress of profits to foreign investors, and the temporary wartime relief from foreign industrial competition were all factors which contributed to more rapid rates of development (Aguilar 1967:51).

The restructuring of Mexico's fiscal policies in favor of greater state participation and of Mexicanization of development became reflected in the structure of investments during the interval 1939 to 1950. The average annual investment during this interval was 2,889 million pesos. The relative contributions of specific sectors to this total were as follows: internal public, 33.4; internal private, 58.8; external public, 3.2; and external private, 4.6. Taken together, investments from domestic sources (both public and private) increased, in relative terms, from less than half of the total in 1902 and 1903 to over nine-tenths (92.2) in the 1939–50 interval. The total relative share of private investments also decreased by 17.3 percentage points—from a total of 77.7 per cent in the earlier interval to a total of 60.4 per cent in the later interval. The figures show a drastic increase in the federal government's contributions to the investment funds available and in the actual investments. The same holds true for domestic private sources. There is also a drastic decrease in the participation of foreign private investments. The decrease in loans from external public sources is heavy but less dramatic (Rostro 1965:294).

The most recent year for which this type of data is available is 1963. The total investment during that year amounted to 28,244 million pesos. The contribution of each of the various sectors in relative terms was as follows: internal public, 34.7; internal private, 49.6; external public, 10.4; and external private, 5.3 per cent. The most noticeable change is in the increasing reliance on loans from international credit agencies (Rostro 1965:294). It is evident also that state participation in investments was sustained at a high level, while the private domestic sector's contribution declined.

Figures released recently (1970) by the Banco de México indicate that the absolute size of Mexico's gross investments increased from 747 million pesos in 1940 to 75,000 million pesos in 1970—at 1970 prices. A cursory examination of the bank's coefficient-of-investment figures shows that the trend in gross investments has been steadily upward, except for a sharp drop in 1953 and for relative stagnation in the early 1960's. Over all there was an increase in gross investment rates from 10.0 per cent in 1940 to 17.8 per cent in 1970 (Banco de México 1971b:227). However, data on trends in net investments alter the picture somewhat. Net-investments figures show a rapid climb of a much shorter duration, from 3 per cent in 1940 to 15 per cent in 1947, followed by a slow, steady decline, which approached stagnation at a low of 6 to 7 per cent in the early sixties. Commenting on those figures, Aguilar Monteverde suggests that if the level of net investments reached in 1947 had been maintained for two or three decades, the process of development and expansion of the productive forces would have been decisively influenced. But just as they were reached, they were dropped "as fast as they came up" (Aguilar 1967:45–50).

What happened in 1947? Was some kind of countertrend set in motion, strong enough to offset the direction of the last twelve years? Would this change have anything to do with the rise to power in 1947 of what Carmona has referred to as "a species of *neo porfirismo*" (Carmona 1970:66) in the person of Miguel Alemán? An article dealing with the six years of Alemán's rule (Delgado 1962) throws some light on what this *néoporfirista* political economy was like. One of the characteristics of the regime was that there appeared to be "a sharp contradiction between what it purports to seek and what it in reality manages to obtain" (Delgado 1962:71). All the arguments in favor of "forced savings" can be found in the political economy put in practice by this administration. The slogan appears to have been that of "inevitable sacrifices" required of the population to promote the country's progress (Delgado 1962:70):

> The fundamentals which lay at the bottom of such a political economy are the ones habitual in such cases: Mexico has low levels of income, hence, savings—which are the basis for capitalization—are also very low. Greater *investment* is needed so that the country will develop rapidly, and so that we might soon "emerge out of poverty." Such investments in turn require a higher level of savings. Such savings will come out of the profits accruing to people who have capital, and they must not be substantially touched—whether with the impositive politics, the labor law, or any other instruments—but, on the contrary, they must be surrounded with better warranties and security covenants, while propitiating, by way of "collaboration" the inflow of capital from abroad. [italics mine.]

The share of incomes from labor during this interval ranged from a low of 22.0 per cent in 1947 to a high of 23.8 per cent in 1950; the incomes from capital ranged from a low of 47.4 per cent in 1950 to a high of 50.8 per cent in 1947 (Delgado 1962:73).

Assuming Mexico's typical gross rates of investment to have fluctuated between 1950 and 1970 between 14.9 per cent and 17.6 per cent of the GNP, how do they compare with rates of investment in other nations? Assuming also Mexico's net rates of investment to have fluctuated (1948–63) around 9 and 10 per cent, how do they stack up in the international scene? The typical rates of investment for highly developed industrial capitalist nations are as follows: gross

Table 15.   **Coefficient of Investment in Mexico**

Year	GDP	Investment (millions of pesos)	Coefficient of Investment
1940	7,500	747	9.96
1945	19,900	2,196	11.03
1950	40,600	5,960	14.68
1955	87,300	11,829	13.54
1960	150,500	23,226	15.43
1965	252,000	39,042	15.49
1970	424,000	75,292	17.76

Source: Banco Nacional de México, "Demographic Growth: A Challenge to Economic Development," *Review of the Economic Situation,* 47:227.

rates, 20 to 25 per cent; net rates, 13 to 15 per cent. The rates for socialist nations are: gross rates, 27 to 30 per cent; net rates, 18 to 20 per cent (González Salazar 1971:554–55; Aguilar 1967:50–51). Therefore Mexico's rates of investment are low by comparison to those of industrially developed nations. Its net rates of investment are about two-thirds as large as those prevailing in developed industrial capitalist nations and about half as large as those prevailing in socialist nations. However, in 1960–65 only two Latin-American nations (Chile and Bolivia) had rates of public investment which were higher than those found in Mexico.

Keeping in mind that estimates of the federal government's fiscal intake place this figure between 8 and 15 per cent of the GNP and that this figure is considered to be low by comparison to the 20 to 30 per cent of the GNP collected for fiscal purposes in other nations, and given Mexico's expressed purpose to industrialize itself, certain questions arise as to the alternatives open to it. The following figures on the changed growth-rate patterns of public funds spent on consumption and on investments during the years 1940–50 and 1950–60 place these questions in a more clear perspective. The public sector's average consumption rates changed as follows: 1941–50, 1.9 per cent;

Table 16. **Net Investment Coefficient in Mexico**

Year	Estimate*	Estimate†
1940	3	3
1941	4	4
1942	3	3
1943	5	5
1944	7	7
1945	10	10
1946	12	13
1947	15	15
1948	10	10
1949	9	9
1950	10	10
1951	11	11
1952	9	9
1953	8	8
1954	14	13
1955	9	9
1956	9	9
1957	9	9
1958	8	9
1959	8	8
1960	9	10
1961	7	6
1962	7	7
1963	8	7

*Depreciation estimated as 3 per cent of tangible renewable capital.

†Depreciation estimated as 7 per cent of gross national product.

Source: Alonso Aguilar Monteverde and Fernando Carmona, *México: Riqueza y Miseria* (Mexico City: Editorial Nuestro Tiempo, 1967), p. 49.

1951–60, 7.2 per cent. The corresponding average investment growth rates changed as follows: 1941–50, 11.7 per cent; 1951–60, 2.5 per cent. How is the federal government to provide for its increasing consumption needs and at the same time muster the funds necessary to convert Mexico into an industrial nation (Editorial 1963:345)?

Estimates of how much Mexico needs to invest in order to obtain a 3-per-cent-per-year increase in per capita income vary between 18 per cent and 20 per cent of the GNP (Himes 1965:169; Alvarez 1966:171; LaCascia 1969:77). Keeping in mind Carmona's point that a 2.8-per-cent-per-year increase in real income per capita in Mexico amounts to a scant 5.74 dollars increase per year, one begins to get an idea of the magnitude of investment needed to bring the standard of living of the Mexican population up to the more or less modest standards enjoyed by the West European nations, within a relatively short period of time. Therefore it would appear that even the investment rates prevailing in socialist nations (30 per cent of the GNP) would be insufficient to produce effective and prompt relief for the plight of Mexico's impoverished masses.

Mexico's rulers would appear to be faced with some grim choices. The rhetoric of Mexicanization and more state participation is, very likely, an effective morale booster for a dreadfully abused people. It is another question, however, whether it can muster the kind of public effort needed to deliver on the promise to bring the people out of poverty. Another question that needs answering is whether the Mexican people will be able to find within the richly humanistic tradition of their long and troubled history the strength to carry forward in practice the full implication of the vision which, had it had the backing of a resurgent public force, might have rewritten the 1917 constitution, namely, the view that property is a public function (Mendieta 1946:197–98; Jordan 1927). In the meantime industrial development will continue to mean abundance for the rich and scarcity for the poor.

The view that Mexico's poverty is due to overrapid rates of population growth is clearly one-sided. The investigator who pleads for giving equal weight to deaths and births as a solution to what is perceived as "the problem of people" and who also pleads for a clarification of Mexico's investment policy with a view to promoting economic growth (within a climate of security for private invest-

Graph 3. Trends in the Indexes of Real Wages and Productivity in Manufacturing in Mexico

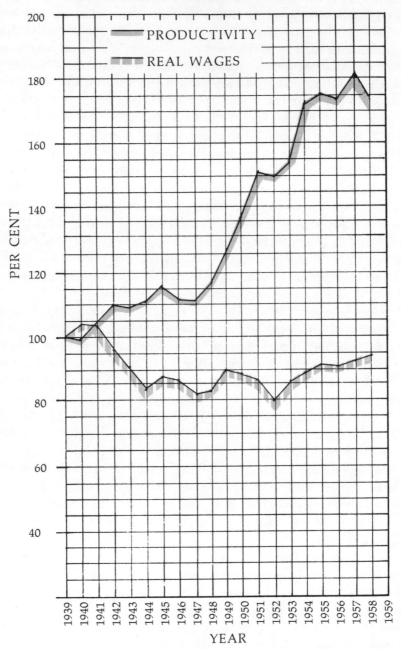

Source: Singer, *Growth, Equality, and the Mexican Experience*, 156.

ments) is clearly not presenting the results of a value-free, ethically neutral social science (Fisher 1964:196, 175, 181–82). His perceptions are limited precisely because the argument is based on value assumptions which view property as an abstract private right.

Mexico's poor have already seen through one generation of *científicos* and, having examined them in the light of historical events, found them wanting. As was the case with the term *sophist* in ancient Athens, the term *científico* ceased to stand for knowledge and became a synonym for folly and cupidity. Man's natural desire for knowledge, science, and the civilization which is thriving upon it deserve a better fate than a repetition of the earlier experience with a new generation of *científicos*.

Nowhere in the literature relevant to this study is talk about the "Mexican Miracle" more ubiquitous than in that concerned with assessments of trends in growth rates of Mexico's gross national product *vis-à vis* trends in population growth rates (Banco Nacional de México 1971b:229; Fisher 1964:181). That Mexico has managed to show an excess of the former over the latter, yielding thus an increment in the GNP per capita (over the course of several decades) is what the miracle is supposed to be about. It is precisely this supposed miracle that Carmona and others have attacked as a carefully glamorized public relations myth designed to disguise the hunger, the rags, the misery, and the inequality that is a daily fact of Mexican life and to distract attention from Mexico's dependence on loans, investments, and aid from the United States—in a word, Mexico's subjection to United States imperialism. The myth is also attacked as an effort to use the historical factors specific to Mexican history to isolate Mexico from the context of common problems that it shares with Latin America and the underdeveloped world (Carmona 1970: 7–8).

Although it is true, as Carmona has noted, that a 2.8 per cent per year increase in Mexico's per capita GNP yields a paltry sum by comparison to what a 1.6 per cent increase yields in the United States, still the fact of an excess of GNP growth rates over Mexico's rapid rates of population growth is significant in itself. An assessment of trends in productivity is essential to obtain one side of a picture, the other side of which is the trend in salaries; both are essential elements of exploitation theory.

Available figures on trends in productivity indicate the following: Stated in terms of 1960 prices, the gross domestic product (GDP) of the Mexican economy increased from 46,400 million pesos in 1940 to 300,800 million pesos in 1970. The growth rate of the GNP during this interval is placed at 6.4 per cent per year. During the same interval the Mexican population increased from 20.1 to 50.4 million inhabitants, a yearly rate of 3.0 per cent. During the same interval the per capita GDP is estimated to have risen from a figure of 2,361 pesos per year in 1940 to 5,965 pesos in 1970. The GDP per capita thus increased at a rate of 3.4 per cent per year. Thus a six-fold increase in the GDP during a thirty-year interval was accompanied by a population growth of two and one half times the original size during the same interval. Hence Mexico's GDP is seen to have increased 2.4 times faster than the population (Banco Nacional de México 1971b:225).

Taking a longer perspective, Reynolds reports a sustained decline in the average growth rate of the Gross Domestic Product from a high of 3.3 per cent per year during the first decade of the twentieth century to a low of 1.6 per cent during the years of reform (1925–40). The decade of the forties showed a very sharp rise in the GDP growth rate to a level over twice as high (6.7 per cent) as that prior to the revolution, followed by a slight decline and stagnation at a relatively high level (6.1 per cent per year through the years 1960–65). On the other hand, average per capita GDP growth rates showed a slight increase from 2.2 per cent during the first decade of the present century to 2.4 per cent during the years of the revolution. This was partly due to a drop of 1.0 per cent per year in population growth rates brought about by the ravages of the revolutionary decade. That is, the increase in average GDP per capita from the first to the second decade of this century appears to have been relative to a shrinking population base. The years of reform (1925–40) reversed the tendency toward population decline, bringing the population growth rate up to 1.6 per cent per year and contributing to total stagnation in GDP per capita growth rates (0.0 per cent per year) during that same interval. The 1940 decade registered a sharp increase (to 3.9 per cent per year) in average per capita GDP growth rates and was followed by a moderate though sustained tendency to decline in subsequent years (to a low of 2.7 in 1960–65). The years since 1940 were years of sustained acceleration in population growth rates. Hence, although Mexico's post-1940 population growth rates were enough to bring about a relative slowdown in average GDP per capita growth rates, still they were not large enough to exceed the average GDP growth rate (Reynolds 1970:22).

Except for the interval 1925–40, when the rates of growth of the GNP per capita averaged zero, the Mexican economy has tended to show positive rates of growth throughout the century. The first decade registered a per capita GDP growth rate of 2.2 per cent per year, despite a relatively low GDP growth rate, due to relatively small population growth rates (1.1 per cent). The revolutionary decade registered a rate of growth in the GDP per capita of 2.4 per cent per year due largely to shrinkage of the population base as a result of the revolution. The highest average rate of growth in the GDP per capita occurred in the 1940's, at which interval it reached 3.9 per cent per year. Since then it has shown a moderate but sustained tendency to decline, reaching a low of 2.7 per cent per year in 1960–65.

Since we devoted some space to the sharp contrasts between rates of investments in the early forties and those in the late forties and early fifties, we should not leave the following decade unexamined. Unfortunately, as happened earlier with gross rates of investment, we run into two sets of figures at variance with one another (Editorial 1963:345; Tello 1971:631) but originating with the same source: the Banco de México. One set of figures which is more in keeping with the data so far assembled reports the following rates of growth of the GDP: 1941–45, 8.6; 1946–50, 5.7. These data appeared in an editorial article of *Revista de Economía*. The other data reports a rate of growth of the GDP amounting to 5.9 in 1940–45 and 6.2 in 1945–50.

With reference to what appears to be growth rates per capita, a student of the years of Miguel Alemán's rule (1947–52) says: "In fact, the mean rate of development obtained during this *sexenio* (of 1.2 per cent) is the lowest registered by the Governments of the Revolution from 1934—an interval for which measurements are now available—to the present" (Delgado 1962:71). The foregoing data and the over-all trend of the evidence presented thus far strongly suggest that trends in productivity during the forties were not uniform and that the sharpest advances were made during the earlier part of the decade. However, indications are that during the Alemán administration, great strides were made in opening up new lands for agriculture through irrigation, though the benefits of this program seem to have strengthened, and perhaps also to have favored, the private, larger-scale holdings (Delgado 1962:77–78).

Because the existing structure of Mexican agriculture is one of the historically specific features of Mexico's capitalist development, its productivity deserves close attention. The slogan of members of the "League of Socialist Agronomers" during the years when Mexico's current system of land distribution was being formed is said to have been, "Neither the *ejido* nor the small property, haciendas without hacendados" (Reyes 1967:198). But Carranza's "revolution" was no more socialist than the Constitution of 1917 written at his bidding. Hence this idea was never put into practice. It currently seems to fall outside the field of vision of most writers on the question, who tend to take sides with the *ejido*, the small property, or both, the key issue apparently being one of the relative efficiency of each.

One student of the question (Reynolds 1970:147) has ranked Mexico's five regions in terms of (1) the rate of increase in the share of the *ejidal* land area to the total land area under cultivation and (2) the rate of growth of agricultural production per rural dweller. Placing the two rankings side by side, he has shown that for the 1940–60 interval, there was a correlation of −1 between the two rankings. The rankings of the regions were as follows (Reynolds 1970:147):

Center	North Pacific
Gulf	South Pacific
North	North
South Pacific	Gulf
North Pacific	Center

A similar ranking for the 1930–40 decade showed the same trend, but the South Pacific and Gulf Regions did not quite reverse positions on the two scales. Prior to 1930 the evidence points in both directions (Reynolds 1970:145–47). Reynolds concludes that the weight of the evidence is in favor of a greater productivity performance on the part of "those regions having a relative increase in private holdings" (Reynolds 1970:147).

On the other hand, official United Nations sources are quoted as saying that "the experience of Mexico proves that 'a frank policy of land redistribution, along with the creation of credit facilities for the small farmer, can contribute to improvement of employment conditions and to the social position of the peasant population'" (Baltra 1960:7).

Is the *ejido* efficient or is it not? The answer seems to depend on whether the question is asked with reference to output per unit of land area or agricultural output per capita. In 1960 Mexico's *ejidal* lands are reported to have taken up 42 per cent of the total tillable land available and to have produced 40.8 per cent of the total value of production. No doubt *ejidatarios* account for all of this production, as the author reporting these figures emphasizes. But what can be inferred on the basis of the data? Since the percentage of *ejidatarios* is not given, the inference would follow that the *ejidal* sector's production per hectare is about as high and very likely no higher than the private sector. However, having said this the question must be, "But at what price in human terms?" The production achieved in the *ejidal* sector is bound to be due to a form of agriculture which is very heavily labor-intensive and consequently associated with low per capita yields relative to capital-intensive units.

How can we explain not only the survival but also the deliberate fostering in the mechanized twentieth century of a type of agriculture carried out on plots ranging in size from .1 hectare to 10.1 hectares? To effectively make use of machinery such as tractor-drawn six-bottom plows, cotton pickers, combined harvester threshers, corn pickers, and so on, farm units of a least 100 hectares are needed. The land area of most *ejidal* units would hardly provide enough parking space for a capital-intensive, mechanized farm of today, especially if the room needed for plant and equipment is included. The formulators of Mexico's dual system of agriculture seem to have foreseen this. Why then did they go ahead with the idea of parceling out the land in small plots? The *ejidal* system shows every evidence of having been fostered not with the view of promoting efficiency in agriculture, but rather to rescue the *latifundio* system from its own consequences: the almost complete destitution, rootlessness, and misery to which the Mexican peasantry had been reduced by the turn of the century through the long process of expropriation which culminated in the *Leyes de Deslindes*. The restored *ejido* system following the revolution simply re-established the traditional patterns of landholding on which *latifundismo* thrives: a few vast tracts which cannot begin to be worked by the "owner" and a large number of small parcels too small to provide full subsistence without supplementary labor in the hacienda. Luis Cabrera, one of the ideologues of the restored *ejido* system, is quoted as saying that the land should be given to the peasants so that "they could live on it and supplement their salaries with it" (Reyes 1967:196–97). In an article dealing with land redistribution, Sergio Reyes Osorio sums up the problem neatly (Reyes 1967:197):

> . . . *the prevailing idea was that the ejido should represent an additional occupation for the ejidatario, a supplement to his salary as wage earner or, at best, an extension of land which would keep them at a subsistence level, with little or no participation in the market.* The preceding is confirmed by the fact that the area fixed for an *ejidal* parcel is 3 to 5 irrigated hectares or its equivalent in other types of land; a fact which, judging in terms of the technology prevailing in those days, could represent no more than production for home consumption.

The secret of the productivity of the so-called small property would appear to lie not in its privacy—not in its functioning as an abstract unit separate from everything else—but in the fact that in that type of unit, operations are carried out on a large enough scale to enable the operator to muster the capital needed to conduct agriculture by modern methods and to allow the effective use of those implements. Moreover, the utilization of those methods, since they have undergone constant improvement to save time and effort, continuously revise upwards the optimum size of the farm unit.

One defender of the *ejido* system has this to say: "The critics of the Agrarian Reform say that it is essentially destructive; that it lowers returns through fractioning. The truth is that it is not possible to obtain lower returns than those produced in the old time haciendas" (Rostro 1964:258). The point however is not to return to the old haciendas but to a type of "hacienda" which would permit optimum utilization of modern technology while making certain that production per capita does become consumption per capita or income per capita. While the small *ejido* plot might assure a measure of the latter, it does seriously restrict the development of productive forces.

A pioneering study of income districution in Mexico (Navarreté 1960) noted that the concentration of income in Mexico was so extreme that a parallel for it could only be found either in countries where there is a rapidly growing industrial and financial bourgeois class or in countries which are still under colonial forms of control. The evidence: 5 per cent of Mexico's families controlled 40 per cent of the income in 1950. In the United Kingdom, 5 per cent of the families controlled 46 per cent of the income in 1880, whereas in 1947 this same percentage of families controlled slightly over half that much (24 per cent). On the other hand, while 20 per cent of Mexico's families controlled 60 per cent of the income in 1950, 20 per cent of India's families controlled 55 per cent, and 20 per cent of Ceylon's families controlled 50 per cent in that same year (Ifigenia Navarreté 1960: 87–88).

Ten years later the economist Reynolds, following an effort to sum up the available data on income distribution, had this to say: "Indeed, by any of the three postwar measures shown, Mexico's income distribution remains less equal than that of India" (Reynolds 1970:75). Writing at nearly the same time (1969), the economist Singer, after considering the phenomenon of massive concentration on one side and massive destitution on the other, commented: "This information serves as a rather chilling reminder of the degree of poverty still to be found in Mexico after a decade of striking economic growth" (Singer 1969:124).

Mexico's income distribution curve is highly skewed (Singer 1969: 126). For that reason median income is more likely to be a measure of central tendency than average income. An estimate of median income is possible on the basis of income figures for the economically active population. Without allowing for persons not reporting, or for unemployment during 1970, median income for that year can be placed at 8,862.72 pesos (Banco de México 1971b:225). Expressed in dollars, at the rate of 12.50 pesos per dollar, Mexico's median income for that same year can be placed at $709 (The American Almanac 1971:828). Per capita income figures would have to include the population dependent upon the economically active population. Since Mexico's labor force includes somewhere between a third and a fourth of the total population, annual per capita median income must fall somewhere between 177 and 236 U.S. dollars, with the actual figures probably being closer to the smaller of the two estimates.

Figures standardized in terms of 1950 pesos indicate that average annual income per capita increased from 1,400 pesos in 1950 to 2,202 in 1966 (LaCascia 1969:80). One estimate places the 1970 average income at 5,965 pesos per year; however, these figures appear to have been obtained by dividing the gross domestic product of 300,800 million pesos for 1970 by a population estimate of 50.4 million inhabitants, a procedure which cannot by any means be taken to yield average income but which should be presented instead as GDP per capita figures (Banco Nacional de México 1971b:225).

More detailed analysis of the distribution of income among the economically active population in 1970 shows that (1) only 0.8 per cent of the population had monthly incomes of 10,000 pesos and over, (2) only 2.8 per cent had incomes higher than 5,000 pesos per month, (3) 86 per cent had incomes below 1,499 pesos per month (110 U.S. dollars), and (4) 10.3 per cent of the preceding figure declared no income at all while the remainder (75.7 per cent) reported incomes somewhere between 1 and 1,499 pesos (Banco Nacional de México 1971c:158).

At the top of this scale, and standing in sharp contrast to the extent of deprivation of the masses we saw earlier, we find the people who live in houses with seven or more rooms, those who send their children to college, and the 16.8 per cent of the population who report eating meat every day (Banco Nacional de México 1971c: 159–65). The latter group corresponds roughly to the population with incomes above 4,250 pesos per month (about 320 U.S. dollars), although it probably includes many people at lower income levels who would not admit that they are unable to afford meat.

Data on family income shares by deciles of the population of families are available for 1950, 1958, and 1963. Data on incomes for 1969, which compare income distribution by strata of family subpopulations across the years specified above, are also available. Data of the former type show the following. Beginning with the families in the wealthiest income tenth of the population, we find their shares of monthly family income to have been as follows: 1950, 49.0 per cent; 1958, 49.3 per cent; 1963, 49.9 per cent. Further refinement is possible for the upper and lower 5 per cent of this decile. The corresponding figures for the top 5 per cent are as follows: 1950, 40.2 per cent; 1958, 38.6 per cent; 1963, 38.3 per cent. For the bottom 5 per cent the figures are: 1950, 8.8 per cent; 1958, 10.7 per cent; 1963, 11.6 per cent. What these figures indicate is that while the over-all income of this top decile remained practically unchanged at a level of nearly half of the nation's income during this thirteen-year interval, there was a noticeable reallocation of the size of the relative shares of the top and bottom half, with the increases accruing to the lower half. Practically all of the change took place during the first eight-year interval so far as the top 5 per cent is concerned (Tello 1971:633).

At the other extreme of the scale, the families in the bottom five deciles, that is, the lower half of the population of families, receive the following shares: 1950, 19.1 per cent; 1958, 16.7 per cent; 1963, 15.7 per cent (Tello 1971:633). Between these extremes, the only decile with shares above 10 per cent is the ninth, with 10.8 per cent in 1950, 13.6 per cent in 1958, and 12.7 per cent in 1963 (Tello 1971: 633).

These figures find support in a study of income distribution in Latin America which gives the following figures for Mexico:

Table 17. **Distribution of Income in Mexico, 1950–64**

Per Cent of Families, from Lowest to Highest Income Strata	Per Cent of Incomes		
	1950	1956–57	1963–64
50	19	16	15
30	21	23	26
20	60	61	59

Source: Carlos Tello, "Notas Para el Análisis de la Distribución Personal del Ingreso en Mexico," *El Trimestre Económico* 38:633.

The trend in the shares of income received by the half of the population of families at the bottom of the distribution is almost identical, with both studies showing a tendency toward relative deterioration in this group's share.

A third source (Reynolds 1970:76) which ought to be considered draws upon Navarreté's figures for the first two years studied and upon the Banco de México for 1963. The sharpest difference between these two original sources is in the estimate of the total share of the top decile in 1963. Navarreté puts this figure at 49.9 per cent, and the bank puts it a 41.5 per cent. The actual figure probably lies somewhere between these two estimates. It is not clear why the date of Navarreté's second analysis year is 1958 in the former set of data and 1957 in the latter. Reynolds reports the following figures for the families in the five deciles at the bottom of the income distribution: 1950, 19.1; 1957, 15.6; 1963, 15.5. The difference between these and the former figures are so small as to be negligible (Reynolds 1970:76).

The latest figures on income distribution by relative income shares show that the lower 50 per cent of the families in the lowest income levels experienced a steady decline from 19.1 per cent of the income in 1950 to 15 per cent of the income in 1969. By contrast, the upper 10 per cent of the families in the wealthiest income levels showed a steady increase in their relative income share from 49 per cent in 1950 to 51 per cent in 1969. These data cast additional doubt on the 1963 estimate released by the Bank and provided by Reynolds. Therefore it must be concluded that there are strong indications that the tendency of income distribution for the last twenty years, in relative terms, has been toward magnifying the degree of income inequality typical of Mexico. Whatever else is true of the trends before and after the revolution, there are strong indications that the trends in income distribution since 1950 have been toward rather than away from greater income inequality (Guzmán 1973:20).

Some points clarified by Navarreté deserve consideration before proceeding futher. She maintains that both those who protest the unjust distribution of income and those who maintain that there has been a general rise in the standard of living are right. With reference to the interval 1940–50 she says (Navarreté 1960:66):

There was an increase of 95% in total income and a 47% increase in average income per worker (entrepreneurial and salaried) in real terms. There was a very unequal distribution of the increases in income. The least favored ones were the salaried workers whose incomes increased by 66%; but since they themselves increased by 25%, their average income increased 33%. A growing group of favored people, the entrepreneurs, increased their total income by 115%, their numbers by 44% and their median income by 49%.

Hence what economic development there was during the decade also brought a widening of the disparity in average incomes between entrepreneurs and salaried workers, with the position of agricultural workers showing the greatest relative deterioration. The income of rural wage workers showed a decline of 33 per cent. Their numbers had decreased (through the *ejidal* program, rural-urban migration, etc.) by 25 per cent. Hence, "their average income only decreased by 11%" (Navarreté 1960:66). It is possible, Navarreté notes, "for the workers' situation to deteriorate in each sector and, nevertheless, for their position as a group to improve, due to the fact that the disparity between urban and rural productivity, and in the productivity of different branches of the economy, permits lucrative transferences of labor power even if at decreasing real salary rates" (Navarreté 1960:63).

The changes which took place in 1950–57 further clarify some of the trends. A conservative estimate of the changes which took place during that interval shows that there was an over-all increase in family income of 23 per cent at 1957 prices. The two population deciles at the bottom of the distribution experienced a deterioration of their incomes which was absolute as well as relative. The relative position of the three population deciles next higher up deteriorated; however, their position improved in absolute terms. The relative position of families in the sixth decile was maintained, while their position in absolute terms improved. With the exception of the 2.4 per cent of the families in the highest income level, the income share of families in the seventh to tenth decile increased in both absolute and relative terms. The top 2.4 per cent experienced a slight decrease in real income in absolute terms and a decline in their relative share (Navarreté 1960:82–87).

The most recent figures, although they are less detailed than Navarreté's analysis, tend to confirm her point that there has been

Table 18.   **Distribution of Income by Families in Mexico**

Strata		1950		1958		1963		1969	
		Percentiles	Cumulative Income	Percentiles	Cumulative Income	Percentiles	Cumulative Income	Percentiles	Cumulative Income
I	Subsistence	20	6.1	20	5.0	20	4.2	20	4.0
II	Lower middle	30	13.0	30	11.7	30	11.5	30	11.0
III	Middle	30	21.1	30	20.4	40	21.7	30	21.0
IV	Upper middle	10	10.8	10	13.6	10	12.7	10	13.0
V	Privileged	10	49.0	10	49.3	10	49.9	10	51.0
	Total	100	100.0	100	100.0	100	100.0	100	100.0

Source: Martín Luis Guzmán Ferrer, "Distribución del Ingreso en Mexico," *Hispano Americano* 64:20.

Table 19.   **Average Monthly Family Income in Mexico**
        (in 1958 pesos)

Family Strata		Percentiles	1950	1958	1963	1969
I	Subsistence	20	292	336	335	367
II	Lower middle	30	415	521	618	672
III	Middle	30	673	1,016	1,160	1,283
IV	Upper middle	10	1,033	1,820	2,049	2,384
V	Privileged	10	4,687	6,605	8,025	9,352

Source: Martín Luis Guzmán Ferrer, "Distribución del Ingreso en Mexico," *Hispano Americano* 64:20.

both a growing inequality of income distribution and a general rise in living standards. The income of the poorest fifth of the nation's families showed a slow but steady increase from 292 pesos per month in 1950 to 367 pesos per month in 1969. The slightly less impoverished thirty per cent of the families just above the poorest experienced income increases of from 415 pesos per month in 1950 to 672 pesos per month in 1969. The richest ten per cent of the nation's families experienced sharp monthly income increases of from 4,687 pesos in 1950 to 9,352 pesos in 1969. By comparison to the latter figures, the income increases experienced by the poorest half of the population are, of course, paltry. The initial incomes were so low that the improvements necessarily amount to very little. Nonetheless, the figures do show an improvement (Guzmán 1973:20).

The foregoing information might be summed up with a simile. If we could think of the whole of Mexico as a family of ten persons gathering to celebrate the revolution and if we could further think of the national income as a pie to be divided up in ten equal parts and eaten in honor of the revolution during the festivities, the end result would then be more or less the following: one rich relative, a gargantuan fellow full of appetite, would make off with about five slices. Five poor relatives, a bit gaunt, toil worn, and four of them suffering from cataracts, end up by having to share only a slice and one-half among themselves. The remaining four relatives, who have been labeled "the in-crowd," make do with three and one-half slices. The obese fellow reports that he thought he had been losing a little weight until very recently. His attempts to reduce took the form of a short morning constitutional stroll along 27th Avenue. He kept readjusting his bathroom scale to improve the accuracy of his readings and perhaps also to set his mood going on a cheery note for the day, for he enjoyed tinkering. His most recent reading turned out to be a little depressing, so he has decided to extend his daily walk up Independence Boulevard, left on Zapata Drive, and then, in honor of the revolutionary tradition, down the Carranza bypass! He was not anything if he was not patriotic! The five poor relatives have been growing a little apprehensive lately, for although the pie has been getting noticeably bigger during the last few celebrations, their cut has been getting smaller, though no doubt also slightly less meager. For three of the remaining four relatives, the cut has remained about the same for the last few years, though also a little more substantial. One of the "in-four," the nearest of kin to the rich one, has been getting a bigger slice for some time now, and he never ceases to praise the revolution for the great democratic accomplishments it made possible. The festivities about over, speeches are made about the "Mexican Miracle," about the united, stable, strong, prosperous, industrialized country that is emerging, about the principles of the revolution, about working class struggles and social justice. The speeches about over, one of the participants shouts, "But we are still hungry here!" Whereupon someone from behind the scenes shouts, "Pity that you have so many children!" Someone from among the circle of relatives looks around and asks, "*What* children?" There is no answer. The intruder is soon forgotten, and the gathering breaks up as they all shout, "¡Viva la Revolución!" All shout except one. Let us say that the silent one's name is Pedro.

We now turn to a consideration of trends in income shares by sources of income. Data for the years 1939–60 show that the lowest share of total income received in the form of wages and salaries was 21.5 per cent in 1946, and the highest was reached in 1953, with 32.0 per cent. By contrast, the lowest property incomes were recorded in 1939, with 34.5 per cent. The highest income from this source was registered in 1946, with 51.5 per cent of the total income. A sizable portion of the annual income is reported in the form of "mixed incomes," and as "incomes imputed to the self-employed" (Singer 1969:136). The highest relative share of income paid in this form is found in 1939, with 35.0 per cent of the total, and the lowest occurred in 1952, with 22.6 per cent of the total (Singer 1969:136).

A breakdown of property incomes by rents and interests and by profits shows that incomes from rents and interests are only between a fourth and a seventh as large as incomes from profits (Singer 1969:136). Also, incomes from interests are only about a fourth as large, in relative terms, as incomes from rents (Navarreté 1967: 136). Therefore, the bulk of incomes from property comes from profits on investments.

From the preceding figures it can be observed that the incomes from labor throughout the interval considered fluctuated between a fifth and a third of the national income. Incomes from capital fluctuated between over a third to a half of the national income. The next-to-highest relative incomes from labor and the lowest relative incomes from capital were registered during the last years of the Cárdenas administration. The lowest relative incomes from labor and the highest relative incomes from capital were registered toward the end of the Avila administration and the beginning of the Alemán administration.

Table 20: Functional Income Distribution in Mexico, 1939–59

Year	(1) Wages and Salaries (%)	(2) Profits (%)	(3) Rents and Interest (%)	(4) Property Incomes (Col. 2 + Col.3) (%)	(5) Mixed Incomes plus Imputed Incomes of Self- Employed (%)
1939	30.5	26.2	8.3	34.5	35.0
1940	29.1	28.6	8.1	36.7	34.2
1941	27.9	30.7	7.8	38.5	33.6
1942	26.5	33.0	7.5	40.5	33.0
1943	25.0	35.3	7.2	42.5	32.5
1944	23.7	37.6	6.9	44.5	31.8
1945	22.6	41.3	6.7	48.0	29.4
1946	21.5	45.1	6.4	51.5	27.0
1947	22.0	44.3	6.5	50.8	27.2
1948	22.9	42.9	6.5	49.4	27.7
1949	23.7	41.5	6.7	48.2	28.1
1950	23.8	41.4	6.0	47.4	28.8
1951	25.0	42.0	6.4	48.4	26.6
1952	27.0	44.0	6.4	50.4	22.6
1953	32.0	38.0	6.4	44.4	23.6
1954	29.0	39.0	6.4	45.4	25.6
1955	26.0	42.5	...	...	...
1956	...	39.0	...	...	...
1957	...	38.0	...	...	...
1958	...	37.5	...	...	...
1959	...	36.5	...	...	...

*The source of the 1939–54 data is Adolfo López Romero, "Desarrollo Económico de México (1934–1959)," *El Trimestre Económico* 29:47. The few figures cited for the years 1955 through 1959 are from successive issues of the Nacional Financiera's annual reports. The Nacional Financiera apparently regards these data as so rough that it cites no statistics as such but merely employs graphs to reveal the broad outlines of changes in functional income distribution.

Source: Morris Singer, *Growth, Equality, and the Mexican Experience* (Austin and London: University of Texas Press, 1969), p. 136.

Table 21.   **Participation of the Factors of Production in the Mexican National Income, 1950–60**

Year	Labor (%)	Capital (%)	Mixed (%)
1950	23.8	47.4	28.8
1951	22.4	48.3	29.3
1952	22.3	48.3	29.4
1953	25.5	46.5	28.0
1954	28.5	44.5	27.0
1955	26.4	45.8	27.8
1956	25.9	46.1	28.0
1957	27.8	44.9	27.3
1958	29.9	43.6	26.5
1959	30.8	43.0	26.2
1960	31.4	42.6	26.0

Source: Morris Singer, *Growth, Equality, and the Mexican Experience* (Austin and London: University of Texas Press, 1969), p. 137.

The ratio between the per cent of income received by, and the per cent of the economically active population employed in, each sector of the Mexican economy can be viewed as an index of the degree of disequilibrium present in that economy. The data available are not reported according to uniform categories; they come from two different sources and deal with two different years.

From the data it can be seen that the largest ratio of income to population, by far, accrues to the commercial or tertiary sector. It can be seen also that a disproportionately small ratio of income to population accrues to the agricultural or primary sector and that an intermediate, though relatively high ratio of income to population accrues to the manufacturing sector. The foregoing statements can be seen to apply to both years for which data are available. Furthermore, it is evident that the ratio of income to population declined for both the agricultural and the manufacturing sectors during the

Table 22. **Relative Income and Population by Broad Occupational Categories in Mexico, 1960**

Occupation or Sector	Per Cent of GNP Received (a)	Per Cent of Economically Active Population (b)	Ratio (a/b)
Agriculture (primary)	20.4	54.2	0.38
Manufacturing	25.7	13.7	1.88
Commerce	20.9	9.5	2.29

Source: Gilberto Rodríguez González, "La Importancia Económica de Los Salarios Minimos," *Revista de Economía,* January, 1966, p. 8.

Table 23. **Relative Income and Population by Broad Occupational Categories in Mexico, 1967**

Occupation or Sector	Per Cent of National Income Received (a)	Per Cent of Economically Active Population (b)	Ratio (a/b)
Agriculture and related activities	16.1	47.0	0.34
Manufacturing	26.9	17.0	1.58
Commerce, finance, and government	29.1	11.2	2.60

Source: Gloria González Salazar, "Crecimiento Económico y Desicualdad Social en Mexico: Una Visión Esquematica," *Revista Mexicana de Sociologia* 33:549.

seven-year interval considered; it is evident also (to the extent that the data are comparable) that the sharpest decrease in this ratio was experienced by the manufacturing sector—the one whose income is most likely to reflect productivity increases. By contrast, the commercial or tertiary sector showed a considerable increase in the ratio of income to population during the interval under consideration.

Both of the sources considered take note of what Gloria González called "the spectacular disequilibrium shown by the agricultural sector" (González Salazar 1971:549), which commands nearly half of the economically active population but less than a fifth of the share of the product received by the other sectors. Industry's greater share is explained in terms of greater productivity and the higher prices of its products. Commerce's relative large share, with only about a tenth of the personnel, is explained as being the result of "the price hikes which intermediaries tag on the products they distribute" (Rodríguez 1966:8).

To round out the picture emerging here, we might consider a comparison of trends in productivity and trends in real wages in terms of index figures. Graph 3 (page 135) shows figures of this type for the years 1939–59. Both sets of figures are taken from the manufacturing sector. The base year for the figures in question is 1939 and equals 100. The trend in the productivity index shows a steady increase from 99.4 in 1940 to 178.7 in 1958. The corresponding trend in the index of real wages is slightly downward, from 103.2 in 1940 to 93.9 in 1958 (Singer 1969:156). Hence during an interval when productivity nearly doubled, real wages declined by nearly a tenth. It is clear that the steadily upward trend in productivity was not being reflected in corresponding increases in real wages. The widening of the differences between these indexes might be compared to the widening of the differences between steady and slowly declining birth rates on the one hand and sharply declining death rates on the other. The widening distance between the birth and death rates has been referred to as "the population explosion." A comparable term is needed to refer to the widening distance between the productivity index and the index of real wages. I suggest the term "profit explosion." As Singer has noted, the implications of the growing disparity between productivity and real wages for property incomes are evident (Singer 1969: 155). Just as the need to explain the behavior of trends related to the

Table 24.   Index of Salaries, Productivity, and Cost of Living
in Mexico

| Year | Cost of Living | Salaries | | Produc-tivity | Purchasing Power of the Peso |
		Nominal	Real		
1940	100.0	100.0	100.0	100.0	100.0
1950	353.7	304.3	86.0	138.3	28.3
1960	724.6	658.0	90.8	185.8	13.7

Source: Editorial, *Revista de Economia* 26:459. See also Luisa Redondo B., *Desocupación y salarios en los paises subdesarrollados,* Ramón Ramírez G., *Tendencias de la Economía Mexicana* (Mexico City: Investigación Económica, 1962).

population explosion gave rise to a theory of population transition, so is there a need to develop a theory of profit transition to account for the behavior of trends related to the profit explosion.

Singer's figures have been confirmed by another study which presents the data shown in Table 24.

On the subject of salaries, the *Centro de Estudios Económicos y Demográficos* has this to say (Centro 1970:233):

The political factors which in many underdeveloped countries tend to make for an accelerated rate of growth in salaries are absent in Mexico. This, combined with a rhythm of rural-urban migration which exceeds the creation of productive employment, is the principal cause of the tendency for real salaries of workers with low skills to show a decline in absolute terms between 1940 and 1950–56, and of their present tendency to grow slowly—above all those of the great majority of low skill workers. This tends to complicate the distribution of income and makes it more difficult for it to grow at a speed greater than the internal market.

This work, however, presents some very interesting features. To begin with it defines "low productivity" in terms of "criteria of minimum monthly income of workers" (Centro 1970:243), low salaries being partly explained in terms of excessive rural exodus to cities. What is and what is not productive would then seem to acquire all the characteristics of the self-fulfilling prophecy, since all that needs to be done in order to classify a worker's productivity as low is to pay that worker a minimum monthly income. Hence, instead of productivity defining income, income comes to define productivity. The plea of "too many migrants" then becomes a convenient excuse for keeping salaries low, and the system that renders their existence redundant goes unchallenged. It is clear that this approach fails to question the redundance of the very system of exploitation which renders a certain portion of the population redundant and that it also fails to question the productivity of that system *vis-à-vis* human life.

I do not mean to suggest that rural migrants are not more likely to be unskilled than urbanites. However, it is plain from the indexes of real wages and productivity that low and even declining real wages exist not because of low productivity but in spite of increasing and relatively high productivity. No doubt the life conditions of the rural population that have been unfolding in this study are such as to inevitably restrict the opportunities for development of the rural population to a level consistently below that of urbanites. However, those conditions are themselves conditioned by the existing economic and political structure of the country, and such structures are themselves subject to change. The institutional conditioning of existing facts cannot be taken for granted without thereby identifying with the structural and evaluative matrix within which these facts take form. It is not possible to determine how productive the Mexican worker potentially is unless that productivity level is open to assessment in terms other than those which account for the existence of a system of minimum salaries in the first place. The Mexican worker is potentially as productive as any other. This fact has been obvious even to plant managers of United States factories in Mexico. It is just such managers who have said: ". . . the Mexican worker is as productive as a worker in the United States if given adequate education and training, the same equipment, and the same working and dietary conditions" (Fisher 1964:197). "Low productivity" is a poor excuse for denying people the means to living more productive lives and, more fundamentally, it is a poor excuse for avoiding the question of the desirability of continuing to produce for ends which render half, if not more, of the population redundant and which deny the great masses of them the hope of ever being able to lift themselves above those conditions.

The rate of savings is reported to have increased from "0.12 and 0.14 to about 0.19 in the last years" (Centro 1970:216). The increasing rate of savings occurring simultaneously with accelerating rates of population growth posed an apparent anomaly. Research on the behavior of savings within the context of the more highly developed industrial nations, where the extent of income inequality is less extreme than in Mexico, has shown a tendency for savings to decline as population growth rates rise. The reason: a larger proportion of family income tends to be devoted to the purchase of nondurable articles of daily consumption. However, in view of what we have learned about the distribution of income by deciles of the population of families, by channels of distribution, and by sectors of the economy, and about the relation of real wages to productivity trends, the apparent anomaly turns out not to be an anomaly at all but rather a predictable consequence of the existing distribution of income and of the rates of exploitation prevailing in Mexico. Thus, what might at first appear to be unique and specific to Mexico turns out to be *unique to the magnitude of income inequality prevailing in Mexico and to the intensity with which capitalist exploitation is carried out.* At the same time we should not discount the possibility that such conditions might tend to encourage, among some people, a positive attitude toward saving as a method of escaping or forestalling some of the tribulations and insecurities which people growing up under such conditions have learned to expect, provided also that they have the wherewithal to make such a possibility worth considering. To a large portion of the Mexican population—46.0 per cent in 1956 (Navarreté 1960:app. 10)—"negative savings," that is, falling into debt, is an everyday fact of life, and a much more realistic possibility than cash in the bank. Growing rates of savings by the few, then, has its counterpart in insolvency, indigence, and destitution on the part of large masses of people. A cursory look at figures showing the distribution of income by states in Mexico (1964) is enough to show where to look for these masses (de la Peña 1966:308).

Mexico's "poverty belt," her valley of misery, runs north and south along the Northern and Central Mesa between the Eastern and Western Sierra Madre, from Southern Coahuila to the proletarian colonies of Mexico City and then on south to Oaxaca, where the so-called "native" or "indigeneous" problem is acute. Another such area could be found in Quintana Roo, on the Yucatan Peninsula. The highest incomes are found in the Federal District and in the states bordering the Sea of Cortes. Other less well off centers (in relative terms) are found in Nayarit, Querétaro, Guerrero, Tabasco, Chiapas, and Campeche. In general also, with the exception of Quintana Roo and the Federal District and immediate vicinity, the tendency was for the areas which showed the most poverty in 1964 to show low to medium rates of population growth in 1970 (Banco Nacional de Comercio 1970:3). The areas which showed the most affluence showed the highest rates of population growth.

Except for Quintana Roo, which appears to represent an isolated rural-type setting, these data seem to be largely explainable in terms of internal migration away from poorer areas and toward better off areas, with the Federal District and the surrounding states of Mexico and Morelos providing the central focus of attention. And little wonder that this migration occurs, for as Gloria González Salazar has written, it is probable "that the accumulated investment in one of the wealthy neighborhoods of Mexico City exceeds all that which corresponds to the wigwams in which 4 to 5 million peasants live, or that what is invested in one great hotel of the capital exceeds all that is applied to the development of the nation's fishing industries" (González Salazar 1971:555).

It should be pointed out that if the data on income distribution presented in this study err in any way, the error is more likely to lie in the direction of underestimation of the wealth of the rich. As Reynolds has noted, there was "systematic underreporting" in the budget studies which collected data on income distribution, ". . . with the upper income groups' share biased downward in the samples [and with] estimates in the middle and lower range [being] much more reliable than those in the top decile . . ." (Reynolds 1970:77).

Mexico's statistics on unemployment are incongruously and curiously low. An unemployment rate of 1.0 per cent is reported for 1970. Yet the same report classifies close to 15 million Mexicans as not sharing "in the benefits derived from the present stage of development" (Banco Nacional de México 1971c:156–57). Among this total are 1.6 million Mexicans who are employed only half the time and about 840 thousand who are employed only seven to nine months out of the year.

One of the points made by the Mexican delegation at the Fifth Latin American Conference on Agriculture and Food (1960) was that disguised unemployment exists in many regions of the country (Delegación Mexicana 1960:349). The same point is made over and over in the literature (Sosa 1964:276; Editorial 1963:348; Tello 1971: 643). At times the concept is used with reference to the *ejido* and the *minifundio*, at other times the reference is to marginal service and commercial occupations as well as to the various forms of hustling that go under the name of "self-employed."

There can be little question that one of the aims of Mexico's program of land reform following the 1910 revolution was to relieve the pressure of rural-to-urban migration as well as the pressure of urban unemployment. The point has been made unequivocally (Durán 1964:251):

> During the hardest moments of national development, when the rate of capital accumulation could not create the job opportunities needed for demographic redistribution, the *ejido* performed the function of retaining in the country the redundant population. This helps explain this particular form of relation of man to land and the peculiar structure of the *ejidos*.

How account for the "redundant population" produced in the countryside on the eve of the revolution? Reynolds finds its source in the inequitable system of land distribution (Reynolds 1970:193).

> Only in this respect did an "excess supply" of labor exist in Mexico in 1910. The unequal landholding system of that time prevented workers from gaining access to extramarginal land that could have provided them with a living wage. Today much of this land has been redistributed, preventing premature urbanization.

Efforts to determine the degree to which human resources are wasted in Mexico must consider the question of disguised unemployment—which is sometimes referred to as "underemployment," "subemployment," "low productivity," "subsistence agriculture," or "autoconsumption." What Marx said of England with regard to pauperism, namely, that it had become institutionalized (Meek 1971: 66–69), also applies to Mexico with respect to these terms, all of which amount to saying that poverty in Mexico is a revolutionary institution. It is something to be fostered, cared for, and nursed, as well as something to be patriotic, nationalistic, conformist, and democratic about. It is the "safe" poverty which takes the revolutionary edge off the poor (for a while) and makes the world safe for the wealthy denizens of the upper class Lomas de Chapultepec, Paseo de la Reforma, and other such centers of "revolutionary fervor." The limits of what has been referred to as Mexico's "impositive politics" lie at the point of complete elimination of poverty, for were that limit to be reached, politics would have ceased imposing upon private property the modalities required by the public interest and would begin to itself embody and live out the principle of property as a public function.

How much unemployment and underemployment is there in Mexico? To begin with, according to one estimate more than 30 per cent of the population of the fields in or around 1960 were affected by rural underemployment. The rural population amounted to 17.2 million people. Hence this estimate would classify approximately 5.2 million rural dwellers as affected by underemployment at the time (Aguilar 1967:72). With respect to the over-all level of unemployment and underemployment there is considerable agreement among three sources (Editorial 1963:348; Sosa 1964:276; Aguilar 1968:72). The over-all level of unemployment and underemployment in 1950 and 1960 has been estimated at 17.6 per cent and 18.2 per cent of the population respectively. In absolute terms, the total number of unemployed and underemployed persons are reported to have been 4.5 million and 6.3 million in 1950 and 1960 respectively.

These figures are reported rather briefly, almost casually, leaving a number of questions unanswered. Aguilar Monteverde says that 18 per cent of the nation's inhabitants in 1960 were "absorbed" by unemployment and underemployment. It is not clear whether "inhabitants absorbed" by unemployment and underemployment includes only persons in the productive age brackets who fit under these categories or whether it also includes the population which is dependent on them.

If we assume the 6.3 million figure includes persons in the productive age brackets who are unemployed or underemployed *and* the population depending on them, and if we assume further that the size of the unemployed and underemployed population stayed at the same level in 1970 as it did in 1950 and 1960 (about 18 per cent), then one could estimate that the total size of the population which was unemployed or underemployed in 1970 was approximately 9 million.

Hence, even if the size of the underemployed population is considered together with the reported unemployed population, the resulting figures are not sufficient to account for the size of the population classified as not sharing in the benefits of Mexico's development. I might add that the bank's estimate of 15 million people not sharing in 1970 seems to underestimate this figure by a wide margin. Those 15 million do not include those persons earning between 500 and 999 pesos per month in 1970, yet already in 1960, 1,000 pesos per month was reported to have been insufficient for a modest existence. The intervening inflation must have effected a considerable reduction in the real purchasing power of that sum by 1970; the bank reports 3.1 million economically active persons in this category. The bank itself uses a conversion factor of three to obtain the total of laborers and dependents (Banco Nacional de México 1971c:156–58). Hence, an additional 9.3 million members would have to be added to the 15 million listed by the bank as not sharing. The total not sharing would then rise to a total of 24.3 million people, approximately half of the 1970 population. Indeed in another article published by the bank (1970), it is specifically recognized that more than half of Mexico's population does not share in the benefits of society. "In the [World's] underdeveloped regions —Mexico is an example—most of the inhabitants are at the fringes of society in every way: they suffer hunger, they are uneducated, sick, and endure many hardships . . ." (Banco Nacional de México 1970b:11–12).

Actually, the latter of the two estimates given by the bank squares better with the fact that Mexico's median income in 1970 amounted to 709 dollars per year, a fact which means that half of Mexico's economically active population received incomes below this figure. Also, the higher of the two estimates given by the bank would come closer to accounting for the fact that over 1.3 million of the economically active did not declare any income in 1970.

Stated in terms of population deciles, the magnitude of the unemployed and underemployed population, and of the population living in poverty, are approximately 2 and 5 respectively, with the former occupying the lower two-tenths of the table of income distribution by deciles and the latter overlapping and including the bottom half of the same distribution. Stated in other terms, these figures mean that nearly two-tenths of Mexico's population suffer from hunger, malnutrition, ill-health, inadequate medical attention, low levels of education, and inadequate shelter because they are either unemployed or underemployed. They mean also that an additional three-tenths (at least) of the remaining population suffer from malnutrition, ill-health, inadequate medical care, and inadequate education and housing despite the fact that they work full time. Therefore, the lot of the unemployed and underemployed is simply a compounding of the problem experienced by the poor who work full time.

The estimate that nearly one-fifth of Mexico's population is either unemployed or underemployed and that half of it is poor corresponds rather well with the fact that the bottom 20 per cent of Mexico's families received only 4 per cent of the nation's income in 1970. It also corresponds well with the fact that the lower half of Mexico's families received less than 15 per cent of the nation's income for the same year. These are the people (the lower 50 per cent of the families) whose incomes are under 709 dollars per year.

The contingent of the unemployed and underemployed must be regarded as constituting a special segment of the impoverished population—a segment whose claim to distinction lies in the fact that it is destitute in both the system of production and the system of distribution. There appear to be forms and degrees of redundancy. The totally redundant are the totally neglected, the pariahs and outcasts whom Marx referred to as the *Lumpenproletariat*. The partially redundant are those who are poor even though they work full time, and many might be thought of as redundant in the sense that they are poor in some ways (even though they work full time) and are better off in other ways. Given the extremes of capital concentration and undercapitalization in the various sectors of Mexico's economy, the high percentage of farm units which have been said to be marginal to the market, and the known defects in Mexico's methods of assessing the magnitude of the problems of unemployment and underemployment, one cannot shake off the feeling that much unemployment remains hidden. What, for instance, would be the effect of including the annual contingent of northbound braceros and wetbacks in Mexico's unemployment figures?

One year for which the absolute size of the labor force and the total number of braceros and wetbacks apprehended is available is 1950. Mexico's labor force for that year included 8,345,240 persons (Banco Nacional de México 1970c:306). The total number of braceros and wetbacks apprehended is given as 542,519 (González Casanova 1970:227). In relative terms the latter figure amounts to 6.5 per cent of the former. One source reports that 0.28 per cent of the population was unemployed in 1950 (Editorial 1963:246). Mexico's 1950 population was 25,791,017 (United Nations 1955:134). The total number of unemployed persons for 1950, therefore, must be placed at approximately 72,215. If this figure is now expressed as a percentage of the labor force for 1950 given above, we end up with a figure of 0.87 per cent unemployed. In conclusion, if the population of braceros and wetbacks apprehended is regarded as part of Mexico's unemployment problem, and if the size of this population is expressed as a percentage of the labor force, the figure we end up with is 7.5 times larger than the percentage figure which supposedly expresses total unemployment for the year 1950. Hence the suspicion that official definitions of the unemployment situation tend to mask the truth of existing conditions (Fisher 1964:191). The 6.5 per cent given above may not begin to tap the true dimensions of the problem. A quite recent report in a conservative daily speaks of rates of unemployment and underemployment ranging as high as 40 per cent, coupled with 20 per cent rates of inflation. Also, two-thirds of a population of 60 million is reported as being poor (Mullen 1975:Secs. 1–16).

The northbound flow of braceros began at a time when the World War II draft was threatening to create a serious farm labor shortage in the United States (Simpson 1971:347–48). As soon as wartime labor shortages were over, the size of the bracero contingent was drastically reduced. According to Loyo the number of braceros increased from about 4,200 in 1942 to a high of over 118,000 in 1944. Then it declined to a low point of 19,000 in 1947. This drastically reduced figure was probably one of the factors which contributed to the 1947 recession in Mexico. After 1947 the size of the bracero force, with the single exception of 1950, began a steady upward climb, reaching an approximate total of 204,000 in 1952 and 436,000 in 1957 (Loyo 1963:29–30). The Korean War probably played a role here. The need for large and even increasing contingents of braceros appears to have continued after the end of that conflict, a fact which is very probably related to the growing importance of corporate or large-scale agriculture in the United States. The very fact that braceros were contract laborers means that their numbers varied as a function of the United States labor market. The absolute size of the bracero contingent is, therefore, of little value in drawing inferences about cyclical fluctuations or about the over-all size of the unemployed labor force in Mexico, although it does say something about the existence of a readily available "floating population" in Mexico as well as about the differences in the standard of living between the two countries. The fact that most United States citizens visit Mexico as tourists while most Mexicans visit the United States as either contract or wetback agricultural laborers speaks very eloquently about how the alignment of international class differences structure the relative position of the two countries.

The relation between the number of wetbacks apprehended and the index of real income per inhabitant in Mexico appears to be of greater significance as an index of the relation between economic conditions in Mexico and the size of Mexico's relative surplus population. On the basis of figures available for the years 1948–57, a −0.84 correlation was found to exist between these variables. This −0.84 correlation clearly indicates that the northbound flow of surreptitious migrants increases as economic conditions in Mexico worsen and that it decreases as those conditions improve. The plight of the Mexican-American is therefore inextricably tied to the conditions of poverty in Mexico, and those conditions are in turn inextricably bound to Mexico's neocolonial dependence on the United States, a dependence which involves such variables as private investments, public loans, the balance of trade, and the balance of payments. The flow of migrants is therefore related to both intranational and international exploitation. No doubt population growth, under existing conditions, also plays a part. The migratory currents of braceros and wetbacks is a subject which deserves special study from different perspectives, particularly from the point of view of their relation to investments, the egress of profits, the balance of trade, payments, and other indicators.

It is plain from the meagerness of the unemployment data available that a systematic analysis of the relation between unemployment and capitalist crises lies out of the reach of this study. Further concern with capitalist crises within the limitations of the available data can only produce insights which are suggestive in nature. A few comments concerning broad historical trends are possible.

The nineteenth century interval between Independence and the Wars of Reform has been described as a time of almost continuous depression and war (Padilla 1968:707–708). The years of Porfirio Díaz' administration are remembered as years of prosperity for the oligarchy and depression for the masses (Padilla 1968:710). Institutional changes which followed the revolution did not take place overnight but were brought about piecemeal over a couple of decades. The land-reform program, for instance, did not acquire full momentum until about a decade and a half after the termination of armed conflict. Changes in the institutions of credit took place in the mid twenties; the expropriation of oil and railways took place in the late thirties. Also, the destruction of the years of revolution was not overcome overnight. Perhaps the most important consequences of these changes were: (1) to place a lower limit on the destitution of the Mexican masses while strengthening Mexico's capacity to feed itself and allowing part of its agricultural production to be deflected to the export market; (2) to increase the participation of the public sector in the regulation, planning, and financing of industry; (3) to place a ceiling on foreign investments while increasing dependency through the export-import market and on foregin sources of public credit; (4) to increase dependence on the export of seasonal labor (*bracerismo*) and on income from tourism; and (5) to develop an industrial and commercial sector which is subsidiary to international conglomerates and chain stores.

Table 25.   Wetbacks Apprehended and
Economic Conditions in Mexico

Year	Wetbacks Apprehended (thousands)	Index of Real Income per Inhabitant [%]
1948	180	99.0
1949	280	96.0
1950	466	97.5
1951	500	99.5
1952	800	92.5
1953	1,000	91.5
1954	1,000	95.5
1955	242	99.5
1956	72	99.5
1957	44	102.0

Sources: Pablo González Casanova, *Democracy in Mexico* (London: Oxford University Press, 1970), p. 227; Enrique Padilla Aragón, *Ensayos sobre Desarrollo Económico y Fluctuaciones Cíclicas en México (1925–1964)* (Mexico City, Universidad Nacional Autónoma de Mexico, 1966), p. 158.

The revolutionary decade was not followed by a period of recovery in the 1920's. The world-wide depression of the 1930's compounded an already difficult situation. The depression of the thirties is reported to have been a deep one. In fact, comparative growth curves for the United States (GNP) and Mexico (GDP) show a sharp curtailment of production at about the same time in both countries (1929) and bottoming out at about the same time (1932–33) in both cases (Padilla 1968:712; Reynolds 1970:242). Bad harvests of corn and beans compounded the difficulties, and heavy quantities of corn had to be imported in 1930. Also, in keeping with a deflationist policy the salaries of public employees were reduced.

Fluctuations of the Mexican economy vary in close relation to fluctuations of the United States economy. Mexico's exports increase during the prosperity cycle and decrease during the depression cycle in the United States economy. Prices drop as exports decrease and related incomes within the Mexican economy decline. This in turn affects production and employment levels. In this connection Padilla says (Padilla 1968:713):

> The mechanism whereby cyclical fluctuations in the U.S. are transmitted to the Mexican economy can be observed with great clarity, both during the depression of 1932 and during the recovery interval which followed. This mechanism is as follows: changes in national income in the U.S. are translated into variation of its import coefficient, primarily in raw materials, since economic cycles rapidly affect the industrial sector. This in turn means changes in Mexico's exports, upwards during prosperity in the U.S. and downwards during depression. Thus it happened that the depression of 1932 in the U.S. meant a landslide in the export prices of Mexico's principal agricultural and mineral exports. The prices of cotton, *henequen*, chickpeas, and tomatoes on the one hand, and principally of silver and industrial metals on the other, dropped abruptly. Internal repercussions spread out rapidly, through a decline in the income of farmers and of all the sectors connected with export industries.

Other related changes included a heavy drop in banking reserves and a one-third reduction in federal income due largely to a decrease in duties received from international commerce (Padilla 1968:713).

About half way through the Cárdenas administration (1937–38) the Mexican economy began to show a sustained tendency to grow, subject to short-term fluctuations. Beginning in 1955 growth rates tended to become either more moderate or stagnant (Padilla 1968: 714, 722).

A recent (1970) review of the economic situation gives the following indicators of the current situation: (1) a GNP growth rate of 6.5 per cent per year, (2) a rate of population growth of 3.5 per cent per year, (3) a per capita GNP growth rate of 3.0 per cent per year, (4) a wholesale price index of 6.1 per cent from January to October, 1970. (5) Sales were down. (6) Import prices had gone up. (7) There was a trade deficit that could go up as high as 900 million dollars. (8) Income from tourism declined. (9) Interest rates on foreign loans

Graph 4.   **Comparative Growth of Mexican and U.S. Economies,
1900–1965**

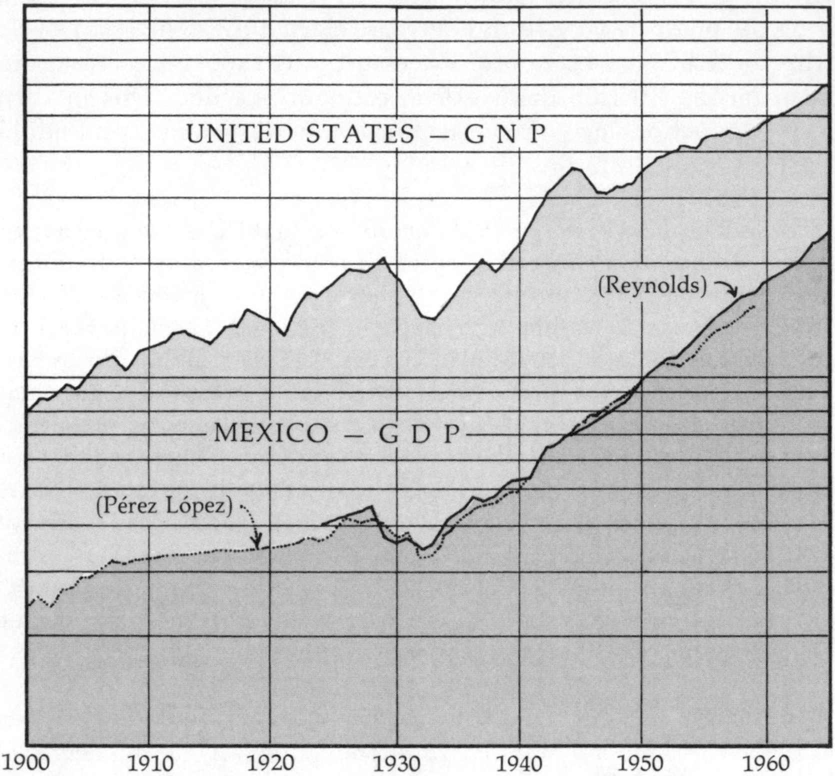

UNITED STATES — G N P

(Reynolds)

MEXICO — G D P

(Pérez López)

| 1900 | 1910 | 1920 | 1930 | 1940 | 1950 | 1960 |

Source: Reynolds, *The Mexican Economy*, 242.

had risen. (10) Increases took place in "practically all wages." (11) In response to a new Federal Labor Law, businessmen were increasing prices in anticipation of rising cost. The uneasiness over inflation and the factors alluded to account for it are suggestive (Banco Nacional de México 1970:303).

> The principal factor causing this inflation was the recession in the U.S. economy and its recurring inflation. Although it did not affect Mexico intensively during the first half of 1970 . . . the recession — aggravated by high unemployment and the strike in the automobile industry — has persisted. The consequences have been noxious for Mexico. . . .

But what of the impact of the distribution of income by sectors? This question is not dealt with by this report. Another report by the same institution has this to say (Banco Nacional de México 1971b: 231):

> From this point forward progress will be closely tied to the over-all organization of the productive activities of the country, because although international markets can absorb part of Mexico's manufactured products, it is not only difficult but also risky to depend on the needs of other nations. The future must be supported by local demand, which will in turn depend on sustained growth of income. The most important requirement is to speed up the redistribution of income in order to increase the number of consumers to strengthen the market.

The field of vision open to investigation here permits awareness of a need to increase incomes so that a market for commodities will be created. The question as to whether the capitalist mode of appropriation is itself in need of change does not arise. Hence, to the extent that the lot of human beings requires improvement, the improvement is viewed as necessary in order that the needs of the market might be better served, rather than the market being in need of improvement so that human life might be better constituted.

14.

Verificative Conclusions

The government of today
keeps watch over our thinking.
And these are not the days of Díaz,
But the story is much the same.
The student is threatened,
repression is a daily occurrence,
and the prestige of our schools
is in the hands of the police.

From the song "Gorilita, Gorilón,"
by Judith Reyes.

Does poverty have its source in overpopulation, as Malthus claimed? Or is it rooted in capitalist exploitation of labor, as Marx maintained? Close study of the basic points at issue between these opposing theoretical perspectives led to a sharp focus on eleven questions. Formulation of these questions was followed by an effort to answer them within a suitable, historically specific setting. Mexico was selected for study due to the sharp polarization found within that setting of the key variables at issue in the study: scarcity and exploitation. To Malthus, overpopulation generates scarcity, which in turn accounts for poverty. To Marx, private ownership of the means of production makes possible the exploitation of living labor through the expropriation of surplus value produced by labor, and this exploitation is in turn the source of poverty. Mexico was known to have one of the fastest rates of population growth in the world as well as one of the most unequal patterns of income distribution.

168

The study of Mexico in light of these questions and from these two opposing perspectives has led to several conclusions.

The first of the eleven questions seeks to establish the extent to which poverty might be said to exist in Mexico, and in so doing it establishes the magnitude of the problem in need of explanation. The remaining ten questions focus attention on the basic issues to which the opposing perspectives address themselves. The questions are:

What portion of the Mexican population lives at or below the margins of subsistence?

What is the balance of forces between population needs and means of subsistence?

What are the respective rates of growth of reproductive and productive forces, past, present, and predicted, and why?

What specific form does private property over the means of production take in Mexico?

What portion of the Mexican population is unemployed or underemployed, and why?

What are the trends in unemployment and underemployment, past, present, and predicted?

What are the trends in land and capital concentration in Mexico?

What are the trends in income derived from profits and rents?

What relation exists between the latter trends and the incidence of business cycles?

What relationship is there between business cycles and the size of the unemployed labor force?

What is the relationship between the unemployed labor force and the population living below the level of subsistence?

Portion of the Mexican Population Living at or below Subsistence Levels. Close consideration and criticism of various estimates of the size of the population living at or below subsistence indicate that somewhere between 50 and 60 per cent of the total population lived under those conditions in 1960 and 1970. It also shows a tendency for the life conditions of that population to deteriorate in relative terms and to improve somewhat in absolute terms. The latter is particularly true among those sectors of that population higher up in the income scale (Sosa 1964:277; González Casanova

1970:109; Guzmán 1973:20; Banco Nacional de México 1970b:11–12). Disagreement across sources hinges on varying concerns with bare biological subsistence and with life-style subsistence. The former view tends to underestimate and the latter to overestimate the size of the population living below subsistence. This study assumes that subsistence of both types varies over a range and that there is a segment of the population in which the two forms overlap. An estimate of 50 per cent of the population living at or below subsistence would err on the safe side.

Balance of Forces between Population Needs and the Means of Subsistence. On or about 1961, Ana María Flores reported 15 per cent of Mexico's population to be hungry (Rodríguez 1966:11). The following minimum standards of daily food consumption for underdeveloped countries were recognized by the United Nations' Food and Agricultural Organization in 1967: calories, 2,600; total proteins, 75 grams; animal proteins, 25 grams (Banco Nacional de México 1970a:165). By 1974 the required minimum daily supply of calories was revised downward to 2,325 per day. The average daily supply of calories available in Mexico during the years 1960–62 exceeded the 1967 FAO minimum by 10 calories and the 1974 FAO minimum by 285 calories. In 1960–62 the average daily supply of proteins from all sources available per capita fell short of the 1967 FAO minimum by 3 grams, while the same figure for 1967 exceeded the same 1967 standards by 1 gram. The average daily per capita supply of animal proteins in 1960–62 fell short of the 1967 minimum by 2.6 grams, while the same figure in 1967 showed a deficiency of 2.1 grams. The 1967 figures show a plentiful per capita supply of vitamins and minerals with the exception of Vitamin A and ribo-flavin, which were each short by 1 milligram. Vitamin C was short 20 milligrams per capita (Banco Nacional de México 1970a:165; FAO 1975:140).

Estimates of the extent of undernourishment in Mexico vary from 50 to 80 per cent of the total population (Súarez 1962:380–81; NACOLA 1973:4). The conclusion warranted is that the magnitude of the population reported hungry and undernourished is far out of proportion to the actual shortages. Part of the problem lies in the fact that twice as much meat per capita is consumed in the Federal District as in the rest of the country. Also, part of Mexico's protein supply is exported: 762.3 million pesos' worth of dairy products, eggs, fish, seafood, and honey in 1968. In 1968–69 Mexico exported 678,000 head of cattle and about 30 million kilograms of processed meat. Further, during 1968–69, Mexico exported 919 million pesos' worth of fruits and vegetables and 780.7 million pesos' worth of cereals, grains, starches, and flour.

Approximately two-thirds of Mexico's 1970 population was reported to be lacking direct medical attention from either private or public sources. The reluctance to spend nearly half the federal funds already appropriated for medical service construction during the sixties suggests, at the very least, official complaisance with existing health standards.

About a fourth of Mexico's population older than ten years was still illiterate in 1970. Three-fifths of the economically active population had less than three years schooling, and only about 15 per cent of that population had completed the sixth grade. Only about 2.1 per cent of Mexico's gross internal product was spent on education in 1965, compared to 3.3 for Argentina and 5.6 for Cuba at that same time.

Close to two-fifths of Mexico's houses had the following characteristics in 1970: They were one-room shacks with dirt floors; walls made mostly of adobe, mud, and makeshift materials; roofs made of wood, palm leaf thatching, and similar materials; totally lacking in electricity and plumbing; cooking done with wood or charcoal. About three in five houses lacked sewers and drainage. Close to seven of ten houses had less than two rooms and lacked bathrooms. Nearly half of Mexico's housing units were renter-occupied. Indications are that nearly two-thirds of the economically active population is excluded from the possibility of having a sanitized, secure, and livable house built by private developers.

Relative Growth Rates of Population Needs and of Means of Subsistence. The results of this study make clear that the relationship between population growth and means of subsistence is not an immediate one-to-one relationship. Rather, it is mediated by the whole body of institutionalized practices, ideological assumptions, and geopolitical concerns which play a role in formulating the policies of the administration in power.

The Díaz regime (1877–1910) followed a policy of promoting

industrialization through heavy reliance on foreign investments and the sale of export crops abroad to provide a source of foreign exchange. The growth of export crop production was encouraged by promoting the growth of large landed estates. This policy was implemented through the so-called surveying laws, which were instrumental in rendering 90 per cent of the inhabitants of Mexico's Central Mesa landless. Over 51 per cent of total investments in 1902–1903 came from abroad, and less than a fourth of the investable public funds were actually invested. Mexico was ruled by a coalition of local and foreign elites who were committed to spreading the gospel of Comtean and Spencerian positivism and who attempted to rule Mexico according to those tenets. Positivist freedom became the freedom of self-enrichment. The "scientific" skills of these positivist *científicos* showed up primarily in the way in which land and capital concentrated in a few hands. Foreign interests controlled 42 per cent of the country's wealth. Seventy-five per cent of the railroads, 64 per cent of the minerals, and 58 per cent of the petroleum was owned by foreign interests, mostly United States based. Mexicans took to speaking of their country as "the mother of foreigners and the stepmother of Mexicans."

The past century of Mexican history shows that periods of relatively low rates of population growth have been accompanied by declining rates of growth in food production, while periods of relatively rapid rates of population growth have been accompanied by even more rapid rates of growth in food production. The years of the Díaz administration were years of relatively low rates of population growth. During the latter part of this administration, the population growth rate averaged approximately 1.5 per cent per year. In 1910, the year of the revolutionary outbreak, it stood at 1.1 per cent per year. Nonetheless, crop production per capita declined at an approximate rate of .8 per cent per year throughout the Díaz regime. The production of food crops such as corn, beans, and wheat declined. Corn production alone dropped from 282 kilograms to 144 kilograms per person during the three Díaz decades. Data specific to Puebla, which was found to typify other areas as well, indicated that during those same years wages increased by 50 per cent, while the price of corn increased by 200 per cent, and the price of *chile* increased by 800 per cent. Close to one in three infants born alive died, chiefly from the parasitic and infectious diseases which are primarily associated with hunger, malnutrition, and general conditions of poverty. Order among the hungry, the ignorant, the sick, and the destitute was kept through the police, particularly the rural police, and through the jails, the army, and the confessional. In the meantime, while total crop production was growing at a rate less than half (.6 per cent per year) the rate of population growth, crop production for export was increasing at a rate of growth four times faster (6 per cent per year) than the rate of population growth. The production of such farm exports as cotton, sugar, tobacco, cattle, and tomatoes was increasing at a per capita rate of 4.6 per cent per year.

The constitution of 1917 laid the legal foundations for the reforms of the late twenties and thirties, and the forces of reform took their greatest impetus during the administration of Lázaro Cárdenas. The years from 1910 to 1940 were characterized by revolution, depression, and reform. Mexico's population increased at an average rate of .9 per cent per year throughout this interval, although during the revolutionary decade (1910–20), the population actually declined by close to 6 per cent. Real per capita crop production throughout these years grew at a very slow average rate of .2 per cent per year. Between 1907 and 1925 per capita agricultural production actually declined at an average rate of .1 per cent per year. This decline was due to the neglect and ravages of agriculture during the armed struggle.

Close to a third of the total land area redistributed between 1915 and 1964 was redistributed during the Cárdenas administration (1934–40). Among the other distinctive acts of this administration are found nationalization of oil industries, establishment of new credit institutions, Mexicanization of insurance companies, and a heavier reliance on internal sources of public funds for investment purposes. Also, the purchasing power of the minimum salary was higher in 1939–40 than in any subsequent year up to and including 1964. Finally, the relative shares of income paid in the form of wages and salaries during the last two years of this administration are high by comparison to those paid in subsequent years.

The years between 1940 and 1970 were years of recovery and industrial development for the Mexican economy. They were also years of rapid population growth. Between 1940 and 1970 Mexico maintained a rate of growth in food production fast enough to permit a steady increase in per capita food production despite a fairly rapid average rate of population increase during the interval.

Between 1940 and 1960 the average rate of population increase might be placed at 2.5 per cent per year. During the same interval food production grew at a rate of 5.6 per cent per year—a rate better than twice the average rate of population increase. The index of food production per capita rose steadily between 1960 and 1973, except for a slight decline in 1972, a decline too unusual to indicate a trend. The figures also indicate that the index of food production per capita increased at a rate considerably slower than that of total food production (FAO 1970:232; FAO 1974:165). Mexico continues to promote agriculture for export. Crop production for export rose at an average rate of 8.7 per cent per year between 1940 and 1960.

Mexico's experience during the years 1940 and 1970 indicate that its food production can increase from two to three times faster than its population, even when that population is doubling during the same interval. Such rapid rates of increase in food production are clearly due to changes of a political, legal, and technological nature, all of which have tended to foster such increases despite the relative barrenness of the soil and climate. Nonetheless, some 15 to 24 million hectares of potentially useful land were reported to be available (subject to prior improvement through irrigation, drainage, etc.) at about the same time that 15 per cent of the population was reported hungry.

Even if it were possible to show that some of Mexico's hunger and malnutrition has its source in diminishing returns on added units of capital investment, the question would still remain as to why the increases that do take place are distributed unequally. The *ejidal* lands are probably as productive as the privately held lands, but at the cost of labor-intensive techniques. Indeed, the evidence indicates that the *ejidal* system was fostered to rescue the *latifundio* system from its expansionist and despoliative tendencies and not to promote efficiency of production. On the other hand, the productivity of the modernized, private sector lies not in its privacy but rather in the fact that larger units are more likely to muster the capital and the resources needed to acquire and to make optimum use of technology. The idea of "haciendas without *hacendados*" has yet to be tried in Mexico.

If the patterns of population growth and food production and distribution which prevailed in 1970–75 continue, the hungry and undernourished population will double by the mid-1990's. The possibility that food output will more than double does exist, but it is becoming more problematic. The dangers of salinization, sinking water tables, overgrazing, soil erosion, and floods will have to be considered. The shrinking supply of fossil fuels will become increasingly problematic.

Mexico faces compound and growing problems in meeting the health, housing, and educational needs of its population. The growing need for medical services has been estimated to require an annual investment of 42 million dollars. If present deficiencies, future deterioration, and growing housing needs are considered, Mexico will have to build one and one-half times as many houses by 1980 as it had in 1969, leaving aside the question of housing quality and distribution. Existing restrictions on Mexico's capacity to invest in education make it highly unlikley that the extent of the population's participation in education can be expanded. Yet growing industrialization will require some such expansion.

Specific Form which Private Ownership over the Means of Production Takes in Mexico. The language of the constitution of 1917 is at times radical: "Property is the right of a man to the products of his personal work." But the full implications of the conception of property as a concrete social function, as contrasted to an abstract private right, were not worked out in full in the constitution. (For such an effort see Jordan, 1927.) The main thrust of Article 27 is the promulgation of the supremacy of public over private interests and a rejection of *laissez-faire* economics (Carmona 1970:57–59).

A number of changes and reforms were carried out under the provisions of this law, among them land reform; nationalization of petroleum, railways, and electric power stations; restrictions on foreign ownership of land, subsoil, and minerals; and state efforts to limit tendencies toward monopolistic concentration. During the interval between the administrations of Carranza and Cárdenas, efforts were made to reduce the extent of foreign indebtedness and to minimize reliance on foreign sources of investments. However, the administration of Avila Camacho (1941–46) marked the beginning of a reversal of this trend. A number of industrial and commercial concerns are now reported to be disguised branches of United States enterprises (Zamora 1960:358).

Portion of the Mexican Population Unemployed or Underemployed and Why. Statistics on unemployment and underemployment in Mexico are difficult to find, and those that are available are of a dubious nature. Official figures on unemployment in particular are implausibly low: 1 per cent for 1970 (Banco de México 1971c:156). Data for a single year (1950), when statistics are available for both unemployment rates and the total contingent of braceros and wetbacks apprehended, indicate that the unemployment situation is much worse than official figures indicate. The percentage relationship between the size of this migratory labor force and the size of the economically active population is 7.5 times the reported unemployment rate.

For a number of reasons, it is best to consider both unemployment and underemployment to properly assess the magnitude of the problem. Among the factors affecting the problem are the large number of infrasubsistence *ejidal* and private holdings, the large contingent of seasonally-hired field hands, and the many forms of marginal unemployment and "hustling" in commerce, services, and manufacturing. Recent estimates of the size of this combined contingent vary from 19 per cent to 40 or 50 per cent. The revolution, such as it was, tended to institutionalize underemployment, low productivity, and poverty. The international economic crisis is compounding the problem.

Trends in Underemployment and Unemployment: Past, Present, and Predicted. The available figures on total unemployment and underemployment for 1950 and 1960 are 17.6 and 18.2 per cent, respectively. These figures, however, are of little use in assessing trends.

According to one estimate (Fisher 1964:190) population growth alone added 300,000 new job seekers to the market between 1950 and 1960. This figure is estimated to have risen to 800,000 per year between 1970 and 1980 (Banco de México 1970b:13). It would be a mistake to take these figures at face value, however. Closer examination reveals that the former figure corresponds very closely to the 1950 population of fifteen-year-old males (284,086). Further, a certain proportion of the available jobs must be vacated through retirement and death. Approximately 50,000 males reached retirement age in 1950. To these must be added roughly 100,000 males aged 15 to 65 who were removed by the death rate. If each of these retirements and deaths left vacated jobs, and we must assume that a large proportion of them did so, then the total number of new jobs needed in 1950 would be cut by close to half the original figure, or by approximately 150,000.

On the exploitation side of the question, there is some evidence that increases in productivity are making for job attrition and displacement. Fisher reports a 29 per cent decrease in employment in textiles coupled with a 177 per cent increase in the value of textile production. An 84 per cent increase in employment in steel production was accompanied by an 876 per cent increase in the value of steel production (Fisher 1964:195). Increases in productivity alone are reported to have eliminated approximately 200,144 jobs in manufacturing between 1950 and 1960 (Trejo 1970:114–18).

The same processes have had similar effects in agriculture. Costs of production on account of machinery rose from 6 per cent in 1940 to 11 per cent in 1960. During the same interval expenditures on salaries declined from 22 per cent to 7 per cent. Agriculture's share of the economically active population declined from 70 per cent in 1940 to less than 50 per cent in 1970. Between 1940 and 1950 alone, some 480,000 workers were transferred from agriculture to other sectors (Reyes 1971:178–80).

If one were to venture the guess that 200,000 to 300,000 workers were displaced in the commercial and service sectors between 1950 and 1960, one would arrive at a figure of close to one million jobs eliminated during the fifties—a rate of about 100,000 a year. The creation of underemployment by increases in productivity would complicate the picture further: the number of effective days worked by 3.5 million workers is reported to have declined from 194 to 100 days between 1950 and 1960 (Banco Nacional de México 1973:169).

We are left with the conclusions that approximately 150,000 new jobs were made necessary by population growth each year during the fifties and that approximately 100,000 jobs per year were being eliminated by increases in productivity during those years. Thus for every three jobs made necessary by population growth, two jobs were eliminated by increases in productivity. Only 13 per cent of the economically active population in 1950 were females. It is unlikely that female unemployment and underemployment would significantly alter this picture within the limits of accuracy permitted by the data.

These data suggest another conclusion: the process of urbanization under capitalist forms of control is a process which creates unemployment and underemployment faster than it creates employment. That is, under capitalism the economy of action made possible by the application of science and technology is transformed into a process of displacement and attrition of jobs and salaries.

Trends in Land and Capital Concentration in Mexico. Despite the program of reforms implemented since the revolution, Mexico remains a country where a relatively small number of persons and corporations control most of the land, wealth, and income of the country. Most of the best farming and grazing lands are concentrated in a few hundred vast estates which are under the control of politicians, bankers, merchants, and industrialists. Sixty-one per cent of the total farm acreage was still in private hands in 1960, and 1 per cent of the total number of haciendas accounted for 75 per cent of the total land area held in private hands. Despite a far ranging program of land reform which redistributed 70 million hectares (about 190 million acres) of land by 1970, the authenticity of both the program of land reform itself and public commitment to the body of law underlying the reform has been questioned (Reyes 1969; Carmona 1970).

The concentration of capital in manufacturing, commerce, and services in 1965 was quite high. One and one-half per cent of the total number of manufacturing establishments accounted for 77 per cent of the total product. Sixty per cent of the total capital and 60.4 per cent of the total gross income in commerce was controlled by 1.3 per cent of the establishments. Sixty-four per cent of the invested capital and 54 per cent of the total income in services was controlled by 1 per cent of the establishments.

Around 1962 approximately 50 per cent of the income received by the 2,000 largest enterprises accrued to the 100 largest corporations. Seventy-seven per cent of that same income accrued to the 400 largest corporations. Among the 400 largest enterprises, 161 were under foreign control and 71 showed strong foreign participation. By contrast, 36 of the 400 largest enterprises were under Mexican state control. About 42 per cent of the total income of the 2,000 largest corporations accrued to corporations showing either foreign control or strong foreign participation. By contrast, the 36 largest state enterprises accounted for 19.2 per cent of the same income (González Casanova 1970:211). The high degree of foreign control and influence in the Mexican economy suggests that fluctuations in that economy are heavily conditioned by international economic fluctuations and that these fluctuations are magnified by the dynamics of the Mexican economy.

The process of capital concentration is primarily an urban phenomenon; that is, capital concentration is the very stuff of which the process of urbanization under capitalist forms of development is made. The evidence can be seen most clearly in the Federal District, which in 1965 showed 320 per cent more production per inhabitant than the rest of the country. Mexico's institutions of private credit showed the Federal District to have the following characteristics in 1967. It accounted for 1,152 per cent more total resources per inhabitant, 200 per cent more capital reserves, and over 90 per cent as many visible cash deposits as the rest of the country. Yet the Federal District accounted for only 17 per cent of the country's population in 1970 (Carmona 1970:42).

Trends in Income Derived from Profits and Rents. Data on profits in any form tend to be scanty and fragmentary. In particular the type of data which could be useful in verifying the Marxian theory of the falling rate of profit are extremely difficult to obtain.

Data which state profits as a percentage of total annual income show a steady rise from 26.2 per cent of total income in 1939 to 45.1 per cent in 1946. This rise is followed by erratic fluctuations around 41 per cent between 1951 and 1955 and by a steady decline to 36.5 per cent by 1959. Now, if commercial profits are seen as a percentage of total profits, we find that commercial profits varied from 53 per cent in 1939 to 61 per cent in 1950 (Singer 1969:136, 139). The same source indicates that incomes from rents and interests showed an over-all decline from slightly over 8 per cent of total income in 1939 to about 6.4 per cent in 1954.

Somewhat more complete data covering the interval 1939–60

(González Casanova 1970:222) show that incomes from capital ranged from one-third to one-half of total annual income. Incomes from labor ranged between slightly over one-fifth to slightly less than one-third of total income. Mixed incomes and incomes imputed to the self-employed ranged between slightly over one-fourth to one-third of total income. The latter showed an over-all downward trend which seems to be indicative of the growth of large-scale industry and a decline in the self-employed sectors.

In Marxian theory the rate of profit is a percentage ratio of surplus value to total capital, i.e., capital which includes both its fixed component (plant and equipment) and its variable component (wages, salaries, etc.). The rate of profit typical of Mexico has been estimated at 20 to 25 per cent (Aguilar Monteverde 1967:74; Singer 1969:109). Aguilar has noted that it is not unusual for such profits to rise as high as 30 per cent of annual invested capital. Indeed, recent reports are that business profits have been averaging 30 per cent and that the government has served notice that those rates are too high (Riding 1976:1, 3). These figures do convey an idea of the profitability of invested capital in Mexico, but they are of little use in assessing trends.

Unfortunately, the data most suitable for a trend analysis fall short in some respects and contain a number of inaccuracies of an arithmetical nature which this study has attempted to correct (Solís 1972:205). These data include estimates of the value of fixed capital in absolute terms, an estimate of the surplus value arising from its operation which is also in absolute terms, and a ratio of the former to the latter. Solís does note that some of the value of the latter arises from living labor. The data cover an eighteen-year interval from 1950 to 1967 and have been converted to the form of running averages by three-year intervals to give a better idea of the trend. To stress the fact that there is doubt about the extent to which variable capital is represented in the figures, the ratio in question will be retained in the form of a ratio, and will be referred to as "the ratio of profit to fixed capital" rather than as "the rate of profit" in the Marxian sense. If each running average is located at the middle of each three-year interval, the trend reads as follows:

Table 26. **Annual Ratio of Profit
to Fixed Capital**

Year	Ratio	Year	Ratio
1951	.30	1959	.24
1952	.29	1960	.24
1953	.28	1961	.25
1954	.27	1962	.25
1955	.27	1963	.25
1956	.27	1964	.25
1957	.26	1965	.24
1958	.25	1966	.23

The data show a gradual but fairly steady decline in this ratio, from a high of .30 in the early fifties to a low of .24 at the end of the decade. At the turn of the sixties, there was a slight increase from .24 to .25, which was sustained for four years and which was followed by a decline to .23 by the end of the interval covered by the data. Concerning the accuracy of the data, efforts to correct it leave uncertainty only about 1965 (unless, of course, other errors preceded the table), where the raw data yield a profit ratio of .32, while Solís records a ratio of .24. The .32 figure represents such an extreme variation as to suggest an error in transcribing the raw figures after the ratio was worked out.

Figures provided by Singer suggest that the rate of return on foreign investments tends to be lower than the rate of return from native sources. In particular, the reported rate of return on total foreign investments between 1939 and 1958 seems relatively low, averaging 7.6 per cent, with a low of 3.4 per cent in 1940 and a high of 13.1 per cent in 1951. The reported rate of return on foreign investments in manufacturing is somewhat higher, averaging 13.1 per cent, with a high of 18.6 per cent in 1943 and a low of 8.8 per cent in 1958 (Singer 1969:109). These data were checked out against two other sources of data for the years 1950–57. Estimates on these bases indicate that Singer's data might underestimate average profits on total foreign investments by as much as 2.15 per cent (Padilla 1969:168–69; González Casanova 1970:109).

Relationship between the Trend in Profits and the Incidence of Business Cycles. The falling ratio of profit to fixed capital was accompanied by a moderate tendency for net investments to fall and for productivity to rise. Estimates 1 and 2 (Aguilar 1967:49) of net investments were correlated to the profit ratio, and *r* coefficients were obtained for both trend data and raw data. Trend data yielded correlations of +.76 and +.64 respectively. Raw data yielded correlations of +.39 and +.36 respectively. A correlation coefficient of −.71 was found between the profit ratio and the productivity index in manufacturing for the years 1950–58. These figures lend moderate support to the Marxian view that as productivity increases with every increase in the total mass of accumulated capital, a point is reached where increasing units of investment in fixed capital yield progressively smaller increases in productivity and a declining rate of profit. Moreover, data on real wages indicate that during an interval when productivity nearly doubled (1940–60) real wages declined about 10 per cent (Editorial 1963:349; Singer 1969:156).

A comparison between the profit ratio and the rate of growth of the gross national product by five-year intervals from 1950 to 1965 shows that the over-all trend of the former is downward, while the latter tends to stagnate at about 6.3 per cent per year. The GNP growth-rate figures were obtained by averaging data from four different sources. With one exception, all of these estimates are within one per cent of each other (Banco Nacional de México 1971b: 226; Reynolds 1970:22; Padilla 1969:154–55; Centro 1970:215).

Rising absolute levels of both private and public investment were found to be highly intercorrelated with rising absolute levels of gross national production, with the public sector showing the greatest correspondence. A +.98 coefficient of correlation was found between the absolute level of public investments and the absolute size of the GNP in Mexico during the years 1939–65. This impressively high coefficient suggests that the public sector exerts an influence on growth which is far out of proportion to its relative size. A +.81

Table 27. **Comparative Trends: Profit
Ratio versus GNP Growth Rates**

Year	Profit Ratio	Year	Rate of Growth of the GNP
1951–54	28.6	1950–54	6.3
1955–59	25.8	1955–59	6.3
1960–64	24.8	1960–64	6.4

coefficient of correlation was found between the absolute level of private investment and the absolute size of the GNP during the same interval (Padilla 1969:176–77).

Throughout the interval 1939–54 the ratio of investments to profit remained at a relatively constant level: about .20. Concerning later trends Singer notes (Singer 1969:181):

> The combination of inflation, exceedingly favorable profits, and the rising inequality in income distribution that occurred from 1939 to the mid-fifties proved to be a wasteful way of inducing savings. . . . Profit recipients apparently allocated one-fifth of their incomes to investment and the remainder to consumption. The economy tolerated a situation in which over 30 per cent of the national income was directed to satisfying the consumption needs of profit earners in order to encourage them to invest at a rate not exceeding 10 per cent of the GNP. These circumstances did not alter in later years.

The years of high net investment levels were also years of relative high shares of income derived from profits rather than years of increasing investments to profits ratios. Correlation coefficients worked out for a fifteen-year interval (1940–54) where data on relative incomes from profits, net investments, and investments to profit ratio are available yielded the results shown in Table 28. Practically no correlation (−.12) was found between the ratio of investments to profits and the percentage share of annual income

Table 28.   **Correlation Coefficients Between Net Investments, Percentage of Annual Income Paid in the Form of Profits, and the Investment–Profit Ratio**

	Net Investments (%)	
	Estimate 1	Estimate 2
Profits as Per Cent of Annual Income	$r = +.84$	$r = +.87$
Per Cent of Total Profits Invested	$r = +.23$	$r = +.21$

paid in the form of profits. (Singer 1969:182, 136; Aguilar Monteverde 1967:49).

The relatively constant GNP growth rates during the years 1951–64 are more likely to have been sustained by increases in the productivity of both accumulated labor and living labor than by any increases in the investment–profit ratio. The public sector's power to influence growth through public investments is also likely to have been a factor.

Mexico's balance of trade—80 per cent of which takes place with the United States—is very highly intercorrelated with the falling ratio of profits to fixed capital. Trend data on the absolute size of the trade deficit and on the ratio of profit to fixed capital yielded a $-.93$ coefficient of correlation. Raw scores for the same variable yielded a lower $-.79$ correlation coefficient. These findings indicate that there is a general tendency for the rate of profit to decrease as the magnitude of the trade deficit increases (Padilla 1969:157).

Relationship between Business Cycles and the Size of the Unemployed Labor Force. For several reasons it is not possible to deal fruitfully with this question given the specific conditions under study. The data are scanty, fragmentary, and of a dubious nature.

Relationship between the Unemployed Labor Force and the Population Living below the Level of Subsistence. For reasons already stated, any effort to understand the unemployment situation in Mexico must also deal with underemployment. A cautious estimate of the relative size of the unemployed and underemployed population in 1970 Mexico is 20 per cent. At this rate, in 1974 approximately 10.8 million people would have been living under conditions where unemployment and underemployment were the dominant influences. However, recent indications are that the decade of the seventies has brought a steady and serious deterioration of the unemployment and underemployment situation so that the actual situation is very likely considerably worse than the above figures indicate.

The unemployed and underemployed population consists of that group of people whose relative share of the national income decreased from 6 per cent to 4 per cent of the total annual income between 1950 and 1969 and whose deaths "from unknown causes" are most likely to hide hunger and malnutrition, since they are the most likely to experience both on a daily basis. These are the people who constitute the bulk of Mexico's remaining illiteracy problem. They are people who are most likely to contract illnesses and least likely to receive medical help of any type. They are the people who would count themselves lucky if they had a rented, one-room shack with a roof over their heads. They are also the people most likely to be pot-bellied in childhood, to be inattentive to any learning which requires much effort, and to become prematurely old. Also, they are the ones who are most likely to live at the margins of society as both victims and perpetrators of every form of degradation and baseness the underworld of misery has in store for them.

To this 20 per cent we must add at least another 30 per cent—16.2 million people in 1974—who together make up the bottom half of the population who are poor. This 30 per cent consists of those people whose hunger is likely to be more palliated than satiated by means of unbalanced diets heavy with starches and fats. They are likely to be malnourished. These are the people whose formal education seldom carries through the third grade. Only one in three might live in something less crowded than a one-room, rented shack: perhaps in two rooms without running water, toilets, or electricity. The rest of them must be satisfied with one-room houses with dirt floors, walls built of adobe, mud, or other makeshift materials, and thatched roofs. Medical attention for these people is also out of reach, though they are more likely to have access to drugs, vaccines, and the like. This is the 30 per cent whose relative share of the national income decreased from 13 to 11 per cent between 1950 and 1969.

All of these taken together are people whose entire lives tend to be an education in the pseudo-art of survival. They must somehow learn to steer clear of the rent man, the tax collector, and the bill collector, or at least to keep them at bay. They are the people who live under the shadow of fate and who capitulate to her sway by unwittingly defining the situation in the only terms they can conceive, i.e., as adjustment. These are people who implicitly feel that human life has a possibility for something different and who long for a higher existence. They are people who cannot, to any significant extent, rise as a people because the burden of the established institutions and the dead weight of the ages is on their backs. They are people whose eyes are veiled by the search for individual salvation and who in seeking it create the assurance that the more things change, the more they will remain the same. It is to them that the world of class exploitation and the lie of the ages preach that they have no one but themselves to blame for their poverty.

The conclusions enumerated in this chapter suggest that data gathered under the guidance of concepts which are taken from ideologically opposing theoretical perspectives on poverty do provide evidence for assessing the relative explanatory power of those theories. Thus it is possible to arrive at knowledge concerning ideologically sensitive issues despite the influence of ideology on political perspectives.

PART FOUR

Critique of
Theories
of Poverty

15.

Critique of Theories:
Scarcity and Poverty in Mexico

We will make him, you and I
We will make him.
Let us take the clay
To make a new man.

His blood will come
From all bloods,
Blotting out the history
of fear and hunger.

From "Canción del Hombre Nuevo."

This study makes clear that the meaning of scarcity or of exploitation theory is not tightly circumscribed within the political or linguistic boundaries of England, Mexico, Latin America, or the United States. The meaning of Malthusian and Marxian ideas is not lost as one leaves the shores of English society and probes into relevant intellectual cross-currents and trends in Mexican life. The language differs, but except for a few items of local folklore (I am still trying to find out what kind of a drink *chincol* is, and what exactly the difference is between *gitomate* and *tomate*), there is no problem finding articulate spokespersons attempting to explain existing poverty in terms of both scarcity and exploitation. A number of them, starting at one pole, end up by trying to clarify another point at the opposite pole.

Malthusianism is definitely one of the theoretical perspectives from which poverty in Mexico is "explained." Its existence and meaning have international dimensions. Since the end of World War II, the influence of Malthusianism has been increasing due to the widening differences in wealth between industrially developed nations, whose reproduction rates are typically lower, and industrially under-developed nations, whose reproduction rates are typically higher.

The best efforts to draw a *cordon sanitaire* around Mexico on the assumption that Mexico must be seen as a closed system come to naught when one finds that some of the strongest arguments on the scarcity side are given by foreign intellectuals, e.g. the president of the World Bank, and that some of the best field studies were carried out by a United States anthropologist. One then begins to run into United Nations data, Latin-American regional conferences speaking to the issues, bishops of the Catholic Church of Latin America concerned with the population explosion and with exploi-tation *vis-à-vis* the traditional church position on the issues. Soon one realizes that to isolate Mexico is to abandon open-mindedness and to lose sight of information which is vital to the life of Mexico. Mexicans themselves pass judgments on their importance by giving these proceedings, position papers, and statements wide publicity in their communication media.

The Banco de México's article, "Fifty Million People: Do We Face Overpopulation?", deserves credit for admitting the extent to which poverty exists in Mexico. It must be noted also that in general the Bank recognizes that Mexico cannot develop a mass-based industry because of a heavily lopsided distribution of income. How-ever, the Bank's criteria for determining whether or not the country is overpopulated must be regarded as naive. The view that overpopu-lation exists as long as a minimum of welfare has not been achieved leaves too much unexplained as to why such welfare minimums have not been achieved. The fact that larger populations require greater expenditures on "social infrastructure" does not exhaust the questions that can be asked regarding investments. For example, what would have been the impact on the welfare of the Mexican population of having maintained a level of net investments equal to 20 per cent of the GNP and a level of gross investments equal to 30 per cent of the GNP for the last thirty or forty years? What changes in the insti-tutional basis of investments, in existing taxation practices, and in the channels of wealth distribution would have been necessary to reach those levels? Since the Bank is a state institution, it is perhaps unavoidable that its questions will be formulated within the restrictions on vision required by the institutional and legal limits set on its operation. This fact should lead to a recognition of the pitfalls of relying on such interpretations rather than to acceptance of the definition of overpopulation in terms of a minimum of welfare. It is precisely the fostering of such welfare that follows practically from a political institution embodying the public will. Hence its absence is more an index of the degree to which government does not embody such a public will than it is an index of overpopulation.

Blanco's article on demographic planning correctly points out that population planning has to be an integral part of Mexico's national planning. However, with so much of Mexico's economy dependent on outside sources, particularly on the United States' economy, such planning cannot stop with a consideration of internal factors. Blanco's attack on those who hope that technological development will prevent a catastrophe is only partly correct in that he emphasizes the dangers of environmental decay and exhaustion of resources. It is incorrect to the extent that it is blind to the creation of a relative surplus population by the growing productive power of technically sophisticated forms of capital equipment. Also, granting that unlimited population growth must end in ecological catastrophe, the question remains how important a conditioning factor of hunger and poverty has population growth been thus far. It should also be noted that ecological problems do not always have an internal source. For instance, the salinization of *ejidal* lands around Mexicali comes from upstream in the United States sector of the Colorado River.

Blanco assumes precisely what needs proving: that population growth is the main scarcity-creating factor. No doubt also a shift in emphasis from quantity to quality of population cannot but issue in an over-all improvement in living standards. However, his mention of the checks as the inevitable alternative to making the shift fails to take notice of the degree to which such checks are manifestations of the limits imposed on population growth by established property distinctions. Finally, if it is true that successive generations of Mexicans of southern origin are growing relatively shorter in stature than successive generations of northerners, then the role played by exploitation in creating the poverty differences between north and south went unexamined, and a one-sided emphasis was given to differential fertility between poor and rich. Thus, if population growth might be said to create scarcity and poverty, then the role of exploitation in encouraging or eliciting higher fertility among the poor, and hence overpopulation, hunger, poverty, and a decline in stature, was not examined. In fact the whole question of evolution stands in need of re-examination from the point of view of exploitation.

The Center for Economic and Demographic Studies must be given credit for its efforts to improve the quality of data, particularly where the quality of the data is lowest: the turn of the century. For instance, their finding that there has been a slight downward trend in the birth rate since the turn of the century should be kept in mind when claims are made of a stable or slightly increasing trend in the birth rate. The Center also deserves credit for taking note of the fact that almost all sectors of the economy tend to absorb the population under condition of underemployment. Credit is also due the center for taking note of the apparent anomaly of increasing rates of savings in the face of rapidly increasing rates of population growth and for pointing to the sources of this anomaly in the magnitude of income inequality in Mexico, in the expansion and consolidation of modern industry and agriculture, and in monetary and fiscal policies. However, the claim that population growth has helped industrial development by making available a wide population with stable or even declining real wages which were attractive to investors, while also providing a wider market for industrial products, looks very much like a bending of the facts to fit structural limitations on perception and ideological preconceptions.

The fairly rigid ratio of investments to profits seems to indicate that investment patterns may be governed more by the exigencies of life style and usage (which are regarded as the indispensable trappings and prerogatives of power) than by perception of low wages. This constancy also suggests that the more significant pressures on financial resources are not those applied by population growth on the public sector (which is the smaller of the two sectors) but rather those applied by a small and wealthy elite (who are accustomed to luxury and power) upon the investable surplus available. These pressures work to limit the size of the invested surplus, thus also limiting the possibilities for development. This study suggests that the impact of declining real wages on investments is more likely to have been felt through the creation of a larger profit fund from which investments are drawn at a fairly constant rate than through the attraction of new investments by low wages.

A number of structural factors in the Mexican economy contribute to the creation of a narrow, capital-intensive industry which lacks a sufficiently large market to permit cutting costs and lowering prices and which tends to be oriented toward the production of luxury items (González Salazar 1971:545). Among these factors are the following: high rates of profit and high incomes from capital; an extremely lopsided distribution of income; a very high ratio of income to population in the commercial sector and to a lesser degree in the manufacturing sector; accumulation of savings in the hands of a relatively small segment of the population at the top, with large sectors of the population at the bottom going into debt; a relatively small portion of the population endowed with purchasing power (defined as incomes weighed in terms of the cost of living index); a relatively high percentage of imports destined for the Federal District; a disproportionate concentration of capital reserves in the Federal District; and a relatively low percentage of exports originating in the Federal District. The size of the market for new industrial products is thus conditioned more by the institutionalized methods and patterns of distribution than by population growth. Even a luxury-oriented industry cannot grow without consumers endowed with purchasing power, to say nothing of an industry which would produce for a mass market. The mere concentration of the population in, say, the Lomas de Chapultepec does not of itself create a consumer's market. Thus it strains credibility to claim that an expanding population which receives constant or even declining real incomes provides an expanding market for industrial development.

Finally, the danger of defining low productivity of rural migrants and other low income workers in terms of the minimum salaries they receive is too obvious to need stressing and too important to go unmentioned. Certainly, if any of the 700,000 agricultural and industrial workers who lost their jobs between 1950 and 1960 as a result of increases in productivity later found themselves on minimum salaries, their minimum salaries are more likely to have been a reflection of increases in productivity under the conditions of capitalist ownership of agricultural and industrial enterprises than a reflection of low productivity. The fact that so much of the new technical equipment is imported in no way alters the fact that it is work that brought such equipment into existence and work which provided the means to purchase it. Also, the close connection between capitalist forms of appropriation and relatively low levels of appropriation for educational purposes cannot go unnoticed. What has to be emphasized is that the institutional conditioning of existing "facts" cannot be taken for granted without thereby identifying our intellectual interests with the ongoing social system and with the limitations it imposes on human life and development.

What will happen to living standards if the population increases in equal or even greater proportion to the rate of increase in resources, services, and social institutions? The answer given to this question by the Population Reference Bureau in its article on "The World's Most Rapidly Growing Countries" is that living standards will either fail to increase or even decline. This answer is elegantly oversimple and naively restricted in its view of the world. If resources are nonrenewable, even a zero growth population, or for that matter even a declining population will eventually exhaust the resources. If resources are renewable and subject to increase through greater technical development of the productive forces, then the rate at which such technical development can increase production has to be considered in relation to the rate of population growth. Greater productivity in agriculture, in manufacturing, and in the services through modernization of the means of production might be sufficient to outweigh a very rapid rate of population growth. This in fact is what has been happening to Mexico's rates of growth in agricultural production, in the modern, industrial sector, and in certain facets of distribution and services. The growing population does not confront the resources, the available services, and institutions with naked hands, nor in an economic, political, legal, and social vacuum. Institutions of public welfare and of private charity are not the only types of institutions whose existence and operation are at issue when considering the balance of population to resources and services. In a deeper sense, the very institutional basis of such institutions has to be considered. Private property and its dynamics in agriculture, industry, and commerce would have to be kept in mind. The degree of conditioning of parliamentary forms of government by established private interests would have to be examined. The degree to which legal forms tend to legitimize exploitative practices should be studied. The extent to which standing armies are instruments of class oppression rather than protectors of national security requires attention. The intermeshing of intranational and international class structures, and the degree to which such intermeshing makes political changes at a national level contingent on much more than political wisdom, courage, and good fortune require consideration. The degree to which dogmatic blindness interferes with effective control over population growth has to be considered. The degree to which abstract rights and private wealth set restrictions on the concrete living requirements of public education has to be investigated. A consideration of all of these questions and more would have to mediate any consideration of the relation of population growth to resources and services, to say nothing of institutions available. The extent to which demographic thought fails to take into consideration all these factors is a measure of the degree to which the so called "population explosion" generates more heat than light, more panic than sanity of vision, more political demagoguery than political wisdom.

Robert McNamara's speech on dynamic misery must be credited with pointing out that the frequency with which the poor seek illicit abortions is an index of the degree of need for family planning. Credit is also due him for pointing out that population growth can no longer be ignored by governments. However, McNamara's one-sided emphasis on population growth as the chief source of the rapidly widening abyss between rich and poor nations is open to a number of criticisms. What would be the effect on this gap of eliminating systems of wealth appropriation which permit ten per cent of the population to appropriate close to half the annual income and where the bottom half of the population receives between one-seventh and one-fifth of the total income? What would be the effect of eliminating a system of wealth appropriation where the index of productivity nearly doubles and the index of real wages declines by about 10 per cent? Is there not something wrong with a social system where food is exported while people are going hungry or are suffering from malnutrition? Is there not something wrong with a social system where there is enough, or very nearly enough food per capita, and yet large segments of the population are going hungry and undernourished? Is there not something wrong with an international economy where nominal fluctuations in prices and exchange cancel out the concrete value of accumulated labor? Is there not something wrong with a political and legal system where the poor, the undernourished, the hungry, and the destitute are taxed so that the rich might save more? Is there not something wrong with a political economy where there is greater respect for the hoarded wealth and the obese bank accounts of the rich than for the education of the young? Is there not something wrong with a social system which is more concerned with protecting the abstract rights of property than with fostering the concrete living requirement that property be right? Would we not be more deserving of being regarded as human if both the hunger and the fullest possible enjoyment of life were shared together?

Arthur Corwin's article, "Mexico Resists the Pill," deserves credit for focusing attention on the fact that Mexico's urge to grow, as well as the tendency shown by its leaders to oppose population control, has something to do with traumatic historical events which have altered the course of Mexican history. The Spanish conquest, the United States takeover of most of the lands west of the Louisiana Territory, the French attempt to establish a monarchy in Mexico —such events cannot but have created among Mexico's leaders a sense of clear, present, and continuous danger from external sources. The many restrictions on foreign ownership of lands, on the ownership of industrial and other enterprises, and on foreign investments which were enacted after the 1910 Revolution are clear evidence that Mexico's rulers have recognized the existence of such dangers.

Corwin seems aware that rural populations tend to be more prolific than urban populations; however, he neglects to mention why this is the case. In a nation which as late as 1970 was still close to 50 per cent rural, the view that children are an economic asset is bound to exert an influence on population growth (Lewis 1967:116). It is also true that Catholic countries have traditionally tended to place the family quite high in the manifest hierarchy of values, i.e., just beneath God and Country, and the family has been an important factor in the delineation and maintenance of class and caste boundaries, despite the church's clear condemnation of racism. It is clear also that despite those boundaries, Mexico has become a predominantly *mestizo* country and that the 1910 Revolution has contributed more than anything else to opening a path to political power for *mestizos*. Corwin also fails to take notice of the degree to which Mexican agriculture remains stratified despite land reform. He thus tends to reduce the explanation for urbanward migration to the pressures of population growth. The displacement of rural workers under the pressures of mechanization and modernization of the private agricultural sector is not considered. Hence the extravagant ease with which Corwin dismisses the explanation of poverty in terms of exploitation as an effort on the part of Mexico's planners to relieve Mexico's impoverished masses of the burden of responsibility for their conduct and to justify the compulsive need to grow despite widespread poverty.

Contrary to Corwin's claims, the exploitative source of poverty in Mexico is not a figment of the imagination of planners anxious to relieve the masses of the burden of individual responsibility. There is no necessary conflict between acceptance of planned parenthood and contraception, and opposition to the exploitative sacrifice of human beings, individually or in masses, at the altar of the god of capital. Exploitation is a fact of Mexican life—a sad, disfiguring, warped, and tragic fact of life in everyday Mexico. Its existence is as real as the 502.4 per cent and the 1,023.2 per cent rates of exploitation in the milk and wheat processing industries found by Aguilar Monteverde. It is as real as the 172 per cent over-all rate of exploitation found by Carmona. It is as real as the fact that 38.1 per cent of the Mexican population, or the equivalent of 18.5 million people, consumed no milk during the week preceding the 1970 Census. A sad and tragic kind of reality, but nevertheless the existing order of things in Mexico.

The history of Mexico is a history of exploitation. Exploitation lies at the core of Mexico's ancient agrarian problem and her modern urban slums. It is as old as the treasures of Montezuma and the gold and silver mines of Potosí and as new as the oil of Tampico and the mines of Anaconda and Asarco. It is as old as the *macehuales* under the control of warlords or the slaves under the control of Cortés' piously hypocritical horde of Gold Trusting conquerors. It is as new as the hacienda peons, migratory farm workers, and denizens of Mexico's proletarian colonies. It is as old as the Marquezado del Valle (Cortés' feudal estate) and as new as the Lomas de Chapultepec. Its operation is insidious, pervasive, widespread, debilitating, callous, brutal, "legitimate," and thereby ultimately lethal. Its march has cast a long shadow on Mexican history. Consciously or unconsciously it "plays for keeps," and it will not stop in its tracks until either the patient is dead or until it is itself confined within the bounds of prehistory.

Its handiwork can be observed in the chronic deficit in the purchasing power of the minimum salary, in the speculation on housing lots in Netzahualcoyotl, in the collections the poor find themselves having to take up in order to bury their dead, in the fees which must be paid for low and high masses that the souls of the poverty-stricken dead might rest in peace, in the neo-*latifundios* of today's "nylon" farmers, in the studied marginal income-producing size of the *ejido* lot, in the view that population has value only when it can be used by capital, in the houses that cannot be built because their building is not profitable enough, in the "unknown causes of death" which are a cover-up for starvation in the midst of enough, in the 45.9 per cent of the houses (most of them hovels) which are renter-occupied, and in the practice of child labor. Exploitation can also be observed in the fact that the rate of savings grows as the population grows and as the poor go into debt; in the fact that the poor are subject to a death rate twice as high as the rich; in what some intellectuals see as an apparent incompatibility between capital accumulation and the well-being of the people; in the "inevitable sacrifices" and forced savings extracted from the people through inflation; and in the fact that the index of productivity increased from 100 index points in 1940 to 186 index points in 1960, while real wages decreased from 100 to 91 index points during the same interval. Exploitation can be seen also in the 20 per cent interest in 24 days which Lewis found the poor paying to loan sharks in Mexico City, in the high interest paid on public loans, in the 20 to 30 per cent rates of profit on capital invested, in the profitable ransoming of bankrupt "private enterprises" by institutions of public credit, in the contemptuous one-fifth to one-third of the national income received by labor in the form of wages and salaries, in the one-third to one-half share of the national income extracted in the name of property, in the fact that the income of the entrepreneurial sector in agriculture is from thirty to fifty times larger than the income paid to the peasantry and to wage workers, and in the 240 per cent rates of exploitation in commerce. The effect of exploitation may be seen further in the ratio of income to population found in the three sectors of Mexico's economy. This ratio is very high (2.60) and was increasing in the commercial sector; it is extremely low (0.34) and was decreasing in the agricultural sector, it was high (1.58) and had been decreasing in the industrial sector.

Further results of exploitation can be seen in the glamorization of the "Mexican Miracle" while 15 per cent of the population is reported actually hungry and 50 to 80 per cent is reported undernourished in the midst of enough food to go around, in the capacity for misery and suffering which has been developed by the Mexican masses, as well as in the fact that—as Rodríguez González has put it—the Mexican laborers who were cannon fodder during the revolution have become the exploitation fodder of today. Finally, exploitation can be seen in the glamorized understatement of unemployment figures and in the fact that increases in productivity result in a decrease in jobs rather than in wage increases or the elimination of hunger, malnutrition, and over-all destitution.

Exploitation is not a new concept invented by Mexico's planners or, for that matter, by Marx and the Marxists. Exploitation was present in Mexico before Marx was ever born and has been around since after his death. It is an inescapable fact of life to the widest sectors of Mexico's population. It is so ubiquitous and heavy-handed that highly trained powers of observation are hardly required to detect its existence.

No, exploitation in Mexico is not a figment of the imagination of the Marxists or of Marxist planners. The facts require another view of things. The evidence reviewed by this study suggests that it is precisely the unthinking, unresearched, and ill-considered dismissal of the explanatory power of the Marxian theory of poverty with reference to Mexican conditions that must be regarded as the product of a class-conditioned political imagination.

Margaret Larkin's article "As Many as God Sends?" brought attention to the fact that Mexico's urban poor have been found to be much more receptive to methods of contraception than their church affiliations and cultural background led many intellectuals to expect. The fact that receptivity increases as economic necessity and the number of children increases means that the poor in urban areas tend to view children, especially a large number of them, as an economic liability.

It is probably true that a sizable number of Mexican intellectuals tend to systematically exclude the question of population growth when discussing how to improve the living standards of the population. But it is also true that a number of them—Ifigenia Navarreté, Francisco Alvarez, Alonso Aguilar, Gilberto Loyo, Pablo González, etc.—are very much aware of population growth as a factor which absorbs capital resources which could otherwise be invested on development.

The tendency for population growth to lead to a relative shrinkage of means and resources can be deduced mathematically from the following formula (Himes 1965:163–76).

$$\frac{Ii}{GNPi} = ICOR\,(P + y)$$

where:

Ii = the gross investment needed in a year i to obtain a desired rate of growth in the per capita income
$GNPi$ = the gross national product in a year i
$ICOR$ = the incremental capital–output ratio
P = the prevailing rate of population growth
y = the desired rate of increase in incomes per capita

If the equation is resolved for the value of y, we find:

$$y = \frac{Ii/GNPi}{ICOR} - P$$

If the value of P is allowed to increase from 2 to 3 per cent per year, while the value of *Ii/GNPi* and the value of *ICOR* are both allowed to remain constant at 18 per cent and at 3 per cent respectively, we find that for the former of the two values of *P* there is a *y* of 4 per cent while for the latter of the two values of *P* there is a *y* of 3 per cent per year, which is the rate of increase in income per capita. Similar results can be shown to follow if net investment figures are used instead of gross investments.

The same point can be made inductively. Keeping in mind the fact that Mexico had a population of 15.2 million in 1910 and a population of 54 million in 1954, then given current rates of hunger, malnutrition, illiteracy, inadequate medical care, and inadequate housing, the following inferences follow. Despite changes which resulted from the revolution, hunger in Mexico today afflicts a contingent between half and two-thirds as large as the total population of 1910. Malnutrition today afflicts a contingent between 1.7 and 2.8 times larger than the total population of 1910. Illiteracy today incapacitates a contingent 86 per cent the size of the total population of 1910 and 1.14 times larger than the total illiterate population of 1910, despite the impressive advances which have been made in absolute terms since that time. Inadequate medical attention today, from both public and private sources, limits the life chances of a population close to 2.3 times larger than the total population of 1910.

It should also be said that if the preceding deductive and inductive arguments strike anyone as being Malthusian or neo-Malthusian in tone, despite the overwhelming weight of evidence to the contrary, then one can only add that *even* the Malthusian and neo-Malthusian theories deserve to be given a full and impartial hearing with a view to finding out to what extent, if any, they measure up to the test of reason and the facts.

Mexico's experience since the revolution might be summed up in the following terms. Many more people in Mexico today are living under conditions which permit relative freedom from hunger, malnutrition, illiteracy, inadequate medical attention, and inadequate housing than before the revolution. However, it is true also that in Mexico today there is a sum of human misery at least as large and in many ways larger than the total sum of misery in 1910. What is unfortunate is that today, as before the revolution, the relative well-being—indeed, the opulence—of a small segment of the population at the top is obtained at the expense of the misery of those at the bottom.

The weakness of Larkin's formulation of the problem of shrinking means, resources, and services is that the tendency toward stagnation in real terms (despite rapid advances in industrialization, in the construction of roads, dams, and schools, and in the availability of health services) is imputed almost exclusively to the "swamping" power of a "proliferating population" (Larkin 1970:319). There is absolutely no awareness in this article of, for instance, the tendency of real wages to decline while productivity increases. Also there appears to be more than just a desire to retain the flavor of Spanish usage in Larkin's handling of the opposing focus on social justice with, as it were, antiseptic gloves: *"justicia social,"* as if the English form of that concept were anathema.

Tadd Fisher's article, "Mexico:The Problem of People," points out that a pattern of steadily high birth rates within a population which has already achieved "death control" has the over-all impact of slowing down development and multiplying the existing misery. On the other hand, those who say that Mexican mothers are second to none in taking care of their children also have a point (Lajous 1968: 62). So does Hector Anaya when he points out that given the extremely unequal pattern of income distribution in Mexico, the over-all impact of birth control might be no more than saving Mexican parents the pain of watching four or five children starve to death in exchange for letting them watch their one and only child starve to death (Lajous 1968:59). Hence Fisher's insistence on the need for a fourth *R* (for reproduction) in Mexican education, though in itself meritorious, is one-sided. It is particularly so if seen in relation to the fact that from Fisher's point of view, the value of a growing population is measured in terms of whether or not the resources and equipment are available to utilize that population (Fisher 1964:181–82).

Of special interest here is the fact that Fisher sees the inverse relationship between productivity and employment as an enigma (Fisher 1964:196). Why? Does exploitation have anything to do with this inverse relationship? Fisher does not consider this question. He notes that growth in employment does not keep up with efficiency, but then he simply assumes that the rate of increase in total employment depends primarily on the size of the labor reservoir. Why is the relationship between exploitation, productivity, and employment not considered? I suggest that this omission has something to do with the point mentioned above, i.e., that from Fisher's point of view the value of a greater population is assessed in terms of whether or not the resources and equipment to utilize such a population are already in existence. It also has something to do with two other facts of which Fisher takes specific note: that many people thought it unwise for the Mexican government to nationalize industries and that foreign investors are concerned about Mexican government restrictions which they do not always find clearly defined. This observation is tantamount to an indirect plea for clarification of Mexico's investment policy (Fisher 1964:182, 196).

What would be the impact of a different way of looking at (1) the relation of resources and equipment to population, (2) the whole question of nationalization, and (3) the nature of investments and their impact on Mexico's capacity to provide jobs for its people? What would be the impact of such a view if it carried authority? Indeed, what would be the impact of such changes on the very concept of employment? What has been happening to the relative increments in the value of production which arise from increasing productivity? What rate of accumulation of truly public capital would be possible under a system of public ownership over the means of production? What rates of investment would be possible under such a system? What rates of growth of the gross national product and of Mexico's capacity to produce jobs follow from them? These and other questions fall outside the field of vision of Fisher's article. The whole article presents a case of tunnel vision in population research. Its field of vision is restricted to the range of questions permitted by scarcity assumptions.

The problem created by capitalist exploitation of the productive process goes beyond merely removing a certain proportion of the value created by labor; it also has a compound decelerating effect on development through the restrictions it imposes on the capacity to invest and to coordinate planning. It goes beyond creating misery; by prolonging misery it creates a milieu of hopelessness and demoralization which becomes a vicious circle of misery and poverty. Hence the fatalism Lewis observed among the poor in Mexico has a basis in fact. It is not that the poor cultivate these values and attitudes by preference or choice. Rather, fatalism results from observing the recurring consequences which arise from the institutional structure of the existing social system. Of course, once developed, that very outlook on life can become an element in compounding the problems and in forestalling change. Thus the problem created by capitalist exploitation of the productive process goes beyond merely rendering a certain proportion of the labor force superfluous as productivity increases. More importantly, it presents an obstacle to the opening up of new levels and forms of productive employment for the population. The problem in the relation of productivity to employment under capitalist forms of control is not merely that increasing productivity becomes reflected in a decrease in jobs rather than in proportionate increases in living standards for the productive population; it is also that through its tendency to limit investments within a low investment-profit ratio, a capitalist form of control puts a brake on development which, under truly public forms of control, would translate into higher living standards for the population as a whole.

While it might be true, as the demographer Jaffe has argued, that the presence of institutionalized low productivity and underemployment in Mexico is of such magnitude that, given a shift of the population from the less productive sectors toward the most productive sectors, the production levels of 1955 could have been achieved by the 1940 population, it does not automatically follow that Mexico did not need more people. There is another way of looking at the matter. If 20 to 30 per cent of the 34.5 to 50.4 per cent of the national income received in the form of property incomes by one-tenth or less of Mexico's propertied classes had been made available for public investments in more productive forms of agriculture, industry, housing, and education, investment levels might have been raised from 30 per cent to 45 per cent of the national income. These in turn would have brought about increases in income per capita of 7 to 12 per cent per year, assuming a rate of population increase of 3 per cent per year. At this rate, per capita incomes would have increased by 2.8 to 4.5 times in fifteen years, or by 7.6 to 21.0 times in thirty years. Estimating very roughly the 1940 per capita income to have been around 1,000 pesos, the 1955 per capita incomes would have ranged from 2,800 to 4,500 pesos, while that of 1970 would have ranged from 7,600 to 21,000 pesos. The latter figure would amount to something on the order of 1,680 dollars. That is, per capita incomes would now be approximating the standards of western Europe. That population which appeared redundant would now be living under more human standards.

The preceding estimates presuppose an average incremental capital-output ratio of 3. There is a possibility that the actual average *ICOR* during the three decades under consideration might have been lower —perhaps somewhere between 2 and 2.5 (Himes 1965:153–76; La-Cascia 1969:162; Padilla 1969:166–67). Two possibilities would follow from a lower *ICOR*. Keeping investments and population growth at the same levels, the rate of increase of the GNP per capita would have been higher and would have led to more dramatic increases in living standards during the same interval. The same results could have been achieved with somewhat lower increments in investments.

The major thrust of the preceding discussion can be formulated in terms of a simple question: What is more important, the rights of property or that property be right? That is, should property continue to be seen as an abstract right of an owner regardless of function performed, or should property now be instituted as a concrete sociopolitical function which is vital to the life of action? There is no apolitical, value-neutral way to answer this question because political questions can only be settled with political answers. The facts we have brought to bear on the theories we have examined are not neutral with respect to the relative explanatory power of Malthusian and Marxian theories. The weight of the evidence with respect to the problem of poverty in Mexico clearly leans more heavily on the side of exploitation theory. Therefore, the resolution of the problem is to be sought primarily in a resolution of the contradiction between the collective nature of production and the private character of appropriation. If anyone wishes to argue that the expropriation of the expropriators is a form of exploitation, the burden of proof for such social and intellectual magic rests on that person. This writer, for one, is of the view that it is neither safe nor expedient to play magic with concepts. They emerge out of social and intellectual history, and it is in those terms that their explanatory power has to be measured.

The question of the relative importance of the two ways of viewing property has been raised in Mexico before, though it has not been fully faced, and history will continue posing it. In the meantime, Mexico will be like a man endowed with a long life span who keeps running into the same questions, keeps making the same mistakes, and is forever returning to a state of crisis.

16.

Critique of Theories:
Exploitation and Poverty in Mexico

Pedro Martínez's views concerning poverty in Mexico have to be appreciated for what they are: the views of a man whose life embodied all of the contradictions of his social milieu and who never quite gave up the struggle to understand and to change his situation. One has to accept what he reveals about his confusion about knowledge: he did not know enough to convince himself that he knew nothing, so his problem became one of deciding what knowledge he could retain. He tried to retain a belief in the prophets. Yet he himself was at his best in summing up his Mexican life situation as he saw it. Scarcity was scarcity for the poor. For the rich there was plenty. Exactly the same insight can be found at the beginning of Engels' criticism of Malthus, that is, Malthus's tendency to isolate poverty from its context of wealth concentration. For a man who had no more than a single year of formal education, Pedro Martínez' insight must be viewed as remarkable. Less complete is his insight that in the past the hacienda owners had exploited the people, while more recently it was the bankers, the opportunists, and the government who did the exploiting, but it is nevertheless suggestive of insights stated more explicitly by others.

Jesús Sánchez's views tell of a man who sought adjustment to life in Mexico by concentrating more on making a living and on providing for his many families than on trying to understand or to change his life situation. He cannot tell left from right in politics, but he is aware of exploitation, which he conceives as a situation where prices increase faster than wages. He is also aware of the coexistence of progress and poverty.

Alonso Aguilar's essay on *Wealth and Misery in Mexico* is clearly the most pointed analysis of Mexican data from a Marxian perspective. He asks theoretically significant questions which sensitize the observer to the kinds of data necessary to test the Marxian view. His work surveys a wide range of data from investments to rates of profit, from unemployment to rates of exploitation. His work is an essential primer for familiarizing oneself with Marxian methods of analysis under historically specific conditions. His analysis does, however, leave some things to be desired. He might have gone beyond pointing out that as Mexico's rates of population growth increase, it becomes more difficult to promote rapid economic development. An analysis of the interplay of demographic and economic factors would have proved invaluable. Solís's data on the ratio of profits to fixed capital for eighteen consecutive years leave one wondering whether trend data on the organic composition of capital (which Aguilar provides for a single year) might not have been possible given direct access to and intensive search through Mexican data. One wonders also whether it is true, as Aguilar seems to suggest, that Mexico's bourgeoisie ever was accustomed to mobilize and spend surplus value productively. Finally, he could have been a little more forthright in stating what specific changes he had in mind under the last of the five measures which he listed as necessary to reverse ongoing trends. I interpret this last measure to call for an abolition of private ownership of the means of production.

Fernando Carmona's essay "The Mexican Miracle" is a valuable analysis and criticism of both what he calls Mexico's state capitalism of underdevelopment and its ideology. His point concerning the relativity of per capita growth figures is a sobering reminder of just how low living standards still are in Mexico. His comparison of such growth rates with those of other nations effectively dampens euphoric claims about the Mexican miracle. His attack on the misuse of the idea of historical specificity for the purpose of isolating Mexico from the context of common problems it shares with the rest of the underdeveloped world is a perceptive warning concerning one of the potential pitfalls of historically specific research. His point concerning the tendency on the part of United States intellectuals to study Mexico with a focus on political economy from a conservative and reactionary perspective should also be a corrective for those who deplore the apparent reticence of Latin-American demographers to accept family planning and contraception (Kahl and Stycos 1964:423). Neither side appears to have a monopoly on tunnel vision. His comparison of rates of exploitation in Mexico with those elsewhere are consistent with what is known about the extreme degree of inequality in Mexico. His analysis of the structural problems of Mexico's economy is illuminating in a number of ways.

Carmona's point that Mexico's growing dependence on the United States for income from a number of sources is indicative of the failure of the revolution deserves closer consideration. No doubt a Mexico which did not *have* to depend on any of the sources of income from the United States mentioned by Carmona would be economically much more self-reliant and self-sufficient and probably healthier. But, one might ask, is dependence as such the problem? Or, rather, is the problem one of exploitative subordination? I do not think that dependence as such is the problem, since the whole thrust toward industrialization is an implicit recognition of the benefits to be derived from the development of mass production technology which is oriented, at least potentially, toward a mass market. Nor is Carmona necessarily unaware of this last point. But what needs emphasis is the point that exploitative subordination is both an index of the failure of the revolution and a factor in bringing on that failure. So the problem of developing a form of dependence which is equitably beneficial to both parties hinges on the development of a political method which transcends national boundaries. Certainly any effort to terminate the existing form of dependence would have to recognize the "external" factor and be prepared to achieve its ends despite that factor.

Pablo González's studies concerning class inequality, development, and politics in Mexico are certainly among the most interesting and informative efforts to confront the facts of poverty in Mexico from two different perspectives, the one radical, the other liberal-reformist. The radical perspective focuses on class exploitation, while the liberal-reformist focuses attention on progress achieved since the revolution despite population growth. Nonetheless, González's thought retains an element of ambiguity. On the one hand he attributes the existence of a large population which is marginal to development to the failure of the revolution to smash the structure from which marginalism arises; on the other hand he explains the continued growth of the marginal population in terms of a rate of population growth which is more rapid than social development. González's detailed use of statistics to lay bare the structure of the problems at hand reflects to his credit. However, his lack of clarity and consistency in conceptual definition at times confuses analysis and creates misconceptions about trends in Mexico.

González's comparison of relative income shares received by labor in a number of countries, including Mexico, provides additional confirmation (along with Carmona's comparison of rates of exploitation) of the extremes of inequality prevailing in Mexico. His point that marginalism is primarily a rural phenomenon is accurate, despite the fact that Mexico is becoming a primarily urban nation. His high estimates of the extent of marginalism and poverty in Mexico should leave no doubt concerning the extent to which marginalism is also an urban phenomenon.

González argues effectively that Mexico is an exploitation colony where poverty is widespread. He argues just as effectively that considerable improvements in education, housing, and other areas have taken place since the revolution. His linkage of the short-term view with a revolutionary perspective and of the long-term view with a perspective which merely recognizes danger is also to his credit.

González is at his best when he attempts to explain why Mexico's exploited population is not ripe for revolution. All of the factors he mentions as contributing to the absence of class consciousness (from migration to nationalization, from government-controlled unions to propaganda) are credible stumbling blocks to the development of class consciousness. No doubt a tendency to seek individual salvation through migration would work to prevent such development. So would the belief that the government is trying to improve things. The same is true of union activity cued from above and of the tendency to confuse thought by shifting the focus of attention from the class struggle to the national struggle. The tendency to confuse class consciousness with "revolutionary ideals" would have the same effect. So would lower-class fatalism and upper-class paternalism.

A problem arises with González's criticism of the Marxists when he takes up the question why they fail to account for the absence of class consciousness. This failure, in González's view, arises from a failure to recognize the priority of the national struggle over the class struggle and to consider the structural differences between the marginal sector and the participating sector of the exploited population. It is not clear whether he expects the Marxists to recognize the priority of the national struggle over the class struggle as a political priority arising out of a clear recognition of the greater weight of international over national sources of exploitation, or whether he expects the Marxists to accept the official version of where the greater weight of exploitation is to be found. Since he recognizes the substitution of the national struggle for the class struggle as a propaganda maneuver directed from above, it would appear unrealistic to expect the Marxists to accept the view without prior examination. Perhaps he means that the greatest source of forcible opposition to fundamental structural changes should be expected to come from across the border. However, he does not make it clear why such an order of priorities should be accepted by the Marxists particularly since class has both national and international dimensions.

González also attacks the Marxists for blindly explaining the absence of class consciousness among the exploited population in terms of their alienation and for not considering the structural differences between the participating sector and the marginal sector. But if alienation in Marxian terms means separation of the worker from the means of production in the sense that the worker's labor under those conditions enriches and strengthens a power which exploits, dominates, and oppresses him, it is hard to see how the participating sector of the exploited poor are not also to some degree alienated. Marx himself drew a distinction between the industrial reserve army (of the unemployed and of the underemployed) and the active labor force, but he placed both under the category of exploited classes.

Official identification of concepts which are not in fact identical is made possible by alienation of the poor from the means of administration, and thus it is a form of deliberately fostered false consciousness. It would appear, then, that González is straining the distinction between the marginal sector and the participating sector of the exploited population. Accepting his view would appear to remove the area of consciousness manipulation from the subject matter of the struggle and convert it into something akin to a *deus ex machina*.

This writer does not find sufficient reason for rejecting alienation as a reason for the absence of class consciousness. Instead, the specific Mexican situation seems to confirm the need to broaden the concept of alienation to include other institutions. In this case one would have to include alienation of the exploited population from the means of administration.

González's use of the term "marginal" leads to two different and widely divergent estimates of the relative size of the marginal population, the one 29 per cent of the total population and the other 60 per cent. Even more confusing and misleading is a statement to the effect that real wages per capita almost tripled between 1929 and 1962 (González Casanova 1964:149). González himself reports elsewhere that the GNP per capita doubled between 1940 and 1965 (González Casanova 1970:109–10). GNP per capita and real wages per capita are not by any stretch of the imagination the same thing. Whether or not GNP per capita will actually become real wages per capita depends upon the pattern of income distribution, and no one is more aware than González himself of the extremes of deprivation to which the laboring classes are subjected in Mexico. Since the years from 1929 to 1940 were an interval of depression and reform, it seems completely out of line to claim a three-fold increase in real wages during the years 1929–62, particularly in view of the fact that the GNP per capita is known to have declined at a rate of one-tenth of one per cent per year during the interval 1925–40 (Reynolds 1970: 104). Another inconsistency is to be found in two differing and divergent claims as to what happened to the GNP during an interval of two decades. One statement is that it quadrupled between 1940 and 1965 (González Casanova 1970:109–10). Another is that it trebled between 1939 and approximately 1964 (González Casanova 1964:149). His claims concerning the trend in real wages might turn out to be either an error in translation or a slip, pure and simple. Whatever the case, it was cited later in an article published by the Population Reference Bureau which must have received wide and influential dissemination (Fisher 1964:181). This is regrettable because it creates a misconception about what is known to be the trend in real wages in Mexico (Singer 1969:156; Editorial 1963:349; Padilla 1966:158). Padilla's data on real income per capita cover the interval 1929–62, and the trend indicates a decline of close to twelve index points, from approximately 111 in 1929 to 99 in 1962. These data are consistent with what is reported by all other sources dealing with real wages. The confusion of GNP per capita with real wages is a serious one which can only compound the difficulty of understanding what is happening.

Finally, González's point that capitalism in Mexico does not conform to the classical capitalist model of development rests on the assumption that Mexico's programs of wealth redistribution tend toward integration of all inhabitants toward full citizenship. This assumption can be questioned on two grounds: the extent to which wealth redistribution has actually led to full citizenship and the extent to which the participating sector continues to grow faster than the marginal sector.

On the first count one might note that a program of land redistribution which has left half of the farming units at an infrasubsistence productive capacity, and half of the rural population landless, can hardly be credited with a tendency to integrate all inhabitants toward full citizenship. Also, in view of the fact that the program of nationalization has left over 90 per cent of the 400 largest corporations in private hands, with 42 per cent of these under foreign control or under strong foreign influence, what basis is there for claiming that the program of wealth redistribution is tending toward the integration of all inhabitants toward full citizenship?

González's point that the participating sector is growing faster than either the total population or the marginal population is the stronger of his two arguments. However, José Rangel's data point toward a reversal of this trend associated with the development of industry in recent years, and these data find support in Carlos Tello's work.

José Rangel's study of the polarization of Mexico's class structure states clearly and concretely what he regards as the specific Mexican conditions which keep capitalist development in Mexico from following classical lines: the modification of the legal system of land tenure and the subsequent government efforts to promote industrialization. What is less clear is how and at what point, in his view, the government efforts to promote industrialization cease being a force directing development away from classical capitalist lines and start being a force directing development toward those lines. His meaning seems to be that government promotion of industrial development constitues in itself a departure from classical, *laissez-faire* lines and that growing industrial concentration is relegating increasing numbers of self-employed (independent) entrepeneurs to the ranks of the proletariat. Hence his argument could be restated to say that the specific conditions which have tended to direct Mexican development away from classical capitalist lines are the program of land reform and the emergence of state capitalism, with the very success of the latter tending to revert development back in the direction of growing proletarianization. With as much justification one could say that the tendency for the rate of savings to increase while the rate of population growth increases is specific to the extent of wealth concentration and to the extreme inequality of income distribution in Mexico. So also it could be said that Mexico's relatively high rates of economic growth are specific to the relatively high levels of public investment for the specific purpose of promoting economic development.

What is being suggested is that historically specific research should be directed precisely at identifying what specific factors exist in a nation to account for variations from the path of development predicted by theory. Repeated references to "specific to Mexico," or "to England," or "to Western Europe" can only mystify and tend to submerge thought into what has been called "the vertigo of relativity" (Berger and Luckman 1967:5). The over-all impact is bound to be a tendency to isolate the specific case under consideration from the context of problems common to the underdeveloped world, on the one hand, and to the industrially developed capitalist countries, on the other. Such an impact would tend to arise from the total absence of precise and concrete research.

17.

Critique of Theories:
*The English Phase of
the Modern Debate*

The facts of Mexican society lend a great deal of support to Godwin's analysis of the sources of poverty and misery. The landed monopolies and their expansion at the expense of the small holdings of the peasantry were the chief source of the destitution and misery of the overwhelming portion of Mexico's population prior to the 1910 Revolution. Despite a rather far-reaching program of land reform, they remain a large source of the problem to this day. Since the land reform program did not aim at equality in land redistribution but sought instead to create a dual system of land tenure, Mexican history since the revolution does not provide a test case for the consequences of a system which meets Godwin's criteria of justice. Other types of ownership concentration were also poverty producing factors, i.e., ownership concentration in extractive industries, in manufacturing, and in commerce. They remain so to this day, despite the development of a state sector.

The legal system in Mexico does favor the wealthy. Article 27 of the Constitution of 1917 did not abolish the institutionalized extremes between wealth and poverty; it merely asserted the right of the state to have an influence on those differences. Government does flout reason. The tendency in official circles to confuse "the class struggle" with "the national struggle" and questions of "class consciousness" with "national unity" are cases in point. Despite the considerably weakened position of the church in Mexico, charity continues to be used as a way to avoid coming to terms with the requirements of justice. Mexico's oligarchy of wealth does consist of about a thousand families by a conservative estimate (Aguilar

1974:65–80). The "revolution" of 1910 destroyed all but the most pliable of the great Porfirista fortunes. Most of the great fortunes of today have been acquired since 1939, and frequent family ties have been observed among them. At the very most, the relative size of the population which can be regarded as the "owners" of Mexico cannot exceed one per cent of the population. In sum, Godwin's point that the established institutions have brought into existence a system of the narrowest selfishness and inequality does apply to Mexico.

Practically the whole range of occupations which Godwin regarded as engaged in the production of luxuries and superfluities can be found in Mexico. There is an industry distorted into the production of luxuries by the established pattern of wealth and income distribution and by the limitations such a pattern imposes on the development of a mass market. There is a commerce which misrepresents the value of what it sells and which hoards a large portion of the wealth and income of the country. There are porters, ushers, government officials, tax collectors, lobbyists, clerks, armies, fleets, police forces, and, one might add, air forces. There are also investors and beggars, stock markets and thieves' markets, banks and gambling casinos, wholesale houses and ambulatory street vendors, speculators in futures and sellers of lottery tickets, street musicians and movie stars.

It is true also that opulent luxury and leisure coexist with destitution and health-impairing labor in Mexico. There are infrasubsistence *minifundios* and *ejidos* where production is labor intensive, and there are haciendas larger than any one farmer or farm family can possibly work. Income from the small units must be supplemented with other jobs, such as working for the larger haciendas. There are people whose incomes from capital make possible a leisurely existence, and there are people who must supplement full-time jobs with sideline activities to make ends meet, provided they are lucky enough to be fully employed in the first place.

However, at the turn of the present century, when the extent of concentration of land ownership was highest in Mexico, its impact on the infant mortality rate was not as high as Godwin believed it to have been in the Europe of his time. The estimate Godwin took from Ogilvie indicated that four out of five live births died in infancy.

Mexican data for the latter phase of the Díaz administration indicate that one out of three live births died in infancy.

Godwin estimated that Europe could support a population five times larger than it had in his day. Mexico could probably support a population five times its present size. Such a population would have a density close to halfway between the population densities of Spain and India. The only question can be: to what end and at what cost in ecological and in human terms? Is there really no better way to pursue human happiness than by multiplying the sum of human beings and (given a continuation of existing conditions) the sum of human misery? There seems little prospect of making human problems any easier to solve by merely magnifying their size. If they are resolved for a smaller population then perhaps they might be resolvable for a larger one. But there is little point in waiting until the problem gets larger to attempt to effect a solution.

Accumulation as such is not the problem as regards economic development. Nor can it be said that the development of cooperation or of efficiency are the problem. The problem has more to do with the fact that under the established property system, increases in efficiency are more likely to be reflected in a relative decrease in jobs available per unit of capital invested than in rising living standards for the working population. The problem also has something to do with the kind of habitat that is being developed. How livable is an urban metropolis of 14 million people? How livable would it be if it were to reach the 42 million mark or even the 70 million mark? What would be the impact on the life support system of two, four, or six times the industrial resources per capita in terms of industrial wastes? What will be produced? To what end? Can a population with a density of 300 per square mile realistically hope for a standard of living three, five, or ten times its present level? What resources would it draw upon and how renewable are those resources?

What type of political and legal system, if any, would be capable of coping with such challenges? Godwin's requirement that political organization be confined to the parish level makes no sense in an economic system which has world-wide dimensions and which requires solutions which go beyond national boundaries. The call for a social system where the free development of all is a prerequisite for the free development of each has to take cognizance of the world-wide system of production which is part of everyday life. Such a principle can also be applied to the relations which bind nations. The call for an end to the exploitation of people by people must be extended to include an end to the exploitation of nations by nations. The establishment of such a principle would contribute more than anything else to terminating the organized waste made necessary by the maintenance of standing armies.

Does religion really have to misrepresent questions of justice as questions of charity? Is another world of truth really necessary in order to avoid coming to terms with the truths of this world? Does morality really have to be surrounded with magic, dogma, and mystery? Does sexuality really have to be shrouded in ignorance, secrecy, misinformation, hypocrisy, and mystery?

Lewis's study of five Mexican families does present a kaleidoscope of thwarting, bickering, and unhappiness. However, three of the five unions studied were common-law marriages. Four of the five men had extramarital affairs and three of them were supporting mistresses. The one with no extramarital affairs had been through a previous union. Three of the five wives had children by other men. All of the men had children by other women, during previous unions or on the side. The thwarting, bickering, and unhappiness takes its most pathetic form in the Castro family, where the husband uses money as a means of control and the wife uses sex for the same purpose. The one withholds money, the other withholds sex, and life becomes an earthly hell for both, despite considerable wealth. Lewis speaks of common-law unions as lower class traits (Lewis 1959:28).

Mexico's 170 per cent rate of exploitation means, in rough terms, that three hours of an eight-hour working day are necessary labor (sufficient for subsistence), and five hours are surplus labor. Thus if exploitation were abolished and subsistence were all that were sought for everyone, three hours of daily labor would be sufficient to keep everyone alive. This figure exceeds by one hour Godwin's high estimate and falls short of Malthus's low estimate by one hour. However, it is the development and enjoyment of humanity's full creative potential that is at issue, not just the achievement of bare subsistence for all.

Mexican data provide absolutely no support for the view that the earth has a boundless capacity to support a growing population. Neither do the facts of Mexican society lend much credence to Malthus's views on the sources of poverty. The balance between the human capacity to procreate and the human capacity to provide the necessaries for subsistence cannot be regarded strictly, or even primarily, as a balance between two isolated and exclusive natural laws without thereby assuming precisely what has yet to be proved: that poverty has its source in the nature of humankind. Nor can an argument against the establishment of a different set of social institutions be validly based on observed or imagined trends whose apparent plausibility and credibility might stem precisely from the dynamics of a *status quo ante* whose soundness, desirability, and permanency are precisely at issue. Least of all is it tenable to utilize the presumed unequal operation of the ratios as an *a priori* formula which exempts us from the need to do historically specific research with a view to determining to what degree, if any, existing institutions and policies are a factor in conditioning existing trends. Ignorance about the failure of previous institutions and policies is no justification for advocating their maintenance.

There can be no question that something extraordinary has happened to the growth of Mexico's population in the half century following the revolution. By 1970 it had expanded to three and one-half times its 1920 size, thus nearly quadrupling in fifty years. However, the food supply did not fall short by a fourth the amount needed by the end of those fifty years. No food shortage equivalent to the needs of the 1920 population (14.3 million people) was observed between 1945 and 1970. Rather the evidence suggests that the rate of growth in food production was higher on the average during the latter half than during the former half of the interval. In fact, the data indicate that on the average, food production growth rates advanced better than twice faster than the average rates of population growth during the years 1940–70. These trends in food production are not explainable in terms of the availability of good lands, since most of the new lands opened for cultivation were desert lands.

There is no data on how many people died from famine, epidemics, and plagues during the latter half of the fifty-year interval under consideration. But the index which is most sensitive to conditions of hunger and poverty (the infant mortality rate) indicates that only slightly more than one in ten live births died during the first year in 1944–46 and that by 1964–66 this figure had been reduced to one infant death in approximately sixteen live births (Centro 1970:25). Deaths from war can be regarded as having been few.

The point is that behind both the very impressive rates of growth in food production and the very rapid rates of population growth there looms a factor which Malthus did not regard as particularly important in deciding which of the two would have the greatest relative weight. The factor in question is science and technology. No doubt the reforms of the revolution, particularly the land reform, have contributed to providing a minimum of security for a sizable portion of the population. They contributed also to improving diets and to improving life chances. But among the scientific and technological factors which have had an impact on food production are mechanization (particularly in the private sector), irrigation, the "green revolution" (hybridization), and fertilizers. Among the scientific and technological factors which have had an impact on population growth are improvements in education, sanitation, and hygiene; and vaccines, vitamins, antibiotics, and other wonder drugs.

The key factor which accounts for these changes is not natural law but rather the human capacity to understand and to transform both the environment and human life itself. Food production increased rapidly despite an agriculture which is still primarily privately controlled and highly stratified, and despite an *ejidal* and communal sector which tends to be small in scale and labor-intensive. Thus one can ask how much more productivity might have increased if a system of "haciendas without *hacendados*" had been instituted instead of a dual system of land tenure. One can also ask how much more productivity might have increased if large-scale production had been retained and if the extreme fractioning of the *ejidal* and communal sectors had been avoided.

The population increased as rapidly as it did even though neither marriage, nor towns, nor unhealthy occupations, nor luxury, nor overwork were abolished. This fact should leave no doubt concerning the possibly disruptive consequences which the uncontrolled and unplanned growth of human population potentially has in store for the life support system.

"Free unions" are not as widespread as one might be led to believe from a study of marriage patterns among the poor. Only about 7.6 per cent of a sample of women interviewed in Mexico City in the late sixties lived in free unions (Dinámica 1970:74–75). Earlier data indicate that approximately one-seventh of the potentially marriageable population lived in free union in Mexico in 1940 (Sexto Censo de Población 1943:1–4). However, the preceding data say nothing about the frequency of other types of liaisons of a more transitory nature which are not classifiable as living together in free unions. In recent years the federal government has sponsored mass marriage ceremonies to expedite the formalization of common-law unions among the poor.

Where then is the pressure of population growth applied? On the means of subsistence? If by "applying pressure" we mean that population has been growing faster than the means of subsistence, then the answer must be no. But if "applying pressure" is taken to mean that population growth makes for growing requirements of diverse forms, then it would be much more accurate to say that pressure is being applied on scientific and technological research to develop more efficient and effective methods of food production and family planning. Pressure is also being applied to rethink old and anthropocentric beliefs and attitudes concerning human reproduction in the light of the threat posed to human survival by humanity's own success in breaking through the natural limitations on population growth. Further, it would be more accurate to say that pressure is being applied on life forms used as food sources to increase their adaptability to different climates, their reproductive capacity, their growth potential, and their resistance to disease. Pressure is being applied to discover new sources of food, new sources of fuel, and agricultural techniques more adaptable to small-scale agriculture. Finally, it would be more accurate to say that pressure is being applied to develop an economic, political, and legal system where the introduction of a more efficient technology does not have to mean a relative decrease in jobs with stable and even decreasing real wages; that is, to develop a social system which makes possible the development and fulfillment of the full creative potential of the population. Ultimately, then, pressure is being applied on the means of finance to convert the investment of surplus value into an instrument for the development and satisfaction of truly public ends.

Mexico's poverty cannot be resolved through reliance on the general benevolence until benevolence becomes general. Benevolence will not become general until the "rights of property" are replaced by the institutionalization of rights consistent with the collective nature of labor and the role of labor in the self-creation of human-kind.

Neither can Mexico's problem be resolved by a reduction in the supply of laborers because a solution is precluded in the very manner of defining the problem. It is precisely the view that the value of labor is to be determined in terms of its relative usefulness to ab-stract capital and to the abstract rights of property that is at issue. Problems of human poverty, misery, and degradation are not to be resolved by asserting the right to further impoverish, make miserable, and degrade human beings.

There is no need to prove that interference with the laws of nature is possible because the opulence and dolce vita of a few hundred families is built on interference and justified through interference. Pedro Martínez saw this: "Scarcity is scarcity for the poor, for the rich there is plenty." Their opulence is built on exploitation and it is justified through scarcity.

Is contraception unnatural to human beings? The answer to this question depends on what is meant by "human" and on whether or not we assume that the "natural" is necessarily the good. Human-kind cannot be defined in abstraction from the biotic and socio-cultural landscape the ages have brought into existence. The human person cannot be separated from the ecology of the planet or from the world of cultural objects through which human life is ordered. We live in a finite planet with limited resources. The human capacity for reproduction is great, and the sexual drive in human beings might bear the imprint of, *or* might be positively correlated to, the selective pressures of exploitation which institutionalized class antagonisms force on them. People are known to have had the largest number of children when the chances of each child surviving to maturity were lowest. Both Malthus and Marx agree that poverty and unemployment are poor conditions under which to expect small families.

The idea that human beings must do what is natural in order to be moral has its source in a beautiful ancient idea: that reason has its source in universal law and that a life according to reason is the essence of morality. But exploitation is not natural to human beings. It is not reasonable for human beings to go idle when there is plenty of work to be done. It is not reasonable for human beings to go hungry in the midst of plenty, or in the midst of enough. The Judeo-Christian tradition, and the Catholic church in particular, have seen in sexuality an evil taint, and the latter has attempted to control it through confession and communion. But its efforts have yielded paltry results when measured against the magnitude of the task ahead. It will do humanity little good to wreck the life-supporting capacities of this planet, even if the wrecking is done in a state of grace. It has been said with a certain amount of truth that people who practice the rhythm method are called "parents."

Obviously something is wrong. The opposition to contraceptive methods in the name of natural law is a form of nature worship which has little connection with the facts. Nature itself does not follow the dictum that the function of sex is reproduction. By human standards of production, nature is wasteful. Typically, it produces many millions more seeds than are necessary to insure reproduction. In every male ejaculation there are millions of sperm whose natural end is not reproduction, and for every union that leads to the birth of a child there are many who end in no more than acceptance, affection, warmth, play, and emotional renewal. Where does exploitation begin in human sexuality? In the millions of sperm which do not fertilize the egg? In the scores, hundreds, and thousands of unions which do not lead to the birth of a child?

The effort to develop a safe contraceptive pill is an effort to institutionalize intelligence in reproduction. Contraception has brought humanity closer to the possibility of planned parenthood. It takes more than reasonableness to eat when one is hungry as long as hunger exists in the midst of plenty, or at least enough. It takes more than reasonableness to work when one wants a job as long as there is work to be done and no jobs to be had. Just so it takes more than reasonableness for people to reproduce when they want children as long as they live under conditions where they can find no human fulfillment in any but the most elementary biological functions. Reasonable human beings will allow the sexual act to issue in children when both the ability and the possibility exist to properly care for them. Contraception has brought humanity closer to the possibility of avoiding waste of human life. In this sense its use is a more distinctively human activity than the failure to use it. Sexuality need no longer mean reproduction unless reasonable beings intend it that way.

Malthus's dictum that women who bear out of wedlock should be subject to social ostracism on the grounds that they are the only identifiable parents is a graceless and contemptible bit of male chauvinism. It has received an eloquent answer from the new technology of contraception and from the Women's Liberation Movement.

Malthus's effort to explain poverty in terms of scarcity of land would have to answer the question: "At what point does land become scarce?" When the density of population reaches 5.7 inhabitants per square mile, as in Canada? When it reaches 69.1 inhabitants per square mile, as in Mexico? When it reaches 176.8 inhabitants per square mile, as in Spain? Or when it reaches 438.1 inhabitants per square mile, as in the case of India? It is plain that there are different levels of population density and that the productive capacity of the land varies with different levels and forms of technology, as well as with different geographical endowments. No doubt there is a point beyond which increasing population density would become self-defeating. But there is a range of livability at different density levels which need not be incompatible with plenty, or with environmental health.

Malthus's claim that poverty has its source in the barrenness of the earth's surface can be answered by saying that there are wealthy *hacendados* and relatively poor *ejidatarios* in equally desertic lands in Mexico's Northwest Region, lands which are rendered productive through irrigation. Quite apart from the possibility that irragated desert lands might eventually be lost through salinization, there is an element of relativity in poverty which cannot be explained away by appealing to the barrenness of the earth's surface.

Finally, Malthus's claim that poverty has its source in diminishing returns on capital investments has been answered as follows. Diminished returns on increasing units of capital investment do not explain how it happens that the increases which do occur are distributed unequally.

Godwin's criticism of Malthusian theory, that it is a judicious combination of squandering by the rich and starving by the poor, is fundamentally correct. But the Malthusian view that population cannot increase indefinitely over a limited territory is a sound one, and it has implications for the permanency of human life on this planet which the Industrial Revolution has served to emphasize. Engels agreed that a possibility existed, which appeared remote in his time, that earth's population would reach a saturation point. Where both Marx and Engels took sharp issue with Malthus was in the view that poverty had its source in overpopulation, and their criticism was aimed at exposing the ideological elements in Malthus's thought.

The view that certain types of institutions and certain types of social systems are unsuited to human nature and that they stand in the way of normal development is one of the most fruitful and promising ideas to emerge in modern thought. This insight is usually credited to modern humanism, and particularly to the French *philosophes*. However, this idea has its roots in ancient Greek philosophy (particularly Plato), where the modern Renaissance humanists went for inspiration. Marx carried this idea to a very high point.

There can be little question that private property applies a brake on Mexico's development through the restrictions it imposes on the capacity to invest surplus value. There can be little question also that Mexico's system of state capitalism is only a partially successful effort to compensate for the failures of private finance. It is plain too that Mexico's poor pay a heavy price in hunger, malnutrition, illiteracy, ignorance, ill health, neglect, and destitution. Their children pay a heavy price in inattention and listlessness in school, in low productivity as adults, and in premature old age and death. Moreover, there can be little question that increasing productivity under capitalism has led to a relative decrease in jobs rather than to improvements in living standards.

Modern humans are not satisfied with a mode of life which provides a bare subsistence through a life of endless and unremitting toil. Mexicans want to make full use of the promise of modern science and technology. They would like to raise their living standards to a level which places them at least on a par with Western Europe. Since Mexico's per capita GNP is slightly more than one-fourth the same figure for Western Europe, Mexico must develop its economy just to create the possibility of such a living standard. That is, it must promote growth.

No doubt growth in some form is necessary to lift the nation's per capita product and to raise the standard of living. But the human world of the twentieth century is not the same as the human world of the nineteenth century. The lives of the oceans, lakes, and rivers are endangered by industrial wastes and chemicals which are often non-biodegradable and sometimes poisonous: DDT, mercury, asbestos, PCB, nitrogen, detergents, garbage, plastics, sludge, strontium 90, and so on. Plant and animal forms are threatened with extinction as never before. The air we breathe is contaminated with automobile and factory emissions which combine with heat, light, and other chemicals in ways which are easier to discover than to control and prevent. The very stability of the planet's climate is threatened by hundreds of thousands of tons of waste particles released by modern industry and technology. Chemical aerosols threaten the ozone layer of the atmosphere and increase the hazards of skin diseases and genetic havoc. The living soil is contaminated with chemicals which find their way up the food chain and contaminate the milk in mothers' breasts. The destructive potential of a science and technology which works for short-term, profit-oriented goals is far greater than Marx and Engels could have envisioned.

Capitalism in the twentieth century has become all the more dangerous to human life, to civilization, and to the biosphere precisely because it hides behind the rhetoric and political economy of growth. Growth has become the panacea which wishes away the apparent enigma, the seeming riddle of chronic unemployment which occurs side by side with growing productivity and increasing wealth. What is dangerous is that under these conditions growth becomes an end in itself, quite oblivious of its ultimate impact on the life support system, on the quality of life, and on the human beings which grow up within this tangle of decay and unknown effects. Thus there is a need for a sociology and a political economy which is mindful, informed, and ever watchful of the potential hazards of a science and technology which is insensitive to questions of meaning, value, and history, and which is gradually laying the basis for its own undoing.

A political economy which has abolished institutionalized class antagonisms cannot continue to adhere to the fetish of growth for growth's sake. It might well be that during the period of its struggle with capitalism, it will have no alternative but to seek growth. But in the long run it must come to terms with the problem of developing an agriculture and an industry which are compatible with the life-support system. The conscious pursuit of this end will become a factor in the outcome of the struggle, since the very earth and life itself will be on its side.

There is no universal and inevitable law of overpopulation in operation in Mexico. The industrially developed nations of the world have led the way in the development of both mortality and fertility control through science and technology. Human control of both mortality and fertility means that population growth is subject to human influence and policy. The sharp decline in mortality is the key to population growth in Mexico and in the modern world as a whole. The relative decline in deaths from infectious and parasitic diseases and the relative increase in deaths from diseases of a degenerative type (cancer and cardiovascular diseases) is a trend which is typical of the modern and the modernizing portions of the world. The technology of mortality control was developed earlier and has transferred more rapidly to Mexico. The technology of fertility control was developed later and seems to be transferring less readily, although there are indications that the resistance to their adoption has been exaggerated. Higher levels of education and higher living standards appear to be far more effective correlates of lower fertility than church attendance. Thus the problem of regulating population growth is primarily an economic and political problem: the problem of how to raise living standards, the problem of defining what to educate the future generations for, and the problem of developing an educational system which achieves those goals. Ultimately population growth depends on the decisions of particular couples. But couples cannot be expected to decide wisely if they lack the necessary information, if they lack the means to implement their decisions, and if they live under conditions where wise personal decisions are precluded by the lack of institutionalized wisdom in public life. Arguments about an iron law of population growth can only play into the hands of blind interests which all too willingly accept the inevitability of their institutionalized private motives, and which would rather allow social life to drift in the name of natural law.

Human beings *are* starving in Mexico, in the midst of enough if not in the midst of plenty. The possibilities for plenty do exist. Their realization depends on the abolition of class antagonisms on a national and international level and on the establishment of fair and just institutions.

Despite official figures which tend to hide the reality of both unemployment and underemployment in Mexico, both of these are present, though there is no lack of work to be done. There is land which stands in need of improvement; there are factories which are working at less than capacity; there is a need for more schools, health centers, and housing units. There are slums which need to be torn down; there is a need to install drainage and fresh water pipes. There are sources of electric power that need developing, a need to educate more teachers, a natural habitat which needs cleaning up. What is lacking is the institutionalized public will to carry out these public tasks.

The fundamental reason for the lack of such a public will is the fact that in agriculture, in industry, and in commerce, capital and its accumulation, rather than the well-being of the producers of wealth and the development and protection of the habitat, are the dominant motives and ends of production. The system of production involves the whole nation and beyond. Control over the wealth lies with a few hundred families at home and abroad.

Thus there is a contradiction between the productive and distributive facets of Mexican society. Private ownership of the means of production is the basis for the exploitation of collective labor. The development of the productive powers of labor in all facets of economic activity, under the conditions of capitalist exploitation, does give rise to an industrial reserve army. Part of this army makes an annual migration in search of work in the United States. However, underemployment in Mexico is a more widespread problem than unemployment.

Mexico's population is increasing faster than the capacity of the existing system of private and state capitalism to employ it. Population growth does put pressure on the means of employment, but ultimately the pressure is applied to the system which puts a break on development: the system of private finance, private profit, and public irresponsibility.

Marx and Engels wrote at a time when the agricultural revolution had just begun. Marx's account of the creation of a relative surplus population is formulated in the language of development within the manufacturing process. Data from Mexico indicate that the agricultural sector yielded the greatest contingent of displaced workers. To the extent that agriculture is being transformed by modern methods of production, greater attention needs to be given to transformations within the agricultural sector. Furthermore, urbanization under capitalism appears to be a process of creating rural unemployment faster than the urban sectors are able to provide employment. Marxian theory must be brought to bear on, and grow and be enriched by, the challenge of developing an urban theory capable of explaining the urbanization process and free from the rhetoric of competition of classical economics. We must move from a vulgar to a profound view of the urbanization process. These pages are being written at a time when there is a real question whether or not, given the shortage of currently used fossil fuels, it will be possible to continue transferring the fuel-costly technology of the industrially developed world to the underdeveloped nations. If such a transfer is not possible, then the concern with displacement in agriculture might be short-lived, or it might turn out to be less important than the Mexican experience suggests. In any case the proletarian colonies, the *barriadas*, *favelas*, and *callampas*, can no longer be automatically assumed to be a product of overrapid population growth in rural areas. Moreover, the whole problem of lost opportunities for employment imposed by capitalist patterns of investment will have to be considered in weighing the relative explanatory power of exploitation versus scarcity theory. The view that "the rate of increase in total employment depends primarily on the size of the labor reservoir" (Fisher 1964:196) is unacceptable. The quantity of potential opportunities for employment depends on the uses to which surplus value is applied and on the degree to which political organization reflects the public purpose to provide maximum opportunity for development of human resources. That is, the problem of surplus population is both an economic and a political question; it is a question of both economic and political organization. Further studies of currents of international migration should be sensitive to the relationship between the egress of capital and of lost opportunities for internal employment, on the one hand, and the egress of a migratory labor force on the other.

No doubt the reproduction of the next generation of workers is part and parcel of the capitalist process, in that subsistence wages pay not only to replace the worker's energies for another working day but also to reproduce the next generation of workers. However, the fact that surplus labor is appropriated by the capitalist must not blind us to the fact that the capitalist system requires a little help from the population in order for the population to reproduce beyond what is necessary to replace it.

While it is quite true that given the existing pattern of income distribution, the poorest sectors of Mexico's population might be just as hard pressed to subsist with one as with three children, it is also true that the less hard pressed of the poor (and the more modestly situated) would benefit from a shift from quantity to quality of life. They would also benefit from an educational effort directed at helping them attain a clearer grasp of the sources of their poverty, misery, and oppression. While the effort to attain such an awareness under the conditions which make it imperative is almost invariably a very difficult uphill struggle, to the extent that a focus on quality of life would facilitate the task, such a shift in focus would revert to their benefit. If a large enough leadership is produced which does contribute substantially to bringing about the type of fundamental changes needed, the shift from quantity to quality will have made the vital difference. A generation of great, informed, creative, dedicated, revolutionary, and innovative spirits does not grow by itself. It has to be nurtured with care, somehow, somewhere. It takes at least a generation of effort. Without such a leadership, the greatest upheavals come to naught. With such a leadership, relatively small crises can have far-reaching results. We must have the courage to invest in life, even if courage is most of what we have to invest. And we must be willing to do so in full knowledge that we cannot be certain of the results even after the job is done. But try we must. In the end it might be that events will overtake any such efforts. However, it remains true that every additional child per family complicates the task of raising living standards, particularly for urban families. Properly cared for, each new child requires provisions, care, thought, and attention which busy and even harrassed parents find it more and more difficult to provide with each additional child. A reduction in the number of children can go on in the knowledge that their chances of reaching maturity are much greater than in the past. Resources and energies can therefore be concentrated on fewer children with greater effectiveness. Effective technical means for such reduction are now available.

The question of how the existing form of marriage and the family arose is not as important as the role these institutions play in today's social structure. It really matters little whether they arose from inequalities to maintain inequalities, as Godwin thought, or from self-love, as Malthus indicates, or from a gradual widening of the incest taboo coupled with a desire to insure the birth of children of undisputed parentage for purposes of inheritance, as Morgan and Engels believed. These answers are not unrelated, and the common thread in all of them might have more than a kernel of truth in specific cultural and historical traditions. But even within a single historical setting, people are known to marry for a variety of purposes. A few gifted or fortunate ones marry because they find fulfillment in mutual love, shared responsibilities and joys, companionship, and so on. Others marry to escape loneliness or a messy and unhappy family history. Still others marry for money, power, prestige, to climb economically, politically, or socially.

The problem is that we have developed an economic system which brings together the labor of human beings across continents. Its productive efficiency and richness is rooted in a far-ranging regional specialization, a vast market, and the economies of large-scale production, including interchangeable parts, assembly line methods, automation, and even computerization. All of these ultimately have their source in creative, collective effort. On the other hand, control over distribution centers in a few hundred families who hoard most of the wealth, tend to intermarry and form cliques, and tend to become politically powerful because they are economically powerful. Our power to produce goods has outgrown the limits of family, local community, nation; it has developed a world-wide economic system. The power to control those goods and our access to them is in the hands of a few privileged families. Whether or not the bourgeois family is based on private gain, and whether or not the bourgeois see their wives as instruments of production, it remains true that private ownership of the means of production is its source of wealth, power, and influence.

The point is that family identity among the wealthy bourgeois is a means for the transmission of wealth, power, and social position. Therefore, monogamy—particularly as applied to the wife —is important for the transmission of property, power, and privilege. Women get pregnant, and there is never a question who the mother is. Men do not, and one never knows who issues from whom unless the woman has remained "faithful." In a society where economic and political life is dominated by males, this opens the way for the double standard. Men can roam because they are men. Women cannot because they are women, and that is that. One of the reasons why the new technology of contraception was met with resistance from ruling circles in its initial stages was concern that removing the fear of pregnancy from the sexual act would undermine one of the foundations of the institution of marriage and the family, with whatever further ramifications that might have.

It is true the poor in Mexico have very little to lose, in terms of wealth, from moving in and out of unions on the basis of mutual attraction, love, economic necessity, companionship, or whatever. In fact what is known about their family life indicates that their unions tend to be common-law unions. The men often do consort with prostitutes. Adultery is common for both men and women (but more so for men than for women), and an open, serial monogamy is often present. What is more, the data indicate that the poor tend to adhere to the double standard: "I can do as I like because I am a man. You have to watch yourself because you are a woman."

Plato had the wisdom to see that the privatization of pleasure would lead to the privatization of the whole of life. He proposed making it impossible to recognize any child's parents in order to provide an equal chance for each child. Science and the technology of contraception have placed in the hands of modern humanity the possibilities for something quite different from what now prevails. It remains to be seen whether modern men and women will have the wisdom and the courage to work out its implications. Certainly the justification for marriage that it discourages "irresponsible breeding," as Malthus put it, has been placed in serious jeopardy by the technology of contraception. Its use indicates that breeding is precisely not the point, unless the partners involved are deliberately seeking parenthood. One thing is certain, the secret is out, and the future can never be quite the same again. If any women ever were in need of liberation, they are Mexican women in particular and Latin-American women in general.

18.

Sociopolitical Conclusions

The age is giving birth to a heart.
It can not keep going, it is dying of pain
and we must rush to the rescue
because the future is falling.

From the song "La Era Esta Pariendo un Corazón,"
by Silvio Rodríguez.

There can be little doubt that a focus on poverty from the point of view of scarcity and exploitation theory brings attention to at least some of the fundamental questions of sociological theory. There can be little doubt also that a focus on the study of poverty from the point of view of both scarcity and exploitation brings into view at least some of the fundamental structural features of the human habitat. Scarcity theory is at the center of demography; exploitation theory, rather than competition, is at the center of what has been called "human ecology." These two fields together contain what appear to be some of the most important questions for sociological theory. These two fields contain a core of factual information from which a new, truly explanatory theory of urbanization can be constructed.

The preceding study has provided sufficient evidence for saying that if economic events appear to lack an objective quality, it is not because their quality of being economic arises exclusively, or even primarily, from our cognitive interests when we face the problem of *scarcity* of means for the satisfaction of our needs. Our cognitive interests fail to take notice of the objective quality in events which make them economic precisely because we identify our intellectual tasks with existing institutions which create want in the midst of plenty after labor has carried out the objective tasks needed to produce plenty.

The facts of Mexican poverty show that even the rates of investment possible in socialist nations coupled with a drastically reduced birth rate would be insufficient to raise per capita incomes to two thousand dollars per year within a generation, though the most dramatic improvements are to be expected from such an approach. Ownership and effective control of the bulk of Mexico's wealth cannot continue to be left in the hands of less than 1 per cent of its population. Mexico cannot continue to allocate half of its annual income to 10 per cent of its population while half of the population at the bottom of the distribution receives less than a fifth of the total. On the other hand, Mexico's population cannot continue to increase at a rate of 3.25 per cent per year with the expectation that such a population, under such conditions, will grow to be healthy, educated, productive, or that it will live in a habitat consistent with human dignity. The choice is clear. Mexico must choose between two alternatives. The first is to see at least a fifth of its population unemployed, underemployed, and hungry, and half or more of its population poor, working only to eat badly, sick, poorly educated, unproductive, and miserable for a long time to come. The second is to render both capitalist exploitation and unplanned parenthood redundant, expendable, and fit only for the museums of prehistory.

Beyond the twin tragedies of exploitation and scarcity in human life, however, there lurks an even greater tragedy. It takes little effort of the analytic imagination to envision the conditions which would have to be met in order to bring about one, five, or ten-fold increases in per capita income in order to accommodate a population growing at a given rate. The mind staggers when one begins to consider the possible cost of such increases to the life-supporting capacities of the biosphere. What would be the impact of a five-fold increase in the production of cattle, corn, nitrogen fertilizer, petroleum, or automobiles? How much more exploitative pressure can be applied on the web of life of the planet? What is the impact of a single additional human life on that delicate web? What is the impact of one million more, of ten million, or of an additional three hundred million? Will the biosphere be able to bear the strain? Will Mexico eventually go the way of North Africa or Mesopotamia? To what end continued growth? What is the point of it all? Are we turning the planet more and more, slowly but relentlessly, into a desert? Heretofore human social systems have grown at the expense of the life-sustaining capacities of the biosphere. This is especially the case with a social system which is in control of science and technology and which is on its way to becoming industrialized. The fate of man and civilization is ultimately and inextricably tied to the fate of the biosphere. The problems created by population growth are not exhausted when we consider the relative shrinkage of resources from the point of view of human life. The problems created by capitalist concentration are not exhausted when we consider the relative shrinkage of value produced through the economies of scale. The cry for planned parenthood and the cry for social justice both fall tragically short of the mark. The deeper and more fundamental question of what justice means within a natural world increasingly bearing the imprint of human action goes unasked, and the stakes involved are lost by default. What does justice mean within the fabric of a natural world becoming a human world What kind of human world? What does justice mean in the value synthesis of nature-humanity-human world? What is the ultimate cost to humanity itself, and to the world of meaning and value which is the condition and content of humanity, of continuing to play with political fictions and self-fulfilling prophecies of the Malthusian type? Are we today, in the eighth decade of the twentieth century, equipped to deal with these questions? Does our obsession with having value-free, ethically neutral social science, with getting "facts" and dismissing values as unscientific, with forcing the categories of the human world of meaning, value, and history under the categories of natural science, produce in us a trained incapacity to deal with these questions? Does it not leave us as defenseless as babes in a field of battle?

I want to tentatively suggest that our obsession with "facts" at the expense of values and history is a major obstacle in the way of dealing with these questions. Not only are we not prepared to deal with them, but our training has also instilled in us a negative, almost visceral reaction to asking them. Yet, not asking these questions might be tantamount to missing out on the fundamental issues which face modern humanity, whose place in the biosphere is threatened by our own "success" within the ecology of the planet. The permanence of humankind and civilization within the life of the planet requires that humans learn to develop a civilization which grows not at the expense of and through the exploitation of nature but rather through the ever-watchful facilitation of nature's life-creating powers and capacity for beauty.

Plato's warning has to be heeded: we should love the land more than our mothers. It only needs stretching a bit: we should love the planet more than our mothers, civilization more than our fathers, and humankind more than capital. Ultimately, our problems go beyond the question of whether poverty has its source in overpopulation or in private ownership of the means of production. Conditions such as those in Mexico (conditions which are by no means unique) point to a fundamental failure in political institutions and thought and to a fundamental flaw in existing institutions and forms of thought about humankind, nature, the social world, and humanity's relationship to nature and to the social world. The problems include population growth and private property, but they go beyond them into the political and intellectual milieus which could provide guidelines for a way out; part of the reason why such milieus are failing is precisely because of the conditioning influence, the limitations and rigidities foisted on them by old forms of thought and old structures connected with the former problems. But there are structural limitations within the political and intellectual milieus themselves which are obstacles in the way of efforts to move in new directions.

There is no value-neutral, apolitical way of dealing with political questions. One might shift the focus of attention, as Marx did, from the questions: "Is exploitation good or bad?" and "What is the nature of Justice?"—presupposed in his association with the League of the Just—to questions such as "What is exploitation, and how do we explain it?" and "What are the historical consequences of the exploitation of man by man; that is, of capitalism?" One might then conclude, as Marx did, that the essence of exploitation is the expropriation of surplus value in the form of unpaid labor and that the fundamental contradiction between the collective nature of production and the private character of appropriation *is* the crisis of the capitalist system. One might find also, as he did, that this contradiction is the fundamental source of crises in societies which forcibly "legalize" class exploitation and class rule. The ethical and political power of Marx's argument is to be found precisely in the fact that he argues that such a system carries within itself contradictions that will lead to its undoing. Thus, in a letter to Arnold Ruge, Marx says (Marx 1971:515):

> The system of industry and commerce, of property and the exploitation of people, leads, even more quickly than an increase in the population, to a breach inside the present society, which the old system will not be able to heal because none of it either heals or produces, but only exists and enjoys.

One might shift from the former type of question to the latter, but the answers one reaches are nevertheless politically loaded. They are politically loaded because the answers to the questions we ask indicate the direction in which action can or cannot proceed in order to work out a solution. There is no getting around the fact that "man," as Aristotle noted, is among other things, "a political animal." Small wonder, then, that like it or not, Marx's critique of capitalist society is the most powerful political catalyst of modern times.

But if the question "What is Justice?" is faced squarely, as it was by Plato and Godwin, what answer do we get? What does justice mean in terms of the knowledge we have of Mexican society? This question is worth an effort at answering. In attempting an answer, it will be presupposed that value, meaning, and history are found within and that they take place in the form of the synthesis of human-being–nature–human world. The central form of the relation which *is* that synthesis, is action which is both adaptive and transformative; that is, creative action. Creative action, in turn, is labor, work, industry, art in the broadest sense. Work is a precondition for anything that is human.

Justice is a special kind of relation of labor to the human world and to the natural world. The special form of this relation is that justice is its own possibility: the possibility of a permanent relation of transformative, collective action to the natural world, where transformation must mean adaptive transformation.

The permanency of this relation involves, in the first place, the fulfillment and satisfaction of labor taken as aesthetic, intelligent, creative activity and as animal urge to sustenance, expression, and growth. Justice involves, in the second place, a question of development: the development of a population raised to its full creative potential; the development of a social system which is consistent with the purpose to develop and which defines the achievement of that purpose as its central purpose. Justice involves the development of the natural habitat not only in such way that human development does not mean destruction of the natural habitat but also in such way that human life is an active agent in facilitating nature's capacity for creativity, health, and beauty. Justice in this sense is not only the development of the full potential of all that is included under the term human; it also involves the establishment of institutions which are human toward human life itself. Justice involves as well the humanization of human beings' relations to the life of nature.

Justice therefore not only requires the development of a population which is well nourished, strong, healthy, alert, and productive. It also requires the development of a population which has the kind of self-confidence which arises from having grown healthy in every sense; a population which is capable of trust, friendship, sympathy, and joy. Justice requires not only a population educated to its fullest capacity to make use of, appreciate, and enjoy the genuine intellectual, artistic, and moral achievements of the ages in a habitat consistent with health, dignity, beauty, and joy. Beyond that, justice requires social institutions which are wholly and completely committed to the achievement of those ends. It requires institutions which produce healthy human beings, healthy foods, clothing, shelter, and a healthy education in a healthy habitat. Justice requires institutions which bring to an end the exploitation of human beings by human beings. It requires institutions which bring an end to the destruction of nature by human beings bent on converting all of the planet's resources, animate and inanimate, into forms of wealth. Justice also requires population control—control and planning of human population which is consistent with responsibility, freedom, and dignity.

Justice requires also an agriculture which is consistent with the continuing fertility and life of the soil, with the continuity of grass-lands, and with the purity of the water we drink and the air we breathe. Justice requires an industry which is consistent with honesty, full employment, rest, recreation, safety, wholesomeness, education, health, and trust. It requires also an industry consistent with pure food, pure air, pure water, and artistic and natural beauty. Justice requires a system of distribution which measures the worth of things in terms of their significance to humans, to nature, and to the human world, rather than measuring humans, nature, and the human world in terms of their usefulness to accumulated, abstract, and alienated capital.

Justice requires that every child brought into existence is wanted and that each child's surroundings *mean* that he or she is wanted: that the child be surrounded by an environment where he or she can grow to be a creative, productive, friendly, happy, joyful, loving human being. Justice requires that no human being shall go hungry in the midst of plenty, or in the midst of enough. Justice requires that no human being shall go unemployed while there is plenty of work to be done and the means to accomplish it. Justice requires that no human being shall go without medical attention for lack of money to pay for it. Justice requires that human beings have a chance to educate themselves to their fullest potential. Justice requires that human beings shall be clothed and housed in ways consistent with health, dignity, and self-respect. Justice requires that no human being shall be overworked while others have unearned leisure. Justice requires that profit making shall not get in the way of physicians healing, of architects designing, of builders building, of teachers teaching, of lawyers providing legal counsel, of legislators legislating, of judges interpreting the law, and of executives carrying out the intent of the law. Justice requires that the law shall be just and that it shall not get in the way of justice.

Justice requires that no more needs shall be created than can be satisfied and that enough means be produced to satisfy those that have been created. Justice requires that food shall not be exported when there is hunger and malnutrition. Justice requires that the concrete value of human labor shall not be abrogated by abstract market fluctuations in price. Justice requires that increases in productivity contribute to the well-being of the producers of wealth, rather than to their superfluity, degradation, and misery. Justice requires that enough be invested in agriculture, industry, transportation, electrification, education, housing, health, research, planning and environmental protection, and development. Justice requires that these be accomplished in the shortest time possible. Justice requires an open mind to new requirements and new possibilities.

Finally, justice requires a vision of the meaning and value of human life in terms of its impact on the life-supporting capacity of the planet which is our life-source and our home (Ahrens 1957):

> This misty, sapphire jewel of the sky
> this restless, aqueous orb circling the sun
> this improbable condensation of galactic dust
> this fertile neighbor of Venus and Mars
> this temperate combination of elements
> this rocky cup of azure seas and air
> this glory of sunlight, rain, and growth
> this passing scene of extinct creatures
> this matchless mother of mankind
> this graveyard of fallen civilizations
> this demiparadise of promise
> this living planet, this earth
> will not be lasting home to any species
> that knows not how to abide in Justice

Appendix:

*Some Thoughts on Mexican Poverty
Viewed from the Perspective of
the World Population Plan
of Action*

The following is an effort to bring together the results of the study of Mexican poverty and some salient points in the World Population Plan of Action. Such an effort will require first a brief summing-up of the basic concerns and findings of the poverty study and then a consideration of their implications in the light of some of the basic guidelines of the World Population Plan of Action. This supplement was presented as a paper at the General Conference of the International Union for the Scientific Study of Population, held in Mexico City, August 8 to 13, 1977.

The focus on poverty is at once an effort to come to terms with the basic question which gave rise to sociological theory and an effort to overcome that theory's tendency to reduce sociological standpoints to the limits of class-conditioned ideologies. The basic question out of which sociology arose in the West was the social question how to explain poverty and misery in human society, particularly growing poverty amidst an ever increasing capacity to produce wealth. The respondents to this question tended to be of two types: those who viewed poverty as rooted in human nature and those who saw the roots of poverty in institutions which are ill-suited to human nature and which prevent normal development. My study's focus on scarcity and exploitation is an effort to get at the core of both standpoints. On the one hand, Malthus and the Malthusians viewed population growth (with some revisions) as the source of scarcity and scarcity as the source of poverty. On the other hand, Marx and the Marxian school saw exploitation as institutionalized in private ownership of the means of production and poverty as having its source in that exploitation. My study of Mexican poverty was an effort to find out whether or not data gathered under the guidance of concepts taken from those politically opposing standpoints would provide evidence for weighing the relative explanatory power of those standpoints.

Mexico was selected for study because Mexico was known to have one of the fastest rates of population growth in the world, as well as one of the most markedly differentiated class systems. Later research showed that Mexico exceeded India in population growth rates and in the extent of income inequality.

Close study of both theoretical standpoints led to a focus on eleven questions. What portion of the Mexican population lives at or below the margins of subsistence? What is the balance of forces between population needs and means of subsistence? What are the respective rates of growth of reproductive and productive forces, past, present, and predicted, and why? What specific form does private ownership of the means of production take in Mexico? What portion of the Mexican population is unemployed or underemployed and why? What are the trends in unemployment and underemployment, past, present, and predicted? What are the trends in land and capital concentration in Mexico? What are the trends in income derived from profits and rents? What relationship is there between the latter trends and the incidence of business cycles? What relationship is there between business cycles and the size of the unemployed labor force? What is the relationship between the unemployed labor force and the population living below the level of subsistence? The conclusions arrived at under each of these questions are summarized below.

Portion of the Mexican Population Living at or below Subsistence Levels. The question here depends on whether one is concerned with bare biological subsistence or with life-style subsistence. The assumptions I make here are that subsistence of both types varies over a range and that there is a segment of the population where the two forms overlap. An estimate of 50 per cent of the population living at or below subsistence would err on the safe side, based on 1970 figures. The actual figure is probably closer to 60 per cent, particularly in recent years.

Balance of Forces between Population Needs and the Means of Subsistence. The magnitude of the hungry and undernourished population in Mexico is far out of proportion to the actual shortages reported. Ana Maria Florez reported 15 per cent of Mexico's population as being hungry in or around 1961. Yet the average daily supply of calories available per capita in the period from 1960 to 1962 exceeded both the 1967 and the 1974 minimum standards set by the FAO, while the amount of proteins *per capita* available during those same years (proteins from all sources) fell short of the 1967 FAO standards by only three grams. Roughly the same pattern prevailed in 1967, with a total shortage of proteins of only one gram. Aside from relatively small shortages of Vitamins A and C and riboflavin, the 1967 figures show a plentiful supply of vitamins and minerals per capita.

Estimates of the extent of malnutrition in Mexico vary from 80 per cent in 1960 to 50 per cent in 1970. Two possible sources of these discrepancies suggest themselves: the unequal pattern of internal distribution and the practice of production for export. The Federal District consumes twice as much meat per capita as the rest of the country. Also, annual exports include cattle on the hoof by the hundreds of thousands and tens of millions of kilograms of processed meat. The list of exports also includes large amounts of dairy products, sea food, eggs, fruits, and vegetables.

Close to two-thirds of Mexico's population was reported to be lacking in medical attention from either private or public sources in 1970. About a fourth of Mexico's population was still illiterate in 1970, and three-fifths of the economically active population had less than three years of education. In 1970 two-fifths of Mexico's housing units were one-room adobe-and-mud structures with dirt floors, lacking electricity and plumbing. About three in five houses lacked sewers and drainage, and nearly half of Mexico's housing units were renter-occupied.

Relative Growth Rates of Population Needs and of the Means of Subsistence. The relationship between population needs and the means of subsistence is not an immediate, one-to-one relation, but rather it is mediated by the whole body of institutionalized practices, ideological assumptions, and geopolitical concerns which play a role in formulating the policies of the administration in power. Among the mediating factors between population growth and means of subsistence during the Díaz administration were the following: A policy was followed of promoting industrialization through heavy reliance on foreign investments and on the sale of export crops abroad to provide a source of foreign exchange. Foreign interests controlled 42 per cent of the country's wealth. Seventy-five per cent of the railroads, 64 per cent of the minerals, and 58 per cent of the petroleum was owned by foreign interests. Over 51 per cent of total investments in 1902 and 1903 came from abroad. Mexico was ruled by a coalition of domestic and foreign elites whose gospel of "positivist freedom" was the freedom for self-enrichment. The "Surveying Laws" were instrumental in dispossessing the Mexican peasantry, in promoting the growth of large, landed estates, and in encouraging the growth of export crops.

The relation of population growth to growth in the means of subsistence during the past century of Mexican history forces a reconsideration of common-sense assumptions of a simple, inverse, relationship between those two variables. Relatively low rates of population growth during the Díaz administration were accompanied by declining rates of growth in food production and by wage increases which lagged far behind prices. However, while total crop production was growing at a rate less than half the rate of population growth, the production of export crops was growing at a rate four times the rate of population growth.

The years between 1940 and 1970 were years of recovery and of industrial development for the Mexican economy following a long interval of revolution, depression, and reform. Between 1940 and 1970 Mexico maintained a rate of growth in food production better than twice the average rate of population increase, although the figure had nearly doubled since the earlier interval. The growth of crop production for export continued at a high rate: better than three times the average rate of population increase. Mexico's experience during the years 1940 to 1970 indicates that food production can increase from two to three times faster than population, even when the population is doubling during the same interval. Changes of a political, legal, and technological nature have all tended to foster these increases, despite the relative barrenness of the soil and climate.

Even if it were possible to show that some of Mexico's hunger and malnutrition has its source in diminishing returns on added units of capital investment, the question would still remain how it happens that the increases that do take place are distributed unequally.

The hungry and undernourished population will double by the middle 1990's if the 1970–75 patterns of population growth and food production and distribution continue. Mexico faces compound and growing problems in meeting the health, housing, and educational needs of its population.

Specific Form that Private Ownership of the Means of Production Takes in Mexico. The main thrust of the constitutional reforms of 1917 was directed at a rejection of a *laissez-faire* economic system. This rejection was achieved through recognition of the right of the state to give private property the modalities dictated by the public interest. The conception of property as concrete social function was not worked out in full in the constitution, despite language which at times is radical. A number of reforms were carried out under the provisions of this law: land reform; nationalization of petroleum, railways, and some utilities; Mexicanization of some private enterprises; amortization of the foreign debt; and reduction of foreign investments. The administration of Avila Camacho initiated a reversal of the latter trend.

Portion of the Mexican Population Unemployed or Underemployed and Why? Official figures on unemployment in Mexico are scanty, implausible, and incongruously low: for instance, 1 per cent in 1970. Inclusion of the contingent of northward migrants alone would require a sharp upward revision: up to 7.5 times higher than the official figure for 1950. The "revolution" has tended to institutionalize underemployment, marginality, low productivity, and poverty. The underemployed include cultivators of infrasubsistence *ejidal* or private landholdings, migratory field hands, and the many types of hustlers in commerce, the services, and manufacturing. Recent estimates of the size of the unemployed and underemployed population place this figure at 19 to 40 or even 50 per cent.

Trends in Underemployment and Unemployment: Past, Present, and Predicted. It is pointless to attempt to assess trends on the basis of the scanty data available: 17.6 per cent in 1950 and 18.2 per cent in 1960. It is possible to show that claims about the size of the annual contingent of new job seekers contributed by population growth alone—300,000 per year during the 1950's and 800,000 per year during the 1970's—are exaggerated. The 300,000 figure for the 1950's is roughly equivalent to the number of 15-year-olds in 1950. The death rate removed roughly 100,000 males aged 15 to 65 during that year. Approximately 50,000 males reached retirement age. Close to 100,000 jobs were eliminated every year during the 1950's as a result of increases in the efficiency of production in industry, agriculture, and commerce and the services. Thus, for every three jobs needed as a result of population growth, two jobs were eliminated by increases in productivity.

The process of urbanization under capitalist forms of control is a process which creates unemployment and underemployment faster than it creates employment. Under capitalism the economy of action made possible by the application of science and technology to the productive process is transformed into a process of displacement and attrition of jobs and salaries.

Trends in Land and Capital Concentration. Despite its reforms Mexico remains a country where most of the land, wealth, and income are controlled by a few persons and corporations. The authenticity of both the program of land reform and public commitment to the law underlying those reforms have been questioned. Most of the best farming and grazing lands are still concentrated in a few hands, and the *ejidal* program seems to have been most successful in creating infrasubsistence farming units. In manufacturing 1.5 per cent of the total number of establishments in 1965 accounted for 77 per cent of the total product. In commerce and services the situation in 1965 was the following:

	Per Cent of Establishments that Control	Per Cent of Total Capital Controlled	Per Cent of Total Gross Income Controlled
Commerce	1.3	60	60.4
Services	1	64	54

In 1962 half the income of the 2,000 largest enterprises accrued to the 100 largest corporations. Also, about 42 per cent of the total income of the 2,000 largest corporations accrued to corporations under foreign control or to corporations which showed strong foreign participation. The latter figures suggest that cyclical fluctuations in the Mexican economy are heavily conditioned by international economic fluctuations and that these influences are magnified by similar trends in the movement of the Mexican economy.

The process of urbanization under capitalist forms of development is essentially a process of capital concentration: the Federal District shows 320 per cent more production per inhabitant than the rest of the country. Within its institutions of private credit the Federal District also shows extreme concentration in resources per inhabitant, in capital reserves, and in visible cash deposits. Seventeen per cent of the nation's population lived in the Federal District in 1970.

Trends in Income Derived from Profits and Rents. Data on profits in any form tend to be scanty and fragmentary. Profits taken as a per cent of annual income show a steady rise from 26.2 per cent in 1939 to 45.1 per cent in 1946. This trend was followed by erratic fluctuations around 41 per cent between 1951 and 1955 and by a steady decline to 36.5 per cent by 1959. During the same interval commercial profits varied from 53 per cent of total profits in 1939 to 61 per cent of total profits in 1950. Also incomes from rents and interests declined from about 8 per cent of total income in 1939 to about 6.4 per cent in 1954.

Between 1939 and 1960 incomes from capital ranged from one-third to one-half of total annual income, while incomes from labor ranged between slightly over one-fifth and just over one-third of total income. Of special interest is the steady decline during that interval in mixed incomes and in the incomes of the self-employed.

The rate of profit typical to Mexico has been estimated at 20 to 25 per cent, though rates as high as 30 per cent are reported to be not unusual. In fact, recent rates are reported to have been averaging 30 per cent.

Marx defines the rate of profit as a percentage ratio of surplus value to total capital, that is, capital which includes both its fixed and variable components. The best data available for the purpose of assessing trends exists only in the form of a ratio of surplus value to fixed capital for the interval 1950 to 1967. To stress the incompleteness of the data it will be referred to as "the ratio of profit."

Running averages worked out for three-year intervals on the basis of these data show a fairly steady decline in this ratio, from a high of .30 in the early fifties to a low of .24 at the end of the decade. At the turn of the sixties there was a slight increase from .24 to .25, which was sustained for four years and which was followed by a decline to .23 by the end of the interval covered by the data.

Indications are that the rate of return on foreign investments tends to be lower than the rate of return on investments from native sources.

Relationship between the Trend of Profits and the Incidence of Business Cycles. Trend data for the profit ratio and for net investments yielded higher, positive coefficients of correlation with one another than did raw data. The former averages +.70 for two different estimates of net investments. The latter averaged +.37. Also, the profit ratio and the productivity index yielded a −.71 correlation coefficient for the years from 1950 to 1958. Hence, as the profit ratio fell, net investments tended to fall also, while productivity tended to rise. Moreover, during an interval when productivity nearly doubled (1940–60) real wages declined by about 10 per cent.

During the years from 1951 to 1964, as the profit ratio fell, GNP growth rates tended to stagnate at about 6.3 per cent per year. Very high correlation coefficients were found to exist between rising absolute levels of national production and absolute levels of both public and private investment. The former yielded a remarkable +.98 *r* coefficient; the latter +.81.

The ratio of profits invested to profits received tends to be rather low and inflexibile: approximately .20. Thus only about a fifth of the profits received are reinvested. The years of high net investments tended to be years when high income shares were obtained through profits rather than years of increasing ratios of profits to investment. An average *r* coefficient of approximately +.85 was found between the percentage of annual income appropriated in the form of profits and two different estimates of net investments. The correlation between percentages of total profits invested and net investment levels tended to be low: an average $+.22$ for two estimates of net investments. Practically no correlation was found to exist between the ratio of investments to profits and the percentage share of annual income paid through profits: a weak $-.12$. These findings suggest that the relatively constant GNP growth rates from 1951 to 1964 are more likely to have been sustained by increases in the productivity of labor, in both its accumulated and living forms, than by changes in the investment-profit ratio.

A very high $-.93$ correlation coefficient was found to exist between trend data on Mexico's predominantly negative balance of trade and the profit ratio. Raw data yielded a lower but still high $-.79$ r coefficient. Hence the profit ratio tends to decrease as the negative trade balance increases.

Relation between Business Cycles and the Size of the Unemployed Labor Force. Unemployment data are scanty, fragmentary, and dubious in nature. Thus it is not possible to deal fruitfully with this question.

Relation between the Unemployed Labor Force and the Population Living below the Level of Subsistence. Both unemployment and underemployment must be considered in any meaningful effort to deal with this question. A cautious estimate of the relative size of the unemployed and underemployed population in 1970 Mexico is 20 per cent. That is, while the ratio of the poor to the total population is 1 to 2, the ratio of the unemployed and underemployed to the poor population is 2 to 5. Had these rates held, the total contingent of unemployed and underemployed in 1974 would have been 10.8 million people, and 27 million people would have qualified as poor. However, there are indications of a serious increase in unemployment, underemployment, and poverty in the 1970's.

The chief distinguishing features between the unemployed and underemployed population, on the one hand, and the remaining poor population, on the other, are the following. The former consists of those whose share of annual income is about 5 per cent (and is declining), and who make up the hard core of Mexico's hunger problem, its severe malnutrition problem, and most of its illiteracy problem; their medical neglect must be regarded as almost total, while their housing conditions are infrahuman. The remaining poor population consists of those whose share of annual income is about 12 per cent (and is declining also) and whose diets are more likely to assuage hunger than to provide a balanced diet; they tend to attend school less than three years or to be illiterate; their medical attention tends to be confined to the purchase of drugs across the counter; and their living quarters include more than their share of rented one-room shacks with dirt floors, devoid of the most elementary sanitary facilities.

The sum of Mexico's unemployed, underemployed, and employed poor make up the bulk of Mexico's population who live in misery and hopelessness. The burden of the established institutions and the dead weight of the ages is on their backs. It is to them that the world of class exploitation and the lies of the ages preach that they have no one but themselves to blame for their poverty. Their eyes are veiled by the search for individual salvation, a search which assures them that the more things change, the more they remain the same.

This study of Mexican poverty leads to the conclusion that data gathered under the guidance of concepts taken from ideologically opposing theories of poverty are not neutral on the question of the relative explanatory power of those theories and that it is possible to arrive at knowledge concerning ideologically sensitive issues despite the tendency of ideology to influence perception.

We now turn to a consideration of Mexican poverty from the perspective of the World Population Plan of Action with a view to relating some of the background ideas, principles, objectives, and recommendations of the plan to the specific conditions of Mexican society.

There is a need to improve the living conditions of the underprivileged (Article B.k.). There can be no question that any program which would pretend to solve Mexico's problems of development and population growth without considering necessary changes of a social, economic, and political nature which are aimed at significantly improving the life conditions of the poor is doomed to failure from the start. The language of the plan in this connection leaves much to be desired, however; it implies that a system of distribution of the world's goods which is based not on work, but on privilege, is not itself the problem and that what needs to be done instead is to bring the poor within the structure of privilege.

An economy such as the Mexican economy, where the poor have so little and the privileged few have so much, cannot provide the kind of mass market which is needed to promote the development of a mass industry. Instead, it encourages the growth of an import market for luxuries and the channeling of resources into conspicuous consumption for the few who can afford to flaunt the symbols of wealth. On the other hand, family income and levels of education are known to be negatively correlated to family size.

The study of population problems cannot be reduced to the analysis of population trends: intranational and international inequities must also be considered (Article A.4). Both Mexico's achievements and its problems have intranational and international dimensions. The effort to uplift the living standards of Mexico's impoverished masses must overcome a multitude of compound and interrelated obstacles to accelerated economic development: the inertia of exploitative institutions, which makes for declining real wages in the face of rapidly increasing productivity and highly unequal distribution of wealth and income; the inertia of neocolonial forms of power politics which work toward frustrating internal efforts to establish equity and justice; the inertia of class-conditioned forms of thought which find it easier to identify an enemy than to think about fundamental issues; the demographic inertia, which makes for growing populations even after replacement growth rates are reached; and, finally, lurking behind all of these obstacles, the ever-growing possibility of eco-catastrophe.

Economic development in Mexico would be encouraged by upping gross investments to 30 per cent of its GNP per year; by changing wealth and income distribution patterns so as to promote the development of a mass industry responsive to a mass market; by discouraging dependence on costly import items, particularly those which appeal to luxury consumption; by improving nutritional, health, and housing standards of its population; by doubling, trebling, and even quadrupling its rate of investment in education; and by continuing to work toward reducing its rapid population growth rates to replacement levels. What this means is that both capitalist exploitation and unplanned parenthood must be relegated to the museums of prehistory.

Population policies are constituent elements of socioeconomic development policies, never substitutes for them (Article B. d.). Under conditions such as existed during the Díaz regime, even a rate of population growth of 1.1 per cent per year would appear to be overrapid. Such conditions included declining rates in food production; rapidly expanding production of export crops; soaring food prices; lagging salaries; increasing concentration of capital in land, industry, and commerce; and heavy reliance on foreign investments accompanied by heavy concentration of wealth in foreign hands. Due to somewhat changed conditions following the 1910 Revolution and the reforms of the thirties, the average rate of population growth (2.5 per cent per year) in recent decades—speaking relatively—is not quite so rapid, since Mexico's growing capacity to feed itself has rapidly outpaced population growth rates. However, both population and socioeconomic policy must ultimately be judged sound or unsound in terms of their ultimate impact on the natural habitat. It is only a naive exercise in anthropocentric blindness which permits us to focus attention on ways and means to overcome human poverty without becoming sensitive to the pauperization of the natural habitat.

The reduction of morbidity and mortality to a minimum should be achieved in conjunction with massive social and economic development (Article C.b.20). The reduction of human morbidity and mortality has been one of the deepest human aspirations from time immemorial. The human capacity for consciousness and the relative continuity of consciousness through generations is saddened by the transitory nature of life. Death, in particular premature death, leaves us with a sense of tragedy. Our most human motives rebel against the waste of human life, and it is only natural that they should do so. Yet we must consider the problems which will be created by a doubling of the hungry and undernourished population by the middle nineties, a doubling which will take place if existing patterns of population growth and of wealth and income distribution continue as before: added environmental stress on forests and grazing lands; on soil fertility; on the water table; on the purity of air, water, and soil; on the shrinking supply of nonrenewable resources. If we consider the impact of an additional 50, 100, or even 150 million inhabitants in this sunny and colorful land called Mexico, were perforce reach certain conclusions. Only a government systematically committed to the idea that property is not an abstract right of a possessor over a thing but a concrete sociopolitical function vital to the life of action, and one which is free from neocolonial interference, will be able to cope with the most momentous crisis heretofore faced by human beings: the crisis of the biosphere.

Fertility levels must be moderated through the promotion of social justice, social mobility, and social development. Neither the cry for social justice, nor the plea for social mobility, nor the call for social development, nor the advocacy of planned parenthood go to the heart of the problem. The plea for increased mobility in particular tends to be a plea for more of the same when uttered within the context of institutionalized class antagonisms. The cry for social justice is a cry for an end to the misappropriation of wealth by exploitative systems of wealth distribution, and its implications are far-reaching, but it does not go far enough. The cry for planned parenthood is a cry to bring under rational control the human capacity to create needs, particularly at a time when human beings have come to see the possibility of higher living standards and to expect the realization of those standards. But this cry does not go far enough either. The call for social development is one-sided to the extent that we continue to view human society as the independent variable and nature as the dependent one, that is, to the extent that we continue to act on the view that nature is there to be exploited by human beings. At issue is the permanency of human life on the planet. Nothing short of full justice will do: the creation and maintenance of social institutions which foster the development of healthy, alert, educated, productive, loving human beings in a healthy and unpolluted habitat which is in harmony with the creative powers of nature. Justice requires an end to the exploitation of man by man; it requires that no human being shall go hungry where there is food to be eaten; it requires that no human being shall go uneducated when there is knowledge to be had; it requires that no human being shall go jobless when there is work to be done; it requires that no child shall be brought forth unwanted, unloved, or uncared for. Justice requires political and legal institutions which are committed to the fullest possible development of both human and natural creative capacities and the development of each in harmony with the other. We must work toward the creation of social institutions which teach us to love the planet and its life support system more than our mothers, civilization more than our fathers, and humankind more than capital.

Countries which are concerned with the outflow of migrant workers . . . should make particular efforts to create favorable employment opportunities at the national level (Article C.e.54). The Mexican government has recently given public recognition to the fact that its out-migration problem is part and parcel of its unemployment problem. It is less well known that the number of so-called wetbacks apprehended across the Río Grande correlates highly, and negatively ($-.84$), with the index of real income per inhabitant. Mexico needs to have frequent, accurate, and realistic readings of its unemployment and underemployment problem. These figures should include a consideration of the out-migration problem, and efforts should be made to relate the unemployment problem to trends in wealth and income distribution both at home and abroad. Such trends cannot but condition the Mexican economy's capacity to create employment for its people.

Decisions on the introduction of technologies affording significant savings in employment of manpower should take into account the relative abundance of human resources (Article C.f.2.69). The problems here are compounded by a number of factors: neocolonial dependence which sets definite limits on the technology which can be introduced; patterns of wealth and income distribution which condition whether the new technology will benefit the population as a whole or only the few that control it; and existing usages, such as the *ejido* and *minifundio* patterns of land tenure, which heavily restrict the type of labor-saving technology which can be applied. It is not labor-saving or effort-saving technology which is the problem. To the extent that savings in employment mean that the displaced population will become marginal to the production process, it is employment-saving technology rather than labor-saving technology that is the problem. Also, as regards labor-saving technology in agriculture, the typically small size of *ejidal* and *minifundio* holdings preclude the possibility of using the most efficient technology. The old idea of haciendas without *hacendados* has yet to be tried in Mexico.

The problems of urban environment are a consequence not only of the concentration of inhabitants but also of their way of life. . . . to avoid such effects . . . a development pattern favouring balanced and rational consumption is recommended (Article C.1.d.50). Overconsumption and waste of resources on one side, coupled with underconsumption and lack of access to resources on the other, is not exclusively an urban phenomenon, though such disparities tend to be greatly magnified by urban settings. Overconsumption and waste are merely symptoms of a fundamental contradiction in a social system which draws its productive and creative energies from collective, concretely corporate efforts but which distributes its benefits in terms of appropriation criteria which are private in character, corporate only in what passes for "legal" fiction. The effort to regulate consumption and to reduce waste is not enough. Only the reconstitution of social relations along genuine and consistent lines will permit the development of equitable, judicious, and fairer rural and urban settings.

Government should take into account not only short-term economic returns or alternative patterns but also . . . social justice in the distribution of the benefits of development among all groups and regions (Article C.1.d.46.c). Mexico shows serious sectoral, regional, and ethnic imbalances in wealth distribution. Most of Mexico's exports originate in rural areas, while most of her imports converge in the Federal District. Rural incomes tend to be considerably lower than urban incomes, and rural poverty is much more intense than urban poverty. Predictably, the wealthiest zones in Mexico are the Federal District and the states located on the eastern shore of the Sea of Cortes. The poorest zones are found in the southern states and in the North Central Mesa. Also, the indigenous population in such states as Oaxaca remains the most submerged and marginal in Mexican life. Any balanced program of development would have to redress these imbalances.

Training in population dynamics . . . should deal not only with population variables but also with the interrelationship of these variables and economic, social, and political variables. (Article C. 3.c.83). Problems such as those concerning the relationship between cyclical economic fluctuations and the relative size of the impoverished, unemployed, underemployed, and migratory labor force need to be studied in greater detail and depth. This task cannot be accomplished in the absence of trend data on such variables as the organic composition of capital, profit rates, the size of the unemployed and underemployed labor force, and the like. The very serious deficiencies in the availability of such data need to be corrected.

Bibliography

Aguilar Monteverde, Alonso and Carmona, Fernando
  1967. *México: Riqueza y Miseria.* Mexico City: Editorial Nuestro
      Tiempo.
  1974. *México: Riqueza y Miseria.* Mexico City: Editorial Nuestro
      Tiempo.
Ahrens, Erich A.
  1954. Lectures on Social Evolution. Unpublished notes. Urbana:
      University of Illinois.
  1957. Social Factors in Personality: Lectures on Plato's Republic.
      Unpublished notes. Urbana: University of Illinois.
Alba, Francisco, and Alvarado, Ricardo
  1971. "Algunas Observaciones Sobre la Mortalidad por Causas
      en México, 1950–67," *Demografía y Economía* 5:145–68.
Alvarez y Lezama, Francisco José
  1966. "Explosión Demográfica y sus Consequencias Socio-Eco-
      nómicas," *Revista de Economía* 29:160–73.
The American Almanac
  1970. *The U.S. Book of Facts, Statistics, and Information for
      1971.* New York: Grosset and Dunlap.
Aubey, Robert T.
  1966. *Nacional Financiera and Mexican Industry.* Los Angeles:
      University of California Press.
Baltra, Alberto
  1960. "La Reforma Agraria y el Progreso Económico," *Revista
      de Economia* 23:6–12.
Banco Nacional de Comercio, S.A.
  1970. *México 1970: Hechos, Cifras y Tendencias.* Mexico: Banco
      Nacional.

Banco Nacional de México, S.A.
   1970a. "Feeding the Mexicans: Levels Are Still Very Low," *Review
          of the Economic Situation of Mexico* 46 (July, 1970):165–
          71.
   1970b. "Fifty Million Mexicans: Do We Face Overpopulation?"
          Review of the Economic Situation of Mexico 46:10–14.
   1970c. "General Panorama," *Review of the Economic Situation
          of Mexico* 46:303–13.
   1970d. "Netzahualcoyotl City: An Imposing Social Phenomenon,"
          Review of the Economic Situation 46:282–84.
   1971a. "Cities of More than 100,000 Inhabitants: They Can
          Change the Rural Panorama," *Review of the Economic
          Situation of Mexico* 46:23–26.
   1971b. "Demographic Growth: A Challenge to Economic Devel-
          opment," *Review of the Economic Situation of Mexico*
          47:225–31.
   1971c. "Final Census Figures: Indicators of Social Development,"
          Review of the Economic Situation of Mexico 47:153–77.
   1973. "Population and Development: Interdependent Phenom-
          ena," *Review of the Economic Situation of Mexico* 49:
          167–71.
Beals, Carleton
   1971. *Great Guerrilla Warriors.* New York: Tower Publications.
Beals, Ralph L.
   1952– "Social Stratification in Latin America," *American Journal
   53.   of Sociology* 58:327–39.
Benítez Zenteno, Raúl, and Cabrera Acevedo, Gustavo
   1966. "La Población Futura de México — Total, Urbana y Rural,"
          El Trimestre Economico 33:163–70.
Berelson, Bernard
   1974. "World Population: Status Report 1974," *Reports on Popu-
          lation/Family Planning* 15:1–48.
Berger, Peter L., and Luckman, Thomas
   1967. *The Social Construction of Reality.* Garden City, N.Y.:
          Anchor Books.
Blanco Macías, Gonzalo
   1965. "Planeación Demográfica Mexicana en el Sexenio 1965–
          1970," *Revista de Economia* 27:105–107.
Brailsford, H. N.
   1913. *Shelley, Godwin, and Their Circle.* New York: Henry Holt
          and Company.

Brinsmade, R. B.
  1916. *El Latifundismo Mexicano.* Mexico City: Departamento
      de Imprenta de la Secretaría de Fomento.
Bugarín Pérez, Ismael
  1968. "La Vivienda y el Desarrollo Económico," *Revista de
      Economía* 31:15–20.
Bury, J. B.
  1955. *The Idea of Progress.* New York: Dover Publications.

Cabrera, Luis, et al.
  1916. "México y los Mexicanos," In *Tres Intelectuales Hablan
      Sobre Mexico.* Mexico City: N.p.
Camargo Piñuelas, Sergio
  1964. "Nacionalización de Recursos," *Revista de Economía* 37:
      265–72.
  1967. "Vivienda y Población," *Revista de Economía* 30:131–36.
Carmona, Fernando, et al.
  1970. *El Milagro Mexicano.* Mexico City: Editorial Nuestro
      Tiempo.
Carrera, C. Emilio
  1968. "Los Industriales y la Vivienda," *Revista de Economía*
      31:215–23.
Centro de Estudios Económicos y Demográficos
  1970. *Dinámica de la Población de México.* Guanajuato Mexico:
      El Colegio de México.
Chaplin, Davis
  1971. *Population Policies and Growth in Latin America.* Toronto:
      Lexington Books.
Cline, Howard F.
  1962. *Mexico: Revolution to Evolution 1940–1960.* London:
      Oxford University Press.
Commoner, Barry
  1972. *The Closing Circle.* New York: Bantam Books.
Corwin, Arthur F.
  1964. "Mexico Resists the Pill," *Nation,* May 11, pp. 477–80.

de la Peña Cejudo, Ernesto
  1966. "El Problema Urbano como Factor en la Economía Mexi-
      cana," *Revista de Economía* 29:305–11.
Delegación Mexicana
  1960. "Conferencia Sobre Agricultura y Alimentación en Latino-
      américa," *Revista de Economía* 23:346–52.

Delgado Navarro, Juan
  1962. "Desarrollo Económico y Justicia Social," *Revista de Eco-
         nomía* 25:70–86.
Dozer, Donald M.
  1953. "Roots of Revolution in Latin America," In *Readings in
         Latin American Social Organization and Institutions,* edited
         by Chas. P. Loomis and Olen E. Leonard. East Lansing:
         Michigan State University Press.
Durán, Marco Antonio
  1964. "Las Funciones de la Propiedad de la Tierra en la Reforma
         Agraria Mexicana," *El Trimestre Económico* 31:228–42.

Eliecer Ruiz, Jorge
  1968. "La Reunion de Caracas Sobre Población y Desarrollo,"
         Revista de Economía 31:196–201.
Engels, Friedrich
  1972. *The Origin of the Family, Private Property, and the State,*
         edited by Eleanor Burke Leacock. New York: International
         Publishers.
Estados Unidos Mexicanos
  1943. *Sexto Censo de Población, Resumen General.* Mexico:
         Secretaría de la Economía Nacional, Dirección General
         de Estadística.

Ferrer, Martín Luis Guzmán
  1973. "Distribución del Ingreso en México," *Hispano Americano*
         44 (December 31, 1973).
Fisher, Tadd
  1964. "Mexico: The Problem of People," *Population Bulletin*
         20:173–202.
Food and Agricultural Organization
  1970. *The State of Food and Agriculture 1970.* Rome: United
         Nations.
  1975. *The State of Food and Agriculture 1974.* Rome: United
         Nations.
Fromm, Eric, ed.
  1969. *Marx's Concept of Man.* New York: Frederick Ungar Pub-
         lishing Co.

García-Peña, Alvaro
  1969. "La Miseria Dinámica: Report of a Speech by Robert

McNamara," *Revista de Economía* 32:155–57.

Glass, D. V., ed.
1953. *Introduction to Malthus.* New York: John Wiley and Sons.

Godwin, William
1926. *An Enquiry Concerning Political Justice and Its Influence on General Virtue and Happiness.* New York: Alfred A. Knopf.
1949. *Political Justice: A Reprint of the Essay on Property.* London: George Allen and Unwin, Ltd.

Gómez Jara, Francisco
1970. "La Estratificacíon Rural en México," *Revista Mexicana de Sociología* 32:691–707.

González Aparicio, Luis
1963. "El Problema Urbano como Factor en la Formulación de un Problema," *Revista de Economía* 26:90–95.

González Casanova, Pablo
1964. "Mexico Looks to the Future," *Atlantic Monthly* 213: 149–54.
1966. "The Mexico Which Has and the Mexico Which Has Not." In *Is the Mexican Revolution Dead?* edited by Stanley R. Ross. New York: Alfred A. Knopf.
1968. "Dynamics of the Class Structure." In *Comparative Perspectives on Stratification: Mexico, Great Britain, Japan,* edited by Joseph A. Kahl. Boston: Little, Brown and Company.
1970. *Democracy in Mexico.* New York: Oxford University Press.

González Salazar, Gloria
1971. "Crecimiento Económico y Desigualdad Social en México: Una Visión Esquemática," *Revista Mexicana de Sociología* 33:541–62.

Guzmán-Ferrer, Martín Luis
1973. "Distribución del Ingreso en México," *Hispano Americano* 64 (1973):14–21.

Hartley, Shirley Foster
1972. *Population Quantity vs. Quality.* Englewood Cliffs, N.J.: Prentice-Hall, Inc.

Hayner, Norman S.
1968. "Mexico City: Its Growth and Configuration, 1345–1960." In *Urbanism in World Perspective,* edited by Sylvia Fava, pp. 166–77. New York: Thomas Y. Crowell and Co.

Hazlitt, William
1960.   *The Spirit of the Age: Or, Contemporary Portraits.* London: Oxford University Press.
Hernández Alvarez, José
1967.   "Perfil Demográfico de la Immigración Mexicana a los Estados Unidos, 1910–1950," *Demografía y Economía* 1: 18–39.
Himes, James R.
1965.   "La Formación de Capital en México," *El Trimestre Económico* 32:153–76.

Jaffe, A. J.
1959.   *People, Jobs, and Economic Development.* Glencoe, Ill.: Free Press.
Jordan, Elijah
1927.   *Forms of Individuality: An Inquiry into the Grounds of Order in Human Relations.* Indianapolis: Progress Publishing Company.
1952.   *Theory of Legislation: An Essay on the Dynamics of the Public Mind.* Chicago: University of Chicago Press.
1952.   *Business Be Damned.* New York: Henry Schuman.

Kahl, Joseph A., and Stycos, J. Mayone
1964.   "Filosofía de la Política Demográfica en Latinoamérica," *El Trimestre Económico* 31:423–34.
Keynes, John Maynard
1963.   *Essays in Biography.* New York: W. W. Norton and Company.
Kingsbury, Robert C., and Schneider, Ronald M.
1969.   *An Atlas of Latin American Affairs.* New York: F. A. Praeger.

LaCascia, Joseph S.
1969.   *Capital Formation and Economic Development in Mexico.* New York: F. A. Praeger.
La Iglesia y sus Cometidos en la América Latino: Departamento Básico Preliminar para la II Conferencia del Episcopado Latinoamericano (CELAM)
1968.   *Revista de Economía* 31 (9): 281–94.
Lajous de Ballesteros, Evangelina
1968.   "El Crecimiento de la Población y el Desempleo," *Revista de Economía* 31:59–64.

Larkin, Margaret
   1970. "As Many as God Sends? Family Planning in Mexico."
      In *Sociological Essays and Research: Introductory Read-
      ings*, edited by C. H. Anderson, pp. 372–79. Homewood,
      Ill.: Dorsey Press.
Levin, Samuel
   1937. "Marx vs. Malthus," *Papers of the Michigan Academy of
      Arts and Letters.* Ann Arbor: University of Michigan Press.
Lewis, John
   1965. *The Life and Teaching of Karl Marx.* New York: Interna-
      tional Publishers.
Lewis, Oscar
   1959. *Five Families.* New York: Mentor Books.
   1963. *The Children of Sánchez.* New York: Vintage Books.
   1967. *Pedro Martínez.* New York: Vintage Books.
   1969. *A Death in the Sánchez Family.* New York: Random House.
Loyo, Gilberto
   1963. *Población y Desarrollo Económico.* Mexico: Libros Sela.
   1965. "Ante el Problema Agrario," *Revista de Economía* 27:141.
   1966. "Población y Desarrollo," *Revista de Economía* 29:256–58.

Malthus, Thomas R.
   1960. "A Summary View of the Principle of Population." In
      *Three Essays on Population: Thomas Malthus, Julian Hux-
      ley and Frederick Osborn*, pp. 13–59. New York: Mentor
      Books.
   1961a. "Of Systems of Equality." In *Theories of Society*, edited
      by Talcott Parsons, et al, vol 1, pp. 106–12. New York:
      Free Press.
   1961b. "The Division of Society into Classes." In *Theories of
      Society*, edited by Talcott Parsons, et al, vol 1, pp. 415–
      18. New York: Free Press.
   1964. "An Essay on the Principle of Population." In *Population,
      Evolution, Birth Control*, edited by Garrett Hardin, pp. 2–
      20. San Francisco: W. H. Freeman and Company.
Marx, Karl.
   1906. *Capital.* New York: Modern Library.
   1964. *Selected Writings in Sociology and Social Philosophy*,
      edited by T. B. Bottomore and Maximilien Rubel. New
      York: McGraw-Hill Book Company.
   1971a. *Capital: A Critique of Political Economy*, Vol. 3. Moscow:
      Progress Publishers.

1971b. *On Revolution*, edited and translated by Saul K. Padover. New York: McGraw-Hill Book Company.

——— and Engels, Friedrich
1962a. *Selected Works*, Vol. 1. Moscow: Foreign Languages Publishing House.
1962b. *Selected Works*, Vol. 2. Moscow: Foreign Languages Publishing House.

Meek, R. L., ed.
1971.   *Marx and Engels on the Population Bomb*. Berkeley, Calif.: Ramparts Press.

Mendieta y Nuñes, Lucio
1946.   *El Problema Agrario en México*. 5th. ed. Mexico City: Editorial Porrúa.

Morris, Judy K.
1969.   "Professor Malthus and His Essay." In *Population Studies: Selected Essays and Research*, edited by Kenneth C. W. Kammeyer. Chicago: Rand McNally and Company.

Mullen, William
1975.   "The Two Countries of Third World Mexico," *Chicago Tribune*, October 26.

Navarreté, Alfredo R.
1967.   "The Financing of Economic Development." In *Mexico's Recent Economic Growth*, edited by Enrique Pérez López. Austin: University of Texas Press.

Navarreté, Ifigenia
1960.   *La Distribución del Ingreso y el Desarrollo Económico de México*. Mexico City: Instituto de Investigaciones Económicas.

North American Congress on Latin America (NACOLA)
1973.   "Mexico Today," *Mexico: Days of Struggle—Judith Reyes*. Brooklyn, N.Y.: Paredon Records.

O'Farril, Mario Bautista
1966.   "El Problema de la Vivienda," *Revista de Economía* 29: 38–42.

Ortega Martínez, Alfonso
1966.   "La Revolución Mexicana y el Problema Habitacional," *Revista de Economía* 29:49–53.

Padilla Aragón, Enrique
1966.   *Ensayos Sobre Desarrollo Económico y Fluctuaciones*

Cíclicas en México. Mexico City: Universidad Nacional Autónoma de México, Escuela de Economía.

1968. "La Historia de México y los Ciclos Económicos," *El Trimestre Económico* 35:707–29.

1969. *Mexico: Desarrollo con Pobreza*. Mexico: Siglo Veintiuno Editores.

Plato

1928. *The Republic*. New York: Charles Scribner and Sons.

Population Reference Bureau

1963. "Los Paises que Crecen Más Rápidamente en el Mundo," *Revista de Economía* 26:133–35.

1971. *World Population Data Sheet: Population Information for 145 Countries*. Rev. Ed. Washington, D.C.: Population Bureau, Inc.

Pozas, Ricardo

1962. "Enfoque Antropológico de la Población," *Revista de Economía* 25:248–53.

Primera Asemblea Panamericana de Población

1965. *Revista de Economía* 28:276–79.

Ramírez Hernández, Juan and Chávez, Adolfo

1969. "Balance de los Alimentos en México Durante el Año de 1967," *Revista Mexicana de Sociologia*, 31:73–81.

Ramos Pedrueza, Rafael

1936. *La Lucha de Clases a Traves de la Historia de México*. 2d ed. Mexico City: Talleres Gráficos de la Nación.

Rangel Contla, José Calixto

1970. "La Polarización de la Estructura de Clases Sociales en México," *Revista Mexicana de Sociologia* 32:395–416.

Revista de Economía

1963. "Los Salarios y el Desarrollo Económico," *Revista de Economía*, 26:343–50.

1966. "Vivienda y Electricidad; Dos Grandes Problemas Nacionales," *Revista de Economía*, 29:36.

Reyes Osorio, Sergio

1967. "La Redistribución de la Tierra en México," *Revista de Economía* 30:196–205.

1969. "Hacia un Nuevo Enfoque del Problema Agrario Mexicano," *Revista de Economía* 32:145–48.

1971. "El Desarrollo Polarizado de la Agricultura Mexicana." In *Cuestiones Económicas Nacionales*. Mexico City: Banco Nacional de Comercio Exterior.

Reynolds, Clark W.
    1970.   *The Mexican Economy: Twentieth-Century Structure and Growth.* New Haven, Conn.: Yale University Press.
Riding, Alan
    1976.   "Mexico Elects a Symbol July 4," *Milwaukee Journal,* June 20.
Robertson, William Spence
    1930.   *History of the Latin-American Nations.* New York: D. Appleton and Co.
Rodríguez González, Gilberto
    1966.   "La Importancia Económica de los Salarios Mínimos," *Revista de Economía* 29:6–15.
Rostro Placencia, Francisco
    1964.   "Desarrollo Agrícola, Ganadero y Forestal," *Revista de Economía* 27:257–64.
    1965.   "El Financiamiento del Desarrollo Económico de México," *Revista de Economía* 28:290–96.
    1969.   "Perspectivas de Continuidad del Desarrollo Económico de México," *Revista de Economía* 32:81–87.

Sabine, George H.
    1958.   *A History of Political Theory.* New York: Henry Holt and Company.
Serrón, Luis A.
    1957.   "Institutional Developments in American Agriculture." M.A. thesis. Urbana: University of Illinois.
Simpson, Eyler Newton.
    1937.   *The Ejido: Mexico's Way Out.* Berkeley: University of California Press.
Simpson, Lesley Byrd
    1971.   *Many Mexicos.* Berkeley: University of California Press.
Singer, Morris
    1969.   *Growth, Equality, and the Mexican Experience.* Austin: University of Texas Press.
Smith, Kenneth
    1951.   *The Malthusian Controversy.* London: G. P. Routledge and Paul.
Solís, M. Leopoldo
    1972.   *Controversias Sobre el Crecimiento y la Distribución.* Mexico City: Fondo de Cultura Económica.
Sosa Reyes, José
    1964.   "Salarios y Prestaciones," *Revista de Economía* 27:273–80.

Suárez del Real, Enrique
1962. "El Problema Alimentício en México," *Revista Mexicana de Sociologia* 24:367–79.

Tello, Carlos
1971. "Notas Para el Análisis de la Distribución Personal del Ingreso en México," *El Trimestre Económico* 38:629–57.
Trejo Reyes, Saul
1970. "El Incremento de la Producción y el Empleo Industriales en México, 1950–1965," *Demografía y Economía* 4:102–19.

United Nations
1955. *Demographic Yearbook.* New York: United Nations Publications.
1974. *A Student Map of the United Nations: Members of the United Nations—Date of Membership, Area, and Population.* Map No. 2753. New York: United Nations Publications.
Urlanis, B. Z.
1970. "Marxismo y Control de la Natalidad," *Demografía y Economía* 4:144–47.
Urquidi, Victor L.
1969. "El Desarrollo Económico y el Crecimiento de la Población," *Revista de Economía* 32:117–22.

Whetten, Nathan L.
1950. "The Rise of the Middle Class in Mexico." In *Materiales Para el Estudio de la Clase Media.* Washington, D.C.: Unión Panamericana.
1964. "Tendencias de la Población en México," *Revista de Economía* 27:79–81.
Womack, John, Jr.
1968. *Zapata and the Mexican Revolution.* New York: Vintage Books.
Woodward, Ralph Lee, Jr., ed.
1971. *Positivism in Latin America, 1850–1900.* Lexington, Mass.: D. C. Heath & Company.

Zamora Batiz, Julio
1960a. "Algunas Notas Sobre las Inversiones Extranjeras en México," *Revista de Economía* 23:357–60.

1960b. "Algunos Conceptos Sobre el Ingreso Nacional en México," *Revista de Economía* 23:309–16.

Zeitlin, Irving M.
1968.   *Ideology and the Development of Sociological Theory.* Englewood Cliffs, N.J.: Prentice-Hall, Inc.
1971.   *Liberty, Equality, and Revolution in Alexis de Tocqueville.* Boston: Little, Brown, and Company.
1972.   *Capitalism and Imperialism.* Chicago:Markham Publishing Company.
Zenteno, Raul Benítez, and Cabrera Acevedo, Gustavo
1966.   *Proyecciones de la Población de México, 1960–1980.* Mexico: Banco de México.

Index